To Bob,

Many thanks
for everything –
advice, ideas and
support!

All the best,

Miella

The Decembrist Myth in Russian Culture

The Decembrist Myth in Russian Culture

Ludmilla A. Trigos

Studies of the Harriman Institute

The Harriman Institute, Columbia University, sponsors the Studies of the Harriman Institute in the belief that their publication contributes to scholarly research and public understanding. In this way the Institute, while not necessarily endorsing their conclusions, is pleased to make available the results of some of the research conducted under its auspices.

First published in 2009 by
PALGRAVE MACMILLAN®
in the United States—a division of St. Martin's Press LLC,
175 Fifth Avenue, New York, NY 10010.

Where this book is distributed in the UK, Europe and the rest of the world, this is by Palgrave Macmillan, a division of Macmillan Publishers Limited, registered in England, company number 785998, of Houndmills, Basingstoke, Hampshire RG21 6XS.

Palgrave Macmillan is the global academic imprint of the above companies and has companies and representatives throughout the world.

Palgrave® and Macmillan® are registered trademarks in the United States, the United Kingdom, Europe and other countries.

ISBN: 978–0–230–61916–6

Library of Congress Cataloging-in-Publication Data is available from the Library of Congress.

A catalogue record of the book is available from the British Library.

Design by Newgen Imaging Systems (P) Ltd., Chennai, India.

First edition: December 2009

10 9 8 7 6 5 4 3 2 1

Printed in the United States of America.

CONTENTS

PREFACE

The passage of nearly two centuries has not dimmed the Decembrist uprising as a vibrant event in Russian historical consciousness. Recurring anniversary celebrations and frequent depictions of the uprising attest to the Decembrists' hold on Russian cultural imagination. This book examines the fascination with and subsequent mythologization of the Decembrists, which began after their incarceration and continued through the twentieth century. Despite its failure to achieve its immediate goals, the Decembrist revolt had enormous political and cultural impact. Various individuals and groups manipulated the Decembrists' image to further their own agendas and consolidate their power: Nicholas I, nineteenth-century intelligentsia (both liberals and radicals), early twentieth-century activists across political spectrums (Kadets, Social-Democrats and Bolsheviks), the Soviet regime and political parties of the post-Soviet era. For many of these groups, literature served as their only forum since political discussion was not openly encouraged by imperial or Soviet authorities. To elucidate how literature shapes cultural consciousness and historical memory, I discuss the literary renderings of the Decembrist uprising and exile. These representations crossed the boundary from print to other media during the twentieth century when filmmakers and composers used them as inspiration for cinematic and musical explorations of the topic. I concentrate on the most widely available texts and influential representations to illustrate the myth's pervasiveness and adaptability.

The various manifestations of the Decembrists' mythic image shade from the literary to the political, depending on the mythmakers' needs. The words "myth," "cult," and "legend" tend to be problematic, as literary critics, historians and anthropologists have different definitions of these terms. Yet all are appropriate in a discussion of the Decembrists.

By myth and mythologization, I mean the way that a story takes on a life of its own after the event occurs. Two points are crucial to an adequate definition of myth. First, myths are narratives that are believed to be true; whether they are true or not is irrelevant. Second, a myth is told to promote some practical purpose. Any event can become a mythic text, as Henry Tudor suggests; the mythmaker must choose one that serves his ultimate purpose.[1]

The Decembrist myth permeates Russian literature and culture and evolved over time to fulfill different functions. It is a rich and productive one because of its multivocality.[2] It participates in and enriches other Russian cultural myths: of Pushkin, as founding father of Russian literature and great national poet; of Petersburg, which variously appears as city of illusion and hotbed of revolution; and of Siberia, which alternates as an icy realm of eternal exile or an unspoiled paradise. By analyzing the Decembrist uprising and subsequent myth from an anthropological viewpoint, we gain insight into the myth's deeper workings and emotional hold. This new perspective enhances our understanding of the Decembrists' central position in Russian cultural mythology and illuminates how they speak to Russian national identity.

Though many have seen the revolt as a unique event in the history of Russian opposition, it was very much a product of the general European revolutionary experience of the late eighteenth and early nineteenth century. Historians of revolutionary movements such as Franco Venturi, Andrezj Walicki, Philip Pomper, Marc Raeff, and Adam Zamoyski have all demonstrated how the Decembrists' secret societies emerged out of that fertile common ground and saw predecessors in the French Revolution, the Spanish Revolution of 1820, the Tugenbund and the Carbonari, not to mention the influence of Romanticism in general.[3] To avoid repetition, I emphasize that over time, Russian historians and other cultural commentators chose to downplay the similarities with foreign revolutionary movements in order to foreground the singularity of the Decembrists' feat. This strategy speaks to the need of the Russians (and later Soviets) to see themselves as both a part of and apart from Europe, and demonstrates that Russian national identity continued to hold within itself that tension between being unique while also wanting to be considered on the same cultural and developmental level as Europe.

To provide a broader context, I employ Victor Turner's methodology in my examination of the Decembrist revolt as a "social drama," which "manifests the conflict between the modes of communitas and structure," and provides greater understanding of a culture:

> In the social drama, however, though choices of means and ends and social affiliation are made, stress is dominantly laid upon loyalty and obligation, as much as interest, and the course of events may then have a tragic quality. . . . Conflict seems to bring fundamental aspects of society, normally overlaid by the customs and habits of daily intercourse, into frightening prominence. People have to take sides in terms of deeply entrenched moral imperatives and constraints, often against their own personal preferences. Choice is overborne by duty.[4]

The Decembrist revolt illustrates these aspects of social drama. It tested the moral imperatives of participants on the rebels' and imperial sides. At its deepest level, it was an uprising undertaken by a group desiring equality and freedom of all men in opposition to the autocracy's sociopolitical hierarchy and structure.

My approach uses an anthropological framework extrapolated from the works of Turner, René Girard, and Kathleen Verdery to expose the deeper cultural processes in the Decembrists' mythologization. Following Turner's lead, I go beyond the scrutiny of historical documents to investigate the relationship between fact, myth, and societal context. Additionally, I employ a semiotic analysis of the Decembrists' self-dramatization. The scholars Iurii Lotman and Lydia Ginzburg have argued persuasively that the Decembrists consciously fashioned their personalities out of literary and historical models.[5] The Decembrists' behavior figures significantly here, as well as the way that they and others represent it and the way that these representations interact. Therefore, I examine the Decembrists' own representations to contextualize the myth's later versions. Only through a synthetic analysis of the Decembrists' own *mifotvorchestvo* (mythmaking), and the mythologizing of subsequent generations from the mid-nineteenth century on, will we comprehend the myth's foundational role in Russian cultural mythology.

In my first three chapters I discuss the myth's evolution during the imperial era, focusing on how Nicholas I, the Decembrists themselves, and members of the intelligentsia manipulated it for different purposes. The Decembrist myth originated in opposition to Nicholas's imperial mythology and provided a narrative of political opposition and sacrifice. The Decembrists' sense of honor and obligation to the people appealed to later generations of Russian intelligentsia, who modeled themselves in part on the Decembrists. For some revolutionaries it was the Decembrists' sacrifice that was primary; for others it was, variously, their messianism, utopianism, or extremism.[6] The Decembrists' evaluation changed radically after 1917. When the Bolsheviks won the revolutionary struggle, they needed to assert their government's legitimacy as a ruling entity, and resolve their own relationship to the past, reinterpreting it to justify recent events and predict future successes. As many historians and anthropologists suggest, this process is conscious. Eric Hobsbawm links revolutionary movements to "invented tradition," which he defines as "a set of practices normally governed by overtly or tacitly accepted rules and of a ritual or symbolic nature, which seek to inculcate certain values and norms of behavior by repetition, which automatically implies continuity with the past." [7] Hobsbawm emphasizes the selective nature of invented tradition in that it hearkens back to "a suitable historic past": "Revolutions and 'progressive movements' which break with the past, by definition, have their own relevant past, though it may be cut off at a certain date, such as 1789. However, insofar as there is such reference to a historic past, the peculiarity of 'invented' traditions is that the continuity with it is largely factitious."[8] Hobsbawm's invented tradition can be associated with mythmaking in the Soviet authorities' conscious and active attempt to create an official genealogy throughout the 1920s until one particular version became enshrined during the Stalin era.

The ceremonies of the Decembrist anniversaries, especially of the 1925 centennial, demonstrate obvious attempts to shape the Decembrists' image out of numerous and competing elements. The 1925 jubilee serves as my investigation's nexus (chapters 4 and 5) because it marked an important moment in the history of the newly formed Soviet Union, when the Bolshevik regime, established only eight years earlier, could evaluate its successful position. The definitive decision to include the Decembrists uprising into the Russian revolutionary pantheon served as the first step toward an official Soviet historical assessment. In the version resulting from the jubilee, we discern how commemorative rituals elaborated the Decembrist myth for legitimating purposes. This new legitimating myth differed from the intelligentsia's version established in the nineteenth century. The sixth chapter demonstrates how the ideological demands of the Stalin era further refined the myth into a single, authorized version, which brooked no open challenges. At a time when official culture lost its hegemony, new voices emerged to challenge both the official view of the Decembrists espoused by authorized historians and writers and the unofficial views championed by the intelligentsia on the sidelines, as illustrated in chapters 7 and 8. That the Decembrists still figure largely in the discussion of Russia's historical alternatives testifies to the lasting hold of their myth upon the Russian cultural imagination.

ACKNOWLEDGMENTS

I became interested in the Decembrists while reading Alexander Herzen's memoirs during a graduate course in Imperial Russian History at Columbia University with Richard Wortman more than a decade ago. Subsequent study of cultural mythology with him, and of Russian literature and culture under the tutelage of Irina Reyfman, Catharine Nepomnyashchy, the late Robert Maguire and Richard Gustafson, led to my dissertation on centennial representations of the Decembrists. Their scholarship has shaped my approach, and I thank them for their encouragement and mentoring over the years. I am especially indebted to Irina Reyfman for her careful reading of my book manuscript.

The Harriman Institute provided a generous post–doctoral fellowship to expand on my dissertation and to conduct research in Russian archives. Grants from the Harriman Institute and the Department of Slavic Languages and Literatures at Columbia during my graduate career enabled archival research in Russia and dissertation writing as well. The author thanks the University Seminars at Columbia University for their help in publication. Material in this work was presented to the University Seminar on Slavic History and Culture.

I would like to thank Ronald Meyer, the Harriman Institute's publications director, for his invaluable assistance throughout the publication process. Kevin Laney helped me resolve technical problems with recordings of Iurii Shaporin's opera. Jared Ingersoll, Diana Greene, Bob Scott, Edward Kasinec, and the Slavic Reference Service at University of Illinois greatly facilitated my research, for which I am eternally grateful. Alla Rachkov, Tench Coxe, Eric Roston, and Nastya Lebedeva helped obtain Russian sources. Svetlana Pavlova at Moscow's Teatr Iunogo Zritelia kindly provided me with a copy of the director's script for Kama Ginkas's *The Decembrists' Execution*. Lyrics from Bulat Okudzhava's "I am writing a historical novel" appear courtesy of the

Bulat Okudzhava Museum in Peredelkino. Special thanks to Naum Korzhavin, who granted me permission to publish his poems "Envy" and "In Memory of Herzen . . ." in their entirety and to Tatyana Nazarenko, who provided me with a photograph of her painting "The Decembrists. Chernigov Uprising." The film still from *SVD* appears courtesy of BFI.

I am also grateful to many colleagues for their insights. I would like to thank Ellen Chances for her continuing interest and support of this and other projects. Karen Petrone generously shared her archival notes with me on 1937 Pushkin films. Angela Brintlinger, Susan Reid and Natalia Kolodzei facilitated contacts in Russia. The late James Card generously made a copy of *SVD* from his personal film collection when I could not obtain it otherwise. An anonymous reader and Catherine O'Neil (for the Harriman Institute series) made valuable suggestions for making the transition from dissertation to book. Many AAASS, MLA and AATSEEL presentations gave me the opportunity to benefit from interdisciplinary dialogue with the late W. Bruce Lincoln, Abby Schrader, Tom Trice, Doug Smith, Emily Johnson, Hilde Hoogenboom, Anthony Anemone and Eliot Borenstein, among others. Boris Briker, Catherine Hartzell and Nicole Falk assisted me at the final stages of manuscript preparation. Donia Allen has been an all-around writer/ editor/friend and great source of support, as have Hilary Fink, Olga Briker and Jamie Bennett. Tony and Judy Wohl and Thea Alexander have also been encouraging throughout the process. Most of all, I am grateful to my family, my mother, my husband Paul, and my two beloved daughters, Sophia and Olivia, without whose unswerving faith and encouragement none of this would be possible.

An earlier version of the introduction has appeared as "The Spectacle of the Scaffold: Performance and Subversion in the Decembrists' Execution" in Marcus Levitt and Tatyana Novikov (eds.), *Times of Trouble: Violence in Russian Literature and Culture* (University of Wisconsin Press, 2007), reprinted courtesy of the University of Wisconsin Press. Portions of chapter 5 have been published as "An Exploration of the Dynamics of Mythmaking: Tynianov's *Kiukhlia*" in the *Slavic and East European Journal* 46, no. 2 (Summer 2002), 283–300.

INTRODUCTION

Who respects us inspired bards, in a land where worth is measured according to the number of one's decorations and serfs?...It is painful to be an ardent dreamer in the land of eternal frost.
—Alexander Griboedov[1]

Historical Fact

On November 19, 1825 after a brief illness Tsar Alexander I died suddenly in Taganrog, Crimea without leaving an heir to the throne. The news of Alexander's death arrived in Petersburg on November 27 in the early morning while the imperial family and the court attended mass to pray for his health. The ensuing interregnum, lasting until December 14, 1825, proved decisive for Russia's future course. The imperial family's indecision because of the lack of an heir magnified the confusion and the country "found itself in the strange predicament of having two self-denying Emperors, and no active ruler."[2] The assumed heir Constantine, Alexander's younger brother, had contracted a morganatic marriage to a Polish noblewoman, thus barring him from inheriting the throne. In any case, years earlier, he had renounced his right to the throne in a secret document known only to a few members of the imperial family. As Constantine's action had not been made public, his younger brother Nicholas insisted that all take the oath to Constantine as the new tsar.[3] Though by many accounts Nicholas knew that he was next in line to the throne and the rightful heir, his behavior made it seem otherwise. His awkward decision prolonged the confusion regarding the succession, spurring an exchange of urgent missives from the imperial family in Petersburg to Constantine in Warsaw. Despite the family's urgings, Constantine could not be persuaded to quit his home to come to the capital to renounce his right to the throne publicly and formally.

Constantine's perverse behavior provided secret society members—later known as the Decembrists—a pretense to overthrow the autocracy. They appealed to imperial troops' well-known preference for Constantine to gain support, posing the problem as one of legitimacy: Constantine was the rightful heir, and he was being prevented from ascending the throne. They hoped to galvanize the troops to act while eschewing the masses' involvement. Had they proclaimed their true goals—the abolition of serfdom, the foundation of a government assuring the freedom, rights and equality of all men—they feared they would lose control of the rebellion. Above all they wanted to prevent widespread bloodshed and popular revolt.

The uprising on December 14 was perpetrated primarily by members of a secret society originating in 1816 as the "Union of Salvation." Comprised of military officers and noblemen, the group's founders included Alexander and Nikita Muraviev, Prince Sergei Trubetskoi, Ivan Iakushkin, and Matvei and Sergei Muraviev-Apostol. Inspired by the ideas of the Enlightenment, the French Revolution and freemasonry and their experiences in Western Europe during the campaigns against Napoleon, the members desired political and social reform. Specific aims included the eradication of the autocratic system, reform of the courts and the emancipation of the serfs, though as a group they did not agree on the methods that would achieve these goals. The original group disbanded in 1817 and renamed itself the "Union of Welfare," splitting into two sections in 1818. The Northern Society, located in Petersburg, was led by Nikita Muraviev (later aided by Evgenii Obolenskii and Trubetskoi), and the Southern Society, located in present-day Ukraine, was led by Colonel Pavel Pestel. The split occurred because of conflicting programs, inasmuch as the societies could be said to have them, since both sections did not have fully articulated ideas of how to achieve political change nor did they have complete agreement on what form of government to put into place.[4] For the most part, the Northern Society advocated gradual change and constitutional monarchy; the southern group urged a military overthrow that would then allow for the establishment of a republic.[5]

The conspirators had long been planning a coup. An earlier strategy was to assassinate Alexander I while he reviewed his troops. The secret society's members could not agree on the appropriate timing, nor could they organize their actions. On hearing the news of Alexander's death, they decided to take advantage of the circumstances. It was time to act. The members met nightly at the apartment of the poet Kondratii Ryleev, de facto leader of the Northern Society, to plan their coup. They appointed December 14 as the day for the revolt, the day that a second oath of allegiance was to be taken, this time to Nicholas. They planned to gather troops from their barracks and march them onto Senate Square, where they would publicly refuse the oath and instead demand their "rightful" tsar, Constantine. They would also demand a constitution from the State council members and imperial family, which would establish a constitutional monarchy or a republic; they had not yet decided which they preferred. If all else failed, they would fight.

In addition to the succession crisis, betrayals of both branches precipitated their revolutionary action independently of each other. Captain A. I. Maiboroda's testimony led to the arrest of Pestel in Ukraine on the night of December 13, 1825, the eve of the oath-swearing and subsequent uprising in Petersburg. The former Northern Society member, Second Lieutenant Iakov Rostovstev, told his colleagues of his betrayal of the Petersburg conspiracy; it was his confession that led them to enact their plot.

The conspirators mustered their forces and began arraying them on Senate Square in the early morning of December 14. A force of approximately 2,000 strong stood on the square, refusing to swear allegiance to Nicholas. The conspirators and their troops waited for the appearance of their designated "dictator," Trubetskoi, to lead them into action. While loyal troops surrounded the rebels, crowds gathered to watch the spectacle, offering their support to the insurgents. Occasional shouts of "Hurrah for Constantine" were heard. Trubetskoi did not appear; the Northern Society's inspiration, Ryleev, went to find him and did not return. The nonappearance of the revolt's appointed dictator and the disappearance of its charismatic prophet left the conspirators and troops uncertain of their course. Captain Alexander Iakubovich sallied back and forth from the side of the conspirators to the imperial forces, first urging his rebel colleagues to hold fast and then telling the loyal generals that they were ready to give up. The eccentric poet and conspirator Vilhelm Kiukhelbeker recklessly brandished his pistol.

Count M. A. Miloradovich, Metropolitan Filaret and Grand Prince Michael Pavlovich attempted to negotiate with the rebels. In each case they were turned back with taunts, oaths, and random shots. Miloradovich was wounded by a shot from the gun of the insurgent Petr Kakhovskii and died later that day. The conspirator Ivan Pushchin goaded

Kiukhelbeker to take a shot at the Grand Prince. Kiukhelbeker's gun misfired. The crowd became more restless; workmen from St. Isaac's cathedral at the edge of the square began hurling wood at the loyal troops. With twilight approaching, Nicholas decided to attack. As the cavalry charged, their horses skidded across the square on the ice, accomplishing nothing. The Chevalier Guards attacked next and experienced the same. Nicholas finally ordered the artillery to fire. Chaos ensued. The rebels broke ranks and many fled to avoid the grapeshot. Within twenty-four hours most conspirators were in custody.

A second uprising occurred two weeks later when the news of the events in Petersburg reached the south. Already aware of a traitor in their midst after the incarceration of their leader Pestel, the Southern Society began to strategize. When the authorities arrested Sergei Muraviev-Apostol and Mikhail Bestuzhev-Riumin, the remaining members of the Southern Society and United Slavs, an allied secret society, freed them and gathered reinforcements among the southern regiments to come to the aid of their northern colleagues.

The revolt of the Chernigov troops, led by Muraviev-Apostol, began on December 29, with their march on the town of Vasilkov. Playing on the religious appeal of the Orthodox liturgy, Muraviev-Apostol composed a catechism especially for the revolution, hoping to mobilize support and inspire his troops' devotion. On December 31, Muraviev-Apostol persuaded a local priest to read his text to the assembled troops to justify their action against the tsar. While the rebels in the North played on the troops' preference for Constantine over Nicholas, the Southern insurrectionists manipulated religious symbols to gain support. If the Northern revolt was distinguished by its static quality, then the Southern revolt can be categorized by its aimless wandering in search of manpower. Over the course of five days, the troops roamed the countryside, from Vasilkov to Motovilovka then to Belaia Tserkov and Zhitomir. Imperial troops surrounded them on January 3, 1826, at the village of Trilesy. After a brief and bloody battle, the conspirators were routed and taken prisoner. The members of the Northern and Southern Societies and the United Slavs were reunited in Petersburg in Peter-Paul Fortress where they were imprisoned during the investigation into the conspiracy.

Nicholas I personally questioned the conspirators and oversaw the judiciary process. He established an investigative commission, which he directed throughout. The process dragged on until May 30, 1826, when the perpetrators were sentenced without trial or appeal. The five so-called leaders, Pestel, Ryleev, Kakhovskii, Muraviev-Apostol, and

Bestuzhev-Riumin were sentenced to death by quartering. The other 121 men received sentences varying from demotion to the ranks to lifetime exile and penal servitude. Nicholas graciously commuted many sentences; the five leaders would be executed by hanging rather than quartering to avoid bloodshed.

On July 13, 1826, the sentences were carried out. In the middle of the night, the convicted Decembrists were gathered and stripped of their military uniforms, honors, and scabbards. Imperial officers burned the Decembrists' personal effects and broke their swords over their heads. The prisoners were issued convicts' clothes and taken inside to await news of their colleagues' death. At dawn the five Decembrist leaders were hanged on the ramparts of Peter-Paul Fortress. Though scheduled for 3:00 a.m., the ceremony did not begin until 5:30 a.m. because of the scaffold's faulty construction.[6] The five fettered men were led out to the scaffold: Kakhovskii walked alone first, behind him Muraviev-Apostol with Bestuzhev, then Ryleev, and Pestel. After the police captain read their sentence aloud, Ryleev called for his comrades to make their final obeisance to the Lord, and then they walked onto the scaffold. The two executioners first placed nooses and then white hoods on them. When the command was given, the board on which they stood was removed and at that moment three bodies fell, their ropes having broken. Ryleev, Muraviev, and Kakhovskii, in varying stages of consciousness, were helped back up onto the scaffold and hanged again. When a doctor pronounced them dead at 6 a.m., they were removed, thrown onto a cart, and disposed of in an unknown location on Golodai Island, an outlying Petersburg island. The official news of the execution and exile of the state criminals appeared in *The Northern Bee* (*Severnaia pchela*) and other newspapers days later (July 17) and cleansing services (*ochistitel'noe molebstvie*) were held in Petersburg on Senate Square (July 14) and in Moscow in the Kremlin (July 19).

The remaining Decembrists, sentenced to Siberian exile, imprisonment and/or penal servitude, set off in the remaining days of the summer. Several wives petitioned Nicholas for permission to follow their husbands to Siberia. After much deliberation, he allowed a small number to go, as long as they left their children and renounced their former rank and rights. Eleven wives journeyed to Siberia in the years 1826–1831; from 1838–1847 four sisters, two mothers, and one more wife arrived.[7] The women, renowned in Russian literature and history as *dekabristki* (literally, Decembrist women), became famous for their self-sacrifice and *podvig* (moral feat). The wives were the Decembrists' remaining link to Russian society and supported their husbands both spiritually and materially. Though the Decembrists were physically isolated from society from the moment of their incarceration, they resurfaced in 1856 when Tsar Alexander II granted them amnesty and allowed the few survivors to return to western Russia.

Mythic Narrative

In Victor Turner's terms, the Decembrists' outright refusal to take oath to the new tsar enacted "a public, overt breach"[8] against the autocracy. This act played on the loyalties of the perpetrators (would they pledge allegiance to their tsar?) and the authorities (would they take arms against fellow Russians?). In the intervening hours, while the rebels stood on Senate Square in St. Petersburg, a "phase of mounting crisis" occurred, during which the authorities had to determine how to counteract the social/political breach, and the rebels had to decide how to force their hand. Neither side knew what to do, resulting in the derogatory appellation of the revolt as a "standing revolution" (*stoiachaia revoliutsiia*). Since there was no escalation in the conspirators' military force because of their lack of organization and leadership this phase was brief. The authorities' negotiations failed to achieve resolution; a chaotic atmosphere ensued, with the lower classes watching the stand-off while hurling firewood at imperial troops. December 14 coincided with the winter solstice, when mummers entertained the crowds "in a carnivalesque mixture of Christian and pagan symbolism," an atmosphere that certainly influenced the tone of the revolt.[9]

Though carnivalesque elements may have been inherent in the holiday, they also arose naturally from the new tsar's accession. René Girard's discussion of succession rites illuminates the deeper workings of the Decembrist uprising from an anthropological perspective. Girard examines installation rites in societies where violence often accompanies transfers of power. In these settings, the king must commit transgressions violating sacred laws to take on the role of the original victim, who is polluted. (Recall the figure of Oedipus in *Oedipus Rex*.) Because of the violation, the king is subject to ritualistic insults during the succession rites, which may involve a mock attack on his bodyguard or himself. Girard demonstrates the king's function as "the catalyst who converts sterile, infectious violence into positive cultural values."[10] Given the king's marginal status within society—he is not a member of society, but above it—he can take on the sacrificial or surrogate victim's role to expel violence detrimental to the community.

The Decembrist revolt can be seen in this context as an archetype of ritual confrontation in enthronement rites. However, in their case, the ritual crossed from mock attack to genuine opposition with dire consequences. The confrontation's static quality underlines its ritual nature; the conspirators and their troops stood on the square for hours before being compelled to fight after tsarist artillery fired on them. The ritual aspects are also apparent in the authorities' reactions; they hesitated to quash the revolt, instead negotiating with the rebels. The tsar's military and religious representatives tried to convince the conspirators to withdraw with appeals to higher forces of divine and human law. During their attempts to negotiate with the rebels, the tsar's representatives, Grand Prince Michael and Metropolitan Filaret, were insulted and humiliated, and one of the greatest heroes of the era, Miloradovich, was wounded. Only then did Nicholas take action to efface the social breach's effect, ordering loyal troops to fire artillery at the lightly armed insurrectionists.

Unlike ritual confrontations, the Decembrists directly challenged Nicholas's legitimacy and raised the possibility of regicide in two senses. The explicit question of whether the "rightful" ruler (Tsarevich Constantine) had been killed was the Decembrists' pretense for revolt. However, the implicit question of whether to kill the new tsar to overthrow the monarchy served as the primary impetus for the Decembrists' action and strategy. In this case, Nicholas's behavior during the uprising confirmed his legitimacy, paralleling the legitimating process undergone by the ruler during installation rites performed by primitive communities. The revolt's perpetrators, sentenced to death, imprisonment or exile, became marginalized, liminal figures in society's perception.

Nicholas's Mythology of Rule and
Historical Representation

Immediately after the Decembrists' sentencing, Nicholas forbade their mention in all public media. Contemporaries expected that Nicholas would annul the death penalty for the condemned Decembrists at the last minute as a result of the Empress's intercession on their behalf. When this expectation was not fulfilled, "even more conservative members of the elite were shocked."[11] Out of fear of society's reaction to the punishment and future eruptions of opposition to the state, Nicholas strove to erase the conspirators' names and actions from history and their memory from the public consciousness. However, Nicholas's decisions—to ban public mention of the Decembrists, to execute the five leaders in secret, and to exile the remaining rebels to Siberia—backfired because they allowed legends to arise concerning the executed men and survivors. Among certain elite circles, the intelligentsia and the inhabitants of Siberia, the Decembrists gained mythic status.

The imperial prohibition on the Decembrists' representations (in print and portraiture) lasted throughout Nicholas's reign. The exceptions to the ban were the official narratives of the Decembrist uprising: the newspaper account first published in *The Saint Petersburg News* (*Sankt-Peterburgskie vedomosti*) and reprinted elsewhere, references in imperial manifestoes issued regarding the revolt, sentencing, execution, and cleansing services, and Baron Modest Korf's history *The Accession of Nicholas I* (*Vosshestvie na prestol Nikolaia I,* 1857). Though Korf's work was written in 1848, it was publicly issued only after Nicholas's death in Russian, English, and German. Prior to 1857 copies were available exclusively for the imperial family's private use. These official representations need to be evaluated to examine properly the Decembrists' mythic image. The Decembrist myth arose in response to the official narratives of the uprising, the only publicly available information about the movement and its members. The Decembrists and their sympathizers sought to counter the incomplete and skewed accounts by producing their own versions of the events and representations of their participants (see chapter 2).

The newspaper account after the uprising minimized the rebellion's importance as a stand against the autocracy. Written by Dmitrii Bludov at Nicholas's order,[12] it sought to allay Russian and European fears about widespread insurrection. Instead it impugned the perpetrators' and their supporters' characters, claiming the rebel battalions of the Moscow troops were joined by "several people of vile appearance in frock coats,"[13] who were "madmen" (*bezumtsy*), and insinuated that they were drunk.[14] The article insisted the troops were the "blind instrument" (*slepoe oruzhie*) of a few officers who took advantage of them. For this reason, after hearing that rebel troops returned to their barracks, confessed their wrongdoing and took the oath, Nicholas pardoned them and returned their standard.[15] Only with the leaders discredited and the true goals suppressed could Nicholas defuse the revolt's significance. The article never mentioned the rebels' demand for a constitution or their desire to abolish the autocracy and serfdom.

Months later, after the execution of the Decembrist leaders, a religious ceremony was held on Senate Square to cleanse it of the blood, crime, treason, and dishonor against the *tsar-batiushka* (dear father tsar), which the popular imagination perceived as attempted patricide. The fact that Nicholas felt it necessary to purify the uprising's setting highlights his extreme reaction to the crime and the depth of his fear. The service contained two New Testament readings, from Paul and Luke. The latter illustrates Christ's role in cleansing and saving the faithful as long as they believed. This reading provided an allegory for Russia; believing in the tsar, all would be cleansed of their sins, kept safe and protected from "raging revolt...and the destruction of the entire Russian tsardom."[16] The manifesto Nicholas issued that day repeated the rhetoric and affirmed "the fatherland is cleansed of the marks of infection, which it hid within itself for so many years."[17]

Nicholas celebrated his victory over the Decembrists, whom he called "mes amis de quatorze," with a liturgy on December 14 every year of his reign. As Richard Wortman asserts, Nicholas constructed his own myth of the uprising, which glorified his and his supporters' valiant efforts to persuade the rebels to withdraw and then, only when forced to resort to violence, showed their courage in suppressing the rebellion:

> Nicholas I used the Decembrist Rebellion to refurbish the ruler's image as conqueror and to put it at the service of the autocracy's defense, rather than its transformation.... The insurrection made it possible to present conservatism as a radical break, for Nicholas defined the Decembrist Movement as the embodiment of the Western, rationalistic views that his brother, Alexander, had also held.... In crushing the rebellion, he heroically began a new era, loyal to a tradition presumably demonstrated by the failure of the rebellion.[18]

Nicholas created the myth to legitimate his own right to rule, resting his claim on two facts. First, he demonstrated his capacity to rule the empire during the revolt. Second, he already produced a male heir, whom he offered to the troops as a sign of future dynastic stability.[19] Thus, the validation of his power and creation of his own mythic version of events began in the ceremonies occurring on the day of the insurrection and continued until the end of his reign.[20] Given this atmosphere, an alternative vision could not compete openly with the imperial myth. The manifesto and ritual cleansing of the square on the day of the Decembrists' execution sought to affirm Nicholas's version, his "heroic triumph" over evil: "December 14 thus became another event, with the Napoleonic wars, that united the armed forces in the holy cause of defending Russia."[21]

The Decembrist insurrection became a central defining moment for Nicholas's reign, in validating his claims as emperor and charting his course as a conservative and reformer, and also in shaping his future "mythology of rule"[22]: "Nicholas I renewed the image of conqueror, but now as lone and embattled defender of monarchy against the pernicious forces of revolution."[23] Nicholas's myth, however, was countered by the development of the Decembrist myth, a myth against the establishment, an anti–myth challenging the autocracy's version of truth and right to power. Nurtured in the nineteenth century by the poet Alexander Pushkin, the political activist Alexander Herzen and the Decembrists' families and sympathizers as well as the Decembrists themselves, the myth grew clandestinely, through obscure references, unofficial correspondence and word of mouth. Yet in certain circles, it provided a powerful counterweight to official history. Though they strove to overthrow the autocracy and social hierarchy to equalize citizens, in the end the only status reversal that ensued was their own, from high to low. Because of their crime against the tsar, the Decembrists became marginalized figures in society. As Turner suggests, marginalized figures often take on great sacred power while being considered dangerous and polluting. These "mythic types" come to "symbolize the moral value" of rebellion against oppressive rulers, and are seen as "representatives or expressions of universal human values."[24] Though Nicholas's state rituals emphasized the Decembrists' polluting effect in other circles they achieved a sacred status.

The imperial mythology's most enduring representation was *The Accession of Nicholas I* written by Baron Modest Korf, Nicholas's state secretary and issued in a limited first edition (for the imperial family) on December 14, 1848, 23 years to the day of the Decembrist uprising. Korf wrote his book at the request of Tsarevich Alexander,[25] who recognized that the first days of his father's reign must not "fade or pass into history distorted by exaggerated rumors."[26] Alexander Nikolaevich provided Nicholas's notes but instructed Korf to excise all the personal elements. He also suggested that Nicholas correct the text and add any personal reminiscences that were relevant to make it "the most credible whole."[27] The Tsarevich's suggestions exemplify that history is the victors' domain and shows how historical texts concretely demonstrate political power.

Korf's text borders more on the panegyric than on history. Introducing the first public edition in 1857 after Nicholas' death, Korf proclaims he will give not only the full truth but also a valuable example to posterity: "Emperor Nicholas does not need laudatory exclamations, but history requires truth and valiant examples. This purpose will reconcile the illustrious departed to the violation of his modesty's secret!" (v). Korf justifies the publication of the first day of Nicholas's reign to balance the news of Nicholas's last day; he exalts the recently departed tsar for his virtues, portraying him as a good ruler and courageous man from his succession's first moment.

Korf disclaims his medium, calling it a "chronicle" (*letopis'*) rather than a "history"(*istoriia*): "A chronicle ought to relate events and how they occurred: it is history's province to evaluate them and pronounce upon them definitive judgment" (ix). Pronouncing judgment is, however, specifically what Korf does. His work falls more precisely between the "history" and the "portrait." Korf thus follows the genre described by Louis Marin: "If history is made by actors and if, among these actors, there is an agent through whom they receive being, life, and movement, the narrative of History can be only the narrative of this agent and of all he does, says, and thinks. His acts, words, and thoughts—and only they—define the absolute and universal space of History and of the narrative of history: the king must therefore be praised everywhere.[28] In Korf's narrative, Nicholas is the main actor who must be praised and justified; all others are marginalized. His being and worth gain validation through the Decembrist revolt's suppression, the first and most important act of his reign. It cannot be coincidental that the Tsarevich asked Korf to write the book in 1848, given the number of revolutionary uprisings in Europe at the time. Could this narrative originally have been intended as a reminder of Nicholas's past victory over revolution and consolation, or as a promise of future victory over the specter of revolution? In any case, Nicholas's success is twofold; the tale of the revolt's quashing leads to the suppression of the story's other possible versions. Korf represents the conspirators in highly negative terms: "A handful of young madmen, acquainted neither with the demands of the Empire nor with the people's spirit and the true needs, insolently dreamed of the government's reorganization; soon, the thought of reform was also joined by the unholy thought of regicide" (100). The Decembrists' portrayal as madmen echoes the newspaper accounts and many contemporary letters and memoirs of the elite's conservative members.[29] The figures of the revolt have no say in this text. Their narratives are subsumed by the praise of the king.

Though a panegyric in many ways, the work often seems an apologia. Korf answers publicly for Nicholas's treatment of the Decembrists and his actions as tsar in general. He also speaks to criticism from abroad in foreign publications.[30] The entire text legitimizes Nicholas's rule, explaining why he ascended the throne rather than Constantine. In a surprising example of openness, Korf reveals the letters exchanged between Constantine and Alexander I regarding the succession to demonstrate Constantine's earlier renunciation and validate Nicholas's legitimacy.

Korf focuses on Nicholas's noble character and strong sense of duty, stressing that Nicholas took up the post as emperor even though he felt unprepared. He portrays Nicholas as a reluctant leader, much like Moses, who attempts, albeit unsuccessfully, to turn away from his divinely ordained historical role. Korf proclaims that first hearing of Alexander's intention to alter the natural order of succession in favor of Nicholas over Constantine: "the young couple [Nicholas and his wife] was struck as with a thunderbolt by this unexpected news, which to them was full of terror. In tears, they were unable to respond" (9). Nicholas's reaction underlines his modest nature and lack of imperial ambition: "In vain did the Grand Prince represent that he had never prepared himself to occupy the lofty rank of Emperor; that he felt within himself neither the necessary strength for such a great post, nor the necessary firmness of character; that he had but one wish and ambition in the world—forever to serve the Emperor" (10). On hearing of the Emperor's death, Nicholas's first act was to swear allegiance to Constantine, insisting that it was his duty to observe the succession's unchanging order. Once confronted with positive proof of his inheritance, Nicholas continued to refuse, asserting that no one knew of Alexander's will with its change of succession. As Korf portrays it, Nicholas felt he was making the greatest sacrifice in accepting the new role assigned to him:

> Which of us two, He [Nicholas] inwardly asked himself, makes the greater sacrifice here? Is it he who, once determined to renounce his paternal inheritance under the guise of his own unfitness, remains faithful to his word, in the position which he has himself chosen, in conformity with his taste and his desires; or is it he who, never having prepared himself for a dignity from which he was exempt by his very birth, and without knowing positively of the decision decreeing his own destiny, now suddenly finds himself obligated at a most difficult time, when the future appears anything but smiling, to sacrifice himself and all that he

holds dearest—domestic happiness and peace—to obey the will of another? (85)

Repeated references to Nicholas's consciousness of duty and modesty (which would have kept him out of the limelight) represent Nicholas's final decision to take the throne as the ultimate act of self-sacrifice. Extolling Nicholas's action, Korf further sacralizes the tsar: "In inscribing on our history's pages one of the noblest and sublimest of its events, before his sacred debt to his country, Nicholas Pavlovich forced silent in his heart the voice of self-preservation and self-interest: with a soul full of the most pious trust in Almighty Providence he obeyed its design. Nicholas Pavlovich was emperor" (107). Korf quells any suspicion of Nicholas's ambition to become tsar. Korf then cites Nicholas's letter to his brother Michael on the evening of December 12, 1825, when he received Constantine's definitive refusal of the throne: "Finally all is decided... and I must take on the burden of the Emperor" (109). Nicholas appears as the most dutiful imperial servant, for whom the empire is a burden rather than a reward. Korf turns Nicholas into a sacrificial victim relinquishing his own good for society's benefit.

To highlight Nicholas's rightful status, Korf stresses the people's loyalty compared to the rebels' and deceived troops'. To this end, Korf propagates the negative apocrypha of the uprising. He reports the quip about the crowd calling for "Constantine and Constitution" (*Konstantin i Konstitutsiia*) thinking that they meant Constantine and his wife.[31] By demonstrating the crowd's ignorance, Korf shows their inability to side knowingly against the autocracy in the rebels' favor; rather their childlike understanding leads them into error. The *tsar-batiushka*, paternal authority extraordinaire, steps in to protect his citizen-children from the nefarious conspirators' influences.

Korf effectively provides a new justification of Nicholas's reign after his death. Three primary motivations may have spurred this justification. First, Nicholas died after the devastating loss of the Crimean War. The defeat caused many people to question the regime's earlier policies. Korf allays those doubts by depicting Nicholas' crowning moment. Second, Nicholas's justification provided legitimization of his son and heir, the new tsar, Alexander II. Alexander showed mercy by granting the Decembrists amnesty in honor of his coronation. Thus Alexander's noble act follows ironically in his father's footsteps. Nicholas proved himself as a ruler by crushing the revolt. Alexander II, already a legitimate ruler according to the order of succession, could validate himself by being the antithesis of his father and pardoning the Decembrists.

Though showing clemency toward the remaining Decembrists, Alexander did not withdraw all the restrictions imposed upon them. The few returnees to western Russia could not live in the capital cities, though some played an important role in society upon their return, especially during Alexander's reforms enacted in 1861. Alexander realized the double-edged nature of his pardon when he saw the Decembrists' heroic welcome and specifically told Korf: "It seems to me that the time has come to publish your history of December 14. I am aware of the absurd and false rumors circulating about this event not only in Europe but in Russia itself."[32] However, instead of counteracting the returning exiles' acclamation, Korf's publication provided further impetus to their mythologization.

CHAPTER ONE

The Decembrist Myth in the Nineteenth Century

Without the Decembrists, there wouldn't have been Pushkin.
—Natan Eidelman[1]

The cannons' thunder, ringing out on Senate Square, roused an entire generation.
—Alexander Herzen[2]

From the moment of the uprising, the Decembrist myth developed in elite Russian society. It found its form through the literary culture, in allusions and veiled references. It spread through word of mouth and private correspondence among the Decembrists' sympathizers. The myth was nurtured and fostered by the Decembrists themselves in their writings and their memoirs' eventual publication. This chapter traces the Decembrist myth's evolution in the nineteenth century among the intelligentsia, examining literary representations to see how the Decembrists' image changed over time. Certain portrayals later became canonical and propagated the myth more widely. In the twentieth century, these canonical texts resurface in Soviet historical accounts, criticism and literature during the centennial.

My exploration will be divided into three parts. First I analyze the works of the Decembrists' contemporaries, Alexander Pushkin (1799–1837) and Alexander Griboedov (1795–1829), to demonstrate the complex interrelationship of literature, life, and censorship affecting the myth's early evolution. Second I focus on literary representations by Alexander Herzen (1812–1870), Nikolai Ogarev (1813–1877), and Nikolai Nekrasov (1821–1878) to show how the succeeding generation took up the Decembrists' banner and sacralized them in their works. Third, I examine portrayals by Leo Tolstoy (1828–1910) to illustrate how he counteracted the hagiographic depictions of other writers.

The Contemporaries

Alexander Pushkin and Alexander Griboedov were the Decembrists' contemporaries and friends. In their cases, biography and artistic production intersect and impact later interpretations of their literary works. These writers engaged in a lively critical and stylistic dialogue with Decembrist writers such as Ryleev, Bestuzhev-Marlinsky, and Kiukhelbeker before the uprising. Afterward, Pushkin's and Griboedov's earlier works were reinterpreted as either supportive or critical of the revolt and its participants. Certain characters and phrases were taken as emblematic references to the Decembrists by their contemporaries. This rereading brought them under the imperial authorities' suspicion. Hence, both writers discovered that they had to be vigilant to avoid censure for sympathy to the Decembrists' cause. In any case, given the official ban on representations of the Decembrists, there would be little point in writing explicitly about the revolt and its participants. Instead, a few ambiguous references appear because of the personal danger in referring to the revolt. These ambiguous representations allowed for reinterpretation after the 1917 revolution. Thus Pushkin's and Griboedov's works play a central role in the Decembrist myth as much for the way they were read by succeeding generations as for the specific images that they provided.

Though Pushkin never explicitly represented the Decembrists in work published in his lifetime, many scholars argue that he obliquely addressed the issue of revolutionary action and its consequences in his letters, sketches, and literary works. Such popular rereadings of his work began immediately after the Decembrist revolt but appear in prerevolutionary criticism only in the late 1890s. Pushkin's poem, "André Chénier," written in 1824, was excerpted and distributed anonymously as "On December 14" ("Na 14 dekabria") after the uprising. The authorities called Pushkin to account for his authorship and the poem's distribution under the new title. Pushkin knew of the malleability of his poetry, his inability to control its form once it was released to the public and the consequences of political readings of his work, having already been exiled for writing poems critical of the tsarist government. However, Pushkin wrote those works with a specific ideological purpose in mind, whereas "André Chénier" lauded the French poet who was hanged because of his exploits in a pro-monarchist conspiracy during the French revolution. The public and the authorities elided the two eras in their association of the Decembrists with Chénier.[3]

Pushkin's closeness to the Decembrists has long been noted by scholars according to their own political agendas, be it conservative or liberal: to promote an image of Pushkin as a nascent revolutionary or as a staunch monarchist, to illustrate a change in the poet's political values after the revolt, or to make Pushkin's oeuvre ideologically correct for popular consumption. My concern here will be to pinpoint how and when Pushkin became co-opted by the critics as the Decembrists' supporter.

Pushkin's Biography

After the uprising, Pushkin immediately came under suspicion of membership in the secret society because of his close personal ties to many Decembrists. His childhood friends Pushchin and Kiukhelbeker, whom he knew from the Lycée at Tsarskoe Selo, participated in the Senate Square revolt. Pushkin also knew Alexander Bestuzhev and Ryleev because of their publishing ventures. Their almanac, *Polar Star* (*Poliarnaia zvezda*), included some of Pushkin's poetry, most notably, *The Gypsies* (*Tsygany,* 1824). They maintained a regular correspondence regarding literature and criticism. While in civil service in Kishinev, Pushkin was friendly with the so-called First Decembrist, Vladimir Raevskii, whom Pushkin supposedly warned about his imminent arrest in 1822. Pushkin became acquainted with the brothers Nikolai and Alexander Raevskii (unrelated to Vladimir), who introduced him to Southern Society members while he was in exile. Through them he met Pestel, Ivan Iakushkin, Vasilii Davydov, Prince Alexander Odoevskii, General Mikhail Orlov, and Prince Sergei Volkonskii at Davydov's estate in Kamenka. Though he was never included in their meetings, he was part of the general company, as was the renowned General N. N. Raevskii, father of the aforementioned Raevskii brothers.

In his memoirs, Iakushkin described one gathering, where he and other society members attempted to convince the elder Raevskii that they did not belong to a secret society. During a debate on a

secret society's hypothetical usefulness, Pushkin warmly championed its benefits. Speaking of the impossibility of its existence in
Russia, Iakushkin tricked the senior Raevskii into admitting that had
a secret society already existed, he would belong. After proffering
his hand to Raevskii to join, Iakushkin then claimed he was jok-
ing. Iakushkin describes Pushkin's crestfallen response: "The others
laughed...except Pushkin, who was agitated; first he was certain that
either a secret society existed or that it would begin there and he
would be a member; but when he saw that this only came to a joke,
he stood blushing, and said with tears in his eyes: 'I have never been
as unhappy as I am now; I already saw my life ennobled and a lofty
aim before me, and it was all a mean joke.' At that moment he was
quite wonderful."[4]

The Kamenka gathering has become immortalized in later legends
of Pushkin's esteem for the Decembrists. It also spurred speculations
about Pushkin's knowledge of the secret society's existence. Pushchin
addresses this question in his reminiscences when he posits two reasons for not telling Pushkin about the secret society. First, Pushkin's
light-mindedness deterred him: "The question unwillingly arose: why,
besides me, did none of our older members who were closely acquainted
with him ever think about it? That means what stopped them was the
same thing that frightened me: the manner of his thoughts was well
known to everyone, however there wasn't complete trust in him."[5]
Pushkin's purpose in Russian culture arises as the second. Pushchin
propagates the legend that Pushkin's poetic talent kept the Decembrists
from engaging him in their cause. Pondering Pushkin's untimely death,
Pushchin speculated: "What would have happened to Pushkin, if I
had drawn him into our union and if he experienced a life completely
different from the one that fell to his lot?...Only after his death did all
these seemingly trivial circumstances take on the appearance of providence, which, saving him from our destiny, preserved the poet for
Russia's glory."[6]

Iakushkin treats the question of Pushkin's membership differently in
his memoirs. He recounts Pushkin's farewell to Alexandra Muravieva,
Nikita Muraviev's wife, who left for Siberia in 1827 to join her exiled
husband: "Pushkin said to her: 'I well understand why these gentlemen
did not want to take me into their society: I did not deserve that
honor.'"[7] Iakushkin acknowledges Pushkin's ardor for revolutionary
causes while also showing an awareness of Pushkin's mercurial nature.
Iakushkin suggests that Pushkin was conscious of the shortcomings
preventing the Decembrists from accepting him into their group, and

highlights Pushkin's admiration to counter the prevailing view that it was shameful to be associated with the Decembrists.

Perhaps more damning than his personal ties to the Decembrists was the presence of his incendiary verses—his ode "Liberty" ("Vol'nost'," 1817), "The Village" ("Derevnia," 1819), "The Dagger" ("Kinzhal," 1821) and others—among most conspirators' papers. In a letter to Pushkin, Zhukovskii commiserates: "It is true that you are not implicated in anything. But your verses were found in the papers of each of those who acted. It's a bad way to make friends with the government."[8] The situation worsened with the anonymous distribution (in July and August 1826) of the aforementioned excerpt of "André Chénier," attached to a copy of Ryleev's famous letter to his wife written on the eve of his execution.[9] Taken out of context and previously unknown because of censorship restrictions, the verses were read by the public as a direct statement of sympathy for the Decembrist revolt when they were disseminated after the execution.

Pushkin's involvement with the secret society greatly concerned the imperial authorities. On September 4, 1826, Pushkin was summoned from Mikhailovskoe exile and conveyed under guard to Moscow to account for himself. On September 8, Nicholas questioned him personally. To the question of whether he would have participated in the revolt, had he been in Petersburg, he purportedly responded: "Certainly, my lord, all my friends were in the conspiracy and I could not have not participated. Only absence saved me, for which I thank God!" This account and other variations came to light as Pushkin's contemporaries began publishing their memoirs in the late 1860s. F. F. Vigel, Ia. K. Grot, Baron Korf, P. V. Nashchokin, and M. M. Popov, a bureaucrat in the Third Section, added to or confirmed the tale.[10] Pushkin's friends M. P. Pogodin and Prince P. A. Viazemskii, provided a colorful story regarding his absence from the square. Pushkin allegedly told them that on hearing of Alexander I's death, he planned to travel incognito from Mikhailovskoe to Petersburg, but turned back after a hare crossed his path. Being superstitious, Pushkin decided that it was a bad omen. Both Pogodin and Viazemskii affirm that had he been in Petersburg, Pushkin would have planned and participated in the revolt.[11] These apocrypha, given a new life in print, shed more light on Pushkin's involvement with the Decembrists, since their close friendship and sympathy was not well-known among the general public after the revolt's suppression.

Pushkin's unexpected meeting with Kiukhelbeker while the latter was on his way to Siberia also became part of the oral tradition.

Pushkin had stopped at a station outside of Borovichi on October 15, 1827, and noticed three troikas conveying arrested men approaching the station. He decided to see who the military police was escorting and went outside. Kiukhelbeker was among the prisoners and recognized Pushkin before Pushkin realized it was he: "We fell into each other's embrace. The gendarmes dragged us apart. The courier took me by the arm with threats and a curse—I didn't hear him. Kiukhelbeker felt faint. The gendarmes gave him water, seated him in the carriage and galloped away.... At the next station I discovered that they were taking him from Schlisselburg—but where to?" (12: 307).[12] Pushkin memorialized this meeting in his diary rather than in a public medium. The excerpt was published with other biographical materials only in 1876.[13]

These personal anecdotes counteracted Pushkin's image as a political opportunist and a supporter of the autocracy, which had become common currency due to his poem "Stanzas" ("Stansy," 1826) and his treatise "On National Education" ("O narodnom vospitanii," 1827). In "Stanzas" Pushkin made the implicit connection between the Decembrists and the Streltsy and Peter I and Nicholas. Alternately viewed by readers depending on their ideological beliefs as an appeal for mercy or as pandering to the autocracy, the poem serves as a turning point in Pushkin's oeuvre. This sense of radical change of Pushkin's orientation was confirmed in his treatise "On Popular Education," when he stated: "One must hope that the people who shared the views of the conspirators have returned to their senses; that on the one hand, they have realized the futility of their aims and means, and on the other, the boundless power of the government established by the force of circumstances" (12: 298). Thus Pushkin's nonfiction further reiterated what many saw as his capitulation to the government and his appearance as the autocracy's faithful supporter.

Pushkin's Poetry

Pushkin's works published after the uprising shy from direct reference to the Decembrists, though during certain periods of the composition of *Eugene Onegin* (*Evgenii Onegin*, 1823–1831) and *Poltava* (1828) they were not far from his mind. Manuscripts from 1826–1827 bear witness to this fact: on them Pushkin doodled scaffolds with five hanged bodies and several profiles of his Decembrist friends. One sketch of a scaffold on the upper portion of the page had the inscription: "I also could have hung, like a buffoon."[14] (See Figure 1.)

Figure 1 Alexander Pushkin, sketch of the executed Decembrists on the margins of the manuscript of *Poltava* (1828), PD 836, l. 37.

References to hanging recur in his works after 1826, indicating that the revolt and the execution shook the foundations of his world.[15]

Pushkin's "Epistle to Siberia" ("Poslanie v Sibir'," written in 1827 but first published in 1874) emerges as the primary example of Pushkin's continued esteem. Written for the Decembrists' eyes only, the poem clearly states his empathy. Along with a poem dedicated to Pushchin, "My first friend" ("Moi pervyi drug," 1827, published in 1839), it was conveyed to Siberia by Alexandra Muravieva in 1827. The epistle simultaneously picks up on several images used by the Decembrists in their own poetry and anticipates future images for their myth. Many of Pushkin's phrases resurface in writings about the Decembrists as signal words (*slova-signaly*).[16] I cite the poem here in its entirety:

> Во глубине сибирских руд
> Храните гордое терпение.
> Не пропадет ваш скорбный труд
> И дум высокое стремление.
> Несчастью верная сестра,
> Надежда в мрачном подземелье
> Разбудит бодрость и веселье,
> Придет желанная пора:
> Любовь и дружество до вас
> Дойдут сквозь мрачные затворы,
> Как в ваши каторжные норы
> Доходит мой свободный глас.
> Оковы тяжкие падут,
> Темницы рухнут—и свобода
> Вас примет радостно у входа,
> И братья меч вам отдадут. (3: 49)

In the depths of Siberian mines maintain your proud forbearance. Your grim labor and the lofty striving of your thoughts will not be lost. Faithful sister to unhappiness, hope will rouse your courage and cheer in the gloomy dungeon. The desired time will come: Love and friendship will come to you through the gloomy bars as my free voice comes to your convict burrows. The burdensome fetters will fall, the dungeons will collapse—and freedom will gladly welcome you at the entrance, and your brothers will return the sword to you.

Pushkin portrays himself as a lone "free voice," emphasizing the distance between him and the Decembrists while also confirming their solidarity and promising the future success of their cause. The poem's opening line and other phrases—the lofty striving of thoughts, proud forbearance, faithful sister to unhappiness—resonate throughout later works, and frequently serve as titles for twentieth-century critical and historical works about the Decembrists.

In response to Pushkin's missive, the Decembrist poet Alexander Odoevskii composed a poem (from 1828 or 1829) further developing Pushkin's imagery:

> Струн вещих пламенные звуки
> До слуха нашего дошли,
> К мечам рванулись наши руки,
> И—лишь оковы обрели.
> Но будь покоен, бард! –цепями,
> Своей судьбой гордимся мы,
> И за затворами тюрьмы
> В душе смеемся над царями.
> Наш скорбный труд не пропадет,
> Из искры возгорится пламя,
> И просвещенный наш народ
> Сберется под святое знамя.
> Мечи скуем мы из цепей
> И пламя вновь зажжем свободы!
> Она награнет на царей,
> И радостно вздохнет народы!

The fiery sounds of prophetic strings reached our hearing, our hands grabbed for our swords, but found only fetters. But be at peace, bard! We are proud of our chains and our fate, and behind prison bars in our souls we laugh at the tsars. Our grim labor will not be lost, the flame flares from the spark, and our enlightened people will gather beneath the holy banner. We will forge swords from chains and again will light the fire of freedom! It will descend on the tsars and the people will breathe joyously!

Odoevskii echoes Pushkin's choice of imagery—grim labor, sword, fetters, bars—enhancing his portrayal of the Decembrists as dedicated freedom fighters. Bestowing prophetic qualities on Pushkin, Odoevskii depicts his cohort as men of endurance and conviction who are certain of their self-sacrifice's utility.

Only much later did scholars examine Pushkin's oeuvre for sympathy toward the Decembrists. In 1899, the centennial year of Pushkin's birth, the Pushkinist V. E. Iakushkin, grandson of the Decembrist, published a series of essays in which he examines the strong ties between the poet and the Decembrists. First to tackle their complex personal and artistic relationship, Iakushkin is also the first to explore Pushkin's poetry for references to his exiled and executed friends. Iakushkin cites the poem "My first friend" as literary evidence for Pushkin and Pushchin's close bond and elaborates the important moments of Pushkin's past relationship with the group: his grandfather's account of the Kamenka meeting, the reunion with Kiukhelbeker, the poem "19 October 1827," dedicated to the Lycée, and the epistle to Siberia. Iakushkin adds the poem "Arion," written on July 16, 1827 and published anonymously the same year in *The Northern Lyre* (*Severnaia lira*) to the list of Pushkin's "Decembrist" works. The poem invokes the ancient Greek legend of the singer Arion who through a combination of luck and cleverness escapes from his pursuers by singing to them. Asserting that the poem was inspired by the first anniversary of the Decembrists' execution, Iakushkin reads it as Pushkin's credo as "singer of the Decembrists": "He was the only singer of those ideas lying at the foundation of the social movement of the twenties and the secret societies' activity. The catastrophe of December 14 swallowed up the progressive people, the singer survived, the storm spared him by chance."[17]

In such an interpretation, Iakushkin and subsequent scholars emphasize the thirteenth line ("I sing the same hymns") as the poem's central moment. They suggest that it was Pushkin's attempt to show continued support, despite his new strategy of praising Nicholas's government in his literary works. Seeking to clear Pushkin of harsh charges of opportunism, Iakushkin further discusses Pushkin's political pragmatism: "It [the catastrophe] immediately revealed to him a plan for his future action, determined those means by which he could support and spread those ideas left to him by his ruined friends . . . he immediately, almost at the minute of the catastrophe, understood the role which stood before him."[18] This new evaluation coincided with the 1899 centennial of Pushkin's birth, which projected Pushkin's image as "the anointed poet of Holy Russia."[19] Iakushkin alone proclaimed Pushkin's political radicalism in contrast to the tsarist government's appropriation of Pushkin as a national symbol. For his stance Iakushkin was persecuted and sent into internal exile by tsarist authorities.[20]

A. L. Slonimskii echoes Iakushkin's analysis in his article "Pushkin and the Decembrist Movement" included in the distinguished scholar S. A. Vengerov's complete edition of Pushkin's works published in 1908. Slonimskii discusses Pushkin's personal ties and political beliefs, providing the same apocrypha regarding Pushkin's desire to join the secret society and Pushkin's testimony to the tsar. He also cites the same poems in support of Pushkin's involvement with the secret society. Slonimskii's reiteration of Iakushkin's arguments stems from the same desire to defend Pushkin from accusations of opportunism. Yet, Slonimskii adds a twist by asserting that Pushkin's political views had not changed: "There was no break at all—there was an evolution, and its beginning arose by 1823. Pushkin of the Nikolaevan epoch is the former Pushkin, 'the devotee of truth and freedom.'"[21] Both articles rehabilitate Pushkin for a reading public with a less conservative political orientation. From 1899 to 1917, more scholars moved away from norms established by mid-nineteenth-century scholarship, which perceived that Pushkin wrote poetry for poetry's sake. Interestingly, this politicization of Pushkin's oeuvre on the one hand coincided with the Symbolist reclamation of his purely aesthetic orientation on the other.

Greater access to archival documents in the twentieth century opened the field for more critical labor. New documents came to light as the century progressed, providing insight into Pushkin's complicated relationship with both the tsarist government and the Decembrists. With these discoveries came additions to the list of Pushkin's "Decembrist" works, including Pushkin's masterpieces *Eugene Onegin* and *The Bronze Horseman* (*Mednyi vsadnik*, 1833, published posthumously in 1837).

Attention to *Onegin* as a key text came after previously unknown verses depicting the Decembrists were found in the fragmentary tenth chapter of the poem (stanzas XIV–XVII) in 1910.[22] In the fragment, Pushkin places himself among the conspirators' meetings. He mentions Mikhail Lunin's "decisive measures" (XV), Iakushkin's "regicidal dagger" bared (XV), Pestel who "gathered his army" against tyrants (XVI). In the reconstructed seventeenth stanza, Pushkin diminishes the meetings' seriousness at first:

> Сначала эти заговоры
> Между Лафитом и Клико
> Лишь были дружеские споры,
> И не входила глубоко
> В сердца мятежная наука,
> Все это было только скука,
> Безделье молодых умов,
> Забавы взрослых шалунов,
> Казалось......................
> Узлы к узлам................

И постепенно сетью тайной
Россия.....................
Наш царь дремал..........
.... (6: 525–526)

At first these conspiracies between the Lafitte and Cliquot were only friendly debates and rebellion's science did not enter deeply into their hearts. All this was only boredom, the idleness of young minds, the amusements of grown-up rascals, it seemed....Knots to knots...And gradually with a secret net...Russia....Our tsar slumbered...

By the end, Pushkin hints at the serious turn toward revolutionary, perhaps even regicidal, action. The critical legend arose that Pushkin intended to make Onegin a Decembrist in a later work because of this stanza and other anecdotal information. According to one source, Pushkin purportedly told his brother Lev, "Onegin either must die in the Caucasus or fall into the ranks of the Decembrists."[23]

Critics also viewed Pushkin's *Bronze Horseman* as a veiled allusion to the Decembrists. Though Vissarion Belinsky, Valerii Briusov, and Vladislav Khodasevich already discussed the various kinds of revolt to which Pushkin alluded, in the 1920s Andrei Belyi and Dmitrii Blagoi openly made the connection between Evgenii's challenge to Peter I and the Decembrists' uprising at his statue's base.[24] The Decembrist centennial brought these critical interpretations to the forefront of literary scholarship.

Partly because of his biography, partly because of his poetry, Pushkin figures largely in the Decembrist myth, propagating their image as heroes striving for a lofty cause. Russian literary criticism reflected society's increasing political liberalism due to the lessening of censorship after the 1905 Revolt. As interest increased in the Decembrists' memoirs during this period, an upsurge of publications on Pushkin and the Decembrists also occurred. The number of articles dedicated to this topic grew steadily into the Soviet period, when Decembrist scholarship exploded into an industry.

Alexander Griboedov's Chatskii as a Decembrist

The author Alexander Griboedov also attracted the authorities' attention because of his ties to the Decembrists. According to testimony of Trubetskoi and Ryleev, among others, Griboedov belonged to the Northern Society, though he denied membership upon questioning. Arrested in January 1826 and held until June, he was released with an attestation of innocence, the return of his former rank and his yearly salary as part of the diplomatic corps. He was sent back to the Caucasus as a member of General Paskevich's suite and was killed in Teheran shortly after becoming Russian minister to Persia.[25]

Griboedov's *Woe from Wit* (*Gore ot uma*, written from 1820–1824, first published in 1833) has been read retroactively as a text sympathetic to the Decembrists. The Decembrists thought highly of Griboedov's play, which they heard at various literary evenings in Moscow and Petersburg from 1824–1825. Several Decembrists aided in the recopying and distribution of the play in its earliest form. Decembrist D. I. Zavalishin reminisces that he wrote out a full copy from dictation while in Moscow at Odoevskii's apartment.[26] Griboedov's play reached Pushkin in exile at Mikhailovskoe when Pushchin visited him in January 1825. Pushchin recalls in his memoirs: "I brought Pushkin *Woe from Wit* as a present. He was satisfied with this comedy, in manuscript, which was until that time almost completely unknown to him."[27]

The Decembrists made a public show of their support, engaging in polemics after excerpts of *Woe from Wit* were published in *Russian Thalia* (*Russkaia Taliia*, 1824).[28] Alexander Bestuzhev felt genuine sympathy for Chatskii and highly approved of his unusual behavior: "That noble indignation toward everything base, that proud daring in Chatskii's person pierced me to the depths of my soul."[29] Bestuzhev viewed the play as a "lively picture of Muscovite mores" and asserted that the critics denigrated because they were insulted by its truthful portrayal.[30] Though Pushkin enjoyed the play, he did not admire the hero: "Everything he says is very smart. But to whom does he say all this? To Famusov? To Skalozub? At the ball to the Muscovite grandmothers? To Molchalin? It is unforgivable. The first sign of an intelligent man is to know from the first glance with whom he is dealing" (13: 138). In response to other detractors, the critics Orest Somov and Vladimir Odoevskii affirmed Chatskii's intelligence and patriotism. The long-reigning Soviet historian of Decembrism M. V. Nechkina, asserted that the Decembrists saw in Chatskii someone who was of the same mind as they.[31] More important, several Decembrists include Griboedov's play among readings that led them to "free-thinking" and liberal ideas when asked by the Investigative Commission.[32]

Though the play had great success during and after the polemics of 1825, it was largely ignored or viewed negatively by Russian critics until the 1860s. In the foreign press, Herzen was the first to call Chatskii a Decembrist in his article "The New Phase of Russian Literature" (1864): "The image of Chatskii, unhappy, not knowing what to do with himself in his irony, quivering from indignation and devoted to a dreamy idealism, will appear at the last moment of Alexander I's reign, on the eve of the uprising on St. Isaac's square. This is the Decembrist, the man who crowns the epoch of Peter I and tries to see, at least on the horizon, the promised land..."[33] Herzen developed a Russian literary genealogy: "Chatskii is his [Onegin's] older brother. Lermontov's 'Hero of Our Time' is his younger brother" (18: 184), a lineage expanded upon in subsequent literary studies. Apollon Grigoriev, Fyodor Dostoevsky, and Vasilii Kliuchevskii shared Herzen's association of Chatskii with the Decembrists, and disseminated this interpretation in the Russian press.[34]

Perceptions of Chatskii changed in relation to political stance: the more conservative the reader, the more negative their assessment, as Dostoevsky illustrates. In 1863, Dostoevsky remarks: "Chatskii did very well to slip away then again abroad; had he dawdled a bit, he would have ended up in the east and not the west."[35] Associating the literary character with the Decembrists, Dostoevsky elides their fates. At this point, Dostoevsky emphasizes Chatskii's "Russianness" in contrast to other critics, who maintained he was a representative of Western culture: "Chatskii is a type completely particular to our Russian Europe, a dear type, inspired, suffering, appealing both to Russia and to the soil, but meanwhile he nevertheless went back to Europe when it was necessary to find 'a corner for one's hurt feelings.' In one word, a type now completely useless though at one time terribly useful" (5: 61–62). Dostoevsky's condemnation indicates a lack of sympathy for Chatskii's type (that is, the Decembrist), despite his ironic characterization of it as "dear." Thus Dostoevsky sees Chatskii's defects: "his isolation from the people, and his dissatisfaction arising out of his current situation, the striving to change it which is marked for failure."[36] Though Chatskii appeared "attached to the soil," the fact that he quits Russia indicates his alienation and negates any positive characteristics. This perception signals the growing centrality of the Russian soil (*pochvennichestvo*) in Dostoevsky's thinking. For Dostoevsky, Chatskii reflects the problem common to the intelligentsia and elite: a spiritually dangerous separation from the virtues of the Russian people and soil.

In 1870, Dostoevsky further disparaged Chatskii:

Chatskii, like a genuine fool, did not understand to what extent he was stupid.... He was a lord and landowner, and for him, except for his circle nothing existed. So he comes to such despair with Moscow's high society life, exactly as if there is not other life in Russia. He looked past the Russian people like all our progressive people.... The more progressive the lord the greater his hate, not for Russian order, but for the Russian people. He thinks about the Russian people...as he would about an article on taxes. The Decembrists thought exactly the same, as did the poets, the professors, the liberals and all the reformers up to the tsar-liberator.[37]

Dostoevsky's negative reaction results from a growing concern with Russian realities after Alexander II's reforms (which abolished serfdom) and with increased revolutionary activity. Dostoevsky thus consigns Chatskii to the dust heap of literary and revolutionary history as someone who no longer is useful. Despite his consistent association of Chatskii and the Decembrists, Dostoevsky's assessment was more complex; elsewhere he called the Decembrists "the best people" (*liudshie liudi*) and venerated their wives, whom he met while imprisoned in Siberia and to whom he wrote throughout his life.[38]

The Mythologizers—Alexander Herzen, Nikolai Ogarev, and Nikolai Nekrasov

Margaret Ziolkowski draws attention to the Decembrists' canonization in radical and liberal circles because of their own writings and "the concerted propagandistic efforts of Herzen and Ogarev."[39] Numerous scholars call Herzen the primary mythmaker of the Decembrists. Herzen's publication of the Decembrists' memoirs increased the European and Russian reading public's interest in their lives and fates. Yet Herzen's influence did not end there; his own writing also shaped the myth.

Herzen's assessments of the Decembrists span the length of his career, culminating in his memoir, *My Past and Thoughts* (*Byloe i dumy*, 1852–1868), his most influential work on the Decembrists and a literary masterpiece in its own right.[40] In *My Past and Thoughts*, Herzen adumbrates much of his philosophical, emotional, and political development to justify what he became later: a mature and disillusioned revolutionary. Throughout the text, he plots his own historical personality in relation to the Decembrists, reevaluating his life's milestones.

Herzen initially locates his feelings for revolutionary activity in a complex of romantic associations with Schiller in the foreground. Martin Malia posits that Schiller's focus on art, friendship, and love as the only true path to liberty made Schiller so attractive to Herzen, and sees Schiller's heroes as "the primary symbols for [Herzen's] own endless fantasies of self-fulfillment and emancipation."[41] Herzen's longtime friend and editorial collaborator, Nikolai Ogarev also remarked on the seminal role Schiller played in their childhood and adolescence, juxtaposing Schiller and the Decembrists: "I cannot help pausing upon several paramount features, because even in my adolescent reasoning I recall those moments of sublime pleasure which influenced all my later development. Thus, I cannot forget the first impressions which shook me profoundly (and, also you)—that is to say, the reading of Schiller and Rousseau and the Fourteenth of December. Under these three influences, so similar to one another, we accomplished our transition from childhood to adolescence."[42] Ogarev suggests that the Decembrists—along with Schiller and Rousseau, both quintessential representatives of Romanticism—spurred his and Herzen's maturation.

Herzen also links Schiller and the Decembrists: "From the Moor sneaking with his dagger in his sleeve to 'free the city from the tyrant' [Schiller's Die Burgschaft], from Wilhelm Tell waiting for [Governor] Foch...it was easy to pass to December 14 and to Nicholas. These thoughts and convergences were not new to Nick [Ogarev]; he also knew Pushkin's and Ryleev's unpublished poems" (8: 79). The youths formed their friendship on their love for Schiller and his noble heroes. They then transferred their veneration onto the closest living examples, the Decembrists. Herzen even calls Ryleev "The Schiller of the Decembrists," highlighting their similarity as "poets of liberty."[43] Here Herzen confuses Schiller with his characters, much as contemporaries conflated Ryleev with his own literary creations. Herzen then transfers his particular notion of Schiller onto Ryleev, who already had been transformed into a literary persona as part of the Decembrists' mythogenesis.

Malia points out that in Schiller's plays "the edge of revolt is always blunted by an ambiguous longing for reconciliation with authority, and in the end rebellion is invariably punished by failure."[44] Herzen alludes to the heroes' romantic appeal:

Schiller remained our favorite. The characters of his dramas were living persons for us; we examined them, loved and hated them,

not as poetic creations but as living men. Besides we saw ourselves
in them.... My ideal was Karl Moor, but I soon betrayed him
and went over to the Marquis of Posa. In a hundred variations I
devised how I would speak to Nicholas, and how afterwards he
would send me to the mines or to execution. It is a strange thing
that almost all our reveries ended in Siberia or in execution and
hardly ever in victory; can this be the tendency of Russian fantasy,
or is it the reflection of Petersburg with its five gallows and penal
servitude on the young generation? (8: 84)

The Decembrists' self-sacrifice to a noble cause, subsequent failure and,
in some cases, appeasement of the authorities echoed Schiller's motifs.
Herzen and Ogarev proceed further, conflating art and life in their
own lives. Herzen dwells on his impressionable character to show the
full impact of Schiller's lofty ideals and the Decembrists' deeds. He
mentions his childhood role-playing and daydreams to give insight into
his highly emotional, romantic character. Herzen imagines heroic failure as a grand event from reading Schiller. He then transposes the
doomed image onto his imaginings of a future confrontation with
Nicholas, projecting his future career as an opponent of despotism and
tyranny. These readings and daydreams of failed revolt marked him
for his future role as an activist. The hero's evolution in *My Past and
Thoughts* illustrates this progression from unaware youth to opponent
of autocracy.

References to the Decembrists permeate Herzen's text on the levels
of both form and content: the Decembrists' image perceived through
Herzen's romantic idealism shapes the way he writes as well as the
elements he emphasizes in his autobiography. Beyond serving as a deep
structure for the plot, Herzen's view of the Decembrists also influences his self-creation as an evolving revolutionary.[45] In his portrayal
of societal reaction to the uprising, Herzen conceives of Russian history as before and after December 14, 1825. The world before attains
a prelapserian glow and evokes a feeling of the golden age, whereas
the world after exudes a morally bankrupt atmosphere: "The tone of
society changed before one's eyes; a rapid moral fall served as a sad
indication of how little developed was the feeling of personal dignity
among the Russian aristocracy" (8: 58).[46] Herzen also vividly portrays
his reaction to the uprising and its aftermath:

The stories of the revolt and of the trial...deeply impressed me;
a new world was revealed to me which became more the focus of

my moral existence. I do not know how it happened, but having
little understanding, or only a confused one, of what it meant, I
felt I was not on the side of the grapeshot and victory, prisons and
chains. Pestel and his associates' execution definitively awoke the
childish dream of my soul. (8: 61)

The event serves as a rite of passage for him, awakening his still unclear
moral and political consciousness and bringing him into the adult
world. Herzen becomes an initiate into a new realm, entering into a
liminal phase, much as Turner describes the rites of passage from childhood to adulthood. At this point he begins his real education, clandestinely reading copies of Pushkin's and Ryleev's forbidden poems and
histories of the French Revolution.

Before publishing the above account, Herzen recounted his reaction during the religious service celebrated by Nicholas in Moscow
in his journal *The Polar Star* (1855), named after the Decembrists'
almanac:

A boy of fourteen lost in the crowd, I was at that service, and
there before that altar defiled by bloody prayer, I swore to avenge
the executed men, and dedicated myself to the struggle with that
throne, with that altar, with those cannons. I have not avenged
them: the Guards and throne, the altar and the cannons all remain,
but for thirty years I have stood under that banner, which I have
not once abandoned.[47]

The journal featured an engraving of the executed Decembrists, which
became central to revolutionary iconography (see Figure 2).[48] It is not
unusual for a young person to be profoundly moved by a shocking
experience and to profess his dedication to a noble cause. However,
it strains the imagination to believe that Herzen was as politically
conscious and militant as he suggests. In *My Past and Thoughts* Herzen
later emphasizes the vagueness of his political rebellion at fourteen:
"Though political dreams absorbed me day and night, my notions were
not distinguished by any particular insight; they were so contradictory
that I actually imagined that the goal of the Petersburg revolt was,
among other things, to put Constantine on the throne, having limited
his power" (8: 63). Herzen recreates his unclear adolescent thinking,
without forgetting his goal: to show he was destined for a special role
in the revolutionary movement as an adult.

Figure 2 Frontispiece to the first issue of Alexander Herzen's journal *The Polar Star* (1855) with profiles of Pestel, Ryleev, Bestuzhev-Riumin, Muraviev-Apostol, and Kakhovskii.

Herzen's political awakening culminates in the scene of the oath-swearing on Sparrow Hills. The vow, taken under direct influence of Schiller's *Don Carlos,* confirms Herzen and Ogarev's dedication to the political cause begun by the Decembrists. There Herzen and Ogarev, at age 15, "stood, leaned against each other, and suddenly embracing, swore an oath in sight of all Moscow to sacrifice our lives to the struggle we had chosen" (8: 81). This political dedication entered their minds only after their experience of the Decembrist uprising and their reading of Rousseau, Schiller, and Pushkin's and Ryleev's poetry. Not only does Herzen attribute his political awakening to the Decembrists' suppression, but he also looks to them as models for his future path in life. He aspires to emulate their struggle with the autocratic system. His emotional reaction to their fates serves as the spur for his political and moral development. In the "Herzen myth" the Sparrow Hills scene became the focal moment of the birth of Herzen's political consciousness. Herzen proclaims that the site became sacred to him and Ogarev, "a place of worship," which they would visit once or twice a year. In a letter from 1833, Ogarev designates Herzen as their myth's chronicler: "Write how in this place [Sparrow Hills] the story of our lives, yours and mine, began to unfold" (8: 82). Herzen grants the Decembrists an enormous role in his own myth while also creating theirs. Both stories becomes inextricably intertwined so that Herzen becomes both the Decembrists' follower and narrator, thus insuring their remembrance through his own words and deeds. Although the primary text develops Herzen as a revolutionary hero, it resonates with the Decembrists' subtext.

After his initial forays into political activism, Herzen depicts his arrest and exile by tsarist authorities in 1834 as a holy moment: "This first persecution was to serve as our ordination" (8: 184). He uses the religiously charged term "ordination" to signify the value of political suffering. Herzen finally enters the ranks of those martyrs, the Decembrists, with whom he now shares the common experience of persecution by an unjust government, suffering for a political cause, harsh imprisonment and exile's difficulties. Herzen evaluates his success as authority's challenger according to the Decembrists' examples. Ironically, his success repeats their failure; both Herzen and the Decembrists end up in prison without having changed the system. Herzen emerges from the liminal phase of initiatory education to his new role as a tested activist.

Recounting his relationship with Mikhail Orlov, a founding member of the Union of Welfare who later left the secret society, Herzen reveals as much about himself as Orlov. Herzen warmly discusses their affinity: "He saw in me a rising possibility; I saw in him a veteran of our opinions, a friend of our heroes, a noble figure in our life" (8: 176). Though Herzen acknowledges Orlov's heroism and nobility, he highlights his pathetic grandeur, calling him "a lion in a cage:" "Everywhere he knocked himself against the bars; he had no space to move nor cause, and thirst for activity consumed him" (8: 177). Herzen shows awareness of Orlov's difficult position as a man with noble aspirations in a society that did not value free-thinking and initiative. Describing his final meeting with Orlov six years after their first acquaintance, he compares Orlov to a statue of a dying lion (8: 178). Herzen filters the event through his own experience as an exiled revolutionary, compressing narrative time to reevaluate this past event according to recent experience. As if still sitting before the statue, he reflects on Orlov's tragedy with the benefit of new understanding. Perhaps he also reinterprets Orlov's tragedy through his own. Orlov was rendered politically impotent while remaining in Russia. Though politically influential through his journalism, Herzen finds himself abroad, isolated from Russian society, ineffective as a guiding force to new Russian revolutionaries of the later 1860s.

Herzen criticized the contemporary Russian radicals' misperception of the Decembrists (exemplified by Dmitrii Pisarev, who proclaimed the tenets of nihilism) in "Bazarov Once Again" (1868):

> The type of that time, one of the most splendid types is the *Decembrist*, and not Onegin. Russian literature could not touch upon him for a full forty years, but he did not become less because of this. How could the young generation lack the clear perception, tact, and heart to understand all the greatness, all the strength of these brilliant youths emerging from the ranks of the guards, these favorites of the elites and wealth, who left behind their drawing rooms and their piles of gold in demand of human rights, in protest, for a declaration for which—and they knew this—the executioner's noose and prison labor awaited them? It is a sad riddle. (20, 1: 341)

Herzen valorizes the Decembrists' dedication to a lost cause and their social reversal from noblemen to political prisoners. By drawing attention to this reversal, he alludes to their sacral quality as paramount.

By postulating the Decembrist (though which one, he does not specify) as a genuine historical type, Herzen erases their individual personality traits and differences. Herzen concentrates upon the importance of the Decembrists as a symbol: a collective striving for a higher cause and willing to sacrifice everything to attain its goal. Herzen again conflates art and life by equating the Decembrists with literary characters and places them on the same plane as Onegin and Bazarov. Remaking their historical personalities into literary types, he creates a fictionalized history in which they become major characters. In *My Past and Thoughts* and his literary criticism, Herzen allows the Decembrists to transcend the boundaries of history to become the historical personality types of the 1820s. If, as Ginzburg asserts, Herzen's sense of history is the "shared awareness of a common past,"[49] then here he establishes a revolutionary pantheon upon which generations of activists can draw as a source of inspiration: "The Decembrists are our great fathers.... We received from the Decembrists an awakened feeling of human worth, a striving for independence, a hatred for slavery, a respect for the West and revolution, a faith in the possibility of revolution in Russia, passionate desire to participate in it, a youthfulness and a reserve of strength" (20, 1: 346). Herzen not only preserves a record of that common past to which later revolutionary activists refer but also makes himself the Decembrists' direct descendant.

Ogarev also participated in the mythologization of the Decembrists, though secondary to Herzen. Like Herzen, Ogarev viewed himself as the Decembrists' descendant and idealized them. In his mythologization of the Decembrists, Ogarev valorizes two elements: their *podvig* (moral feat) and the executed Decembrists' image. Ogarev employs religious terminology in his early depictions of the Decembrists, calling the Decembrists "holy sufferers" (l. 38) in his poem "I saw you, newcomers of far lands" ("Ia videl vas, prishel'tsy dalnykh stran," 1838). In "From the Other Shore" ("S togo berega," 1858), he weeps "for the martyrs for the righteous / the saints of holy freedom" (ll. 107–108).[50]

The poem "In Memory of Ryleev" ("Pamiati Ryleeva," 1859) illustrates the apotheosis of Ogarev's mythogenic production. Ogarev glorifies Ryleev's "willing exploit" (*svobodnyi podvig*), an important thematic for later mythmakers. Ogarev appears to be the first to employ the term *podvig* referring to the Decembrists' action, casting their deed in a religious or moral light. Ogarev shifts his earlier focus from the executed Decembrists to Ryleev in particular, who provides a living link to Ogarev in spirit and aims: "Ryleev was my first light... / You, my father related to me in spirit. / In this world your name / Became my valiant testament / And guiding star" (ll.21–25).[51] By calling Ryleev his father, Ogarev affirms his legitimacy as a poet and a revolutionary activist. Though earlier he was a "the Decembrists' child," here he posits his direct spiritual descent from Ryleev alone. Moreover, Ogarev designates himself as heir and keeper of Ryleev's poetic legacy: "We will wrest your verse from oblivion, / And on the first free Russian day, / In view of the young generation, / We will resurrect your suffering shade for worship" (ll.26–30). Ogarev posits Ryleev as a poet-martyr worthy of veneration for literary and revolutionary activities, promising: "Your willing feat will be / a sacred object in the people's memory" (1.38–39).

The vivid picture of the five Decembrists on the gallows dominates Ogarev's poetry. In "Matvei Radaev" (1856–1858) the execution receives a passing mention: "The trial is finished—and five / Were hanged, all in strong spirit / They hanged them quietly / You know, just as the sun was rising / So as not to rouse rumor" (ll. 2.247–51, 623–624). In "Confessions of a Superfluous Man" ("Ispovedi lish-nego cheloveka," 1858–1859), the event takes on greater personal significance: "And the living memory still moved me / Of the five hanged men, / My life was constructed along their path, / I was called to work for freedom / And to triumph, or to fall gloriously" (698). "In Memory of Ryleev" also features the execution scene: "Here are the five hanged men... / Our hearts silently trembled, / But the vivid thought was aroused / And the path of our whole life was designated" (ll. 16–20, 291). Here the execution serves as the moment of Ogarev's political consecration. As with Herzen, the vision of the condemned men directs Ogarev to fight for freedom. Ogarev imagines two possible outcomes of his own struggle: either triumph or glorious failure. The Decembrists' execution provided an emblem of that heroic failure and appealed tremendously to Ogarev's and Herzen's romantic imagination, explaining its centrality in Ogarev's oeuvre. Ogarev provided vivid symbols and catch phrases for later mythologizers (the term *podvig* and the Decembrists' appellation as "firstlings of freedom" [*perventsy svobody*]). As much as his poetry, Ogarev's hagiographic tone influenced later generations.

Nikolai Nekrasov worked with a similarly idealized image, also applying the term *podvig* to the Decembrists. Yet Nekrasov went well beyond Herzen and Ogarev in the Decembrists' sacralization in his poem *Russian Women* (*Russkie zhenshchiny*, 1871–1872). Nekrasov focused on the Decembrists' wives to demonstrate their loftiest sacrifice.[52] Often referred to as having "Ryleev's pathos,"[53] Nekrasov created an image that became common currency in works about the Decembrists' wives and reflected populist revolutionary ideas of the late 1860s.[54] Nekrasov emphasizes the wives' sense of duty and love for their husbands in portraying their journey to Siberia, a land already mythologized in the nineteenth century.[55] Here Nekrasov echoes Ryleev, who in "Natalia Dolgorukova" (1824) first idealized a woman following her husband into Siberian exile. Lotman speculates that this literary model so valorized her sacrifice that it motivated the Decembrists' wives to do the same.[56]

Nekrasov politicizes the wives' actions, sidestepping historical accuracy in favor of a compelling dramatic story. Though Princess Ekaterina Trubetskaia was not politically enlightened before her journey to Siberia, Nekrasov transforms her into a full-fledged activist by the end. As she prepares for her departure, she vows not to forget her past. In Nekrasov's words, she condemns the entire imperial court and family:

> Мне не забыть... Потом, потом,
> Расскажут нашу быль...
> А ты будь проклят, мрачный дом,
> Где первую кадриль
> Я танцевала.... Та рука
> Доселе мне руку жжет...
> Ликуйте ж, изверги, пока
> Возмездье не придет. (ll. 53–60)[57]

I will not forget.... Later, later, our story will be told.... And you be damned, gloomy house, where I first danced the quadrille.... That hand still burns my hand now.... Rejoice then, monsters, until retribution comes.

Only after the sentencing does she clearly see high society's hypocrisy and promises vengeance. By the time she reaches Irkutsk, Trubetskaia has become politically educated. When the governor of Irkutsk suggests that she return to St. Petersburg, she refuses, pronouncing a scathing indictment of Russian society of the 1820s:

> И прежде был там рай земной,
> А ныне этот рай
> Своей заботливой рукой
> Расчистил Николай.
> Там люди заживо гнเюют—
> Ходячие гробы,
> Мужчины—сборище Иуд,

А женщины—рабы.
Что там найду я? Ханжество,
Поруганную честь,
Нахальной дряни торжество
И подленькую месть....
Нет, нет, я видеть не хочу.
Продажных и тупых,
Не покажусь я палачу
Свободных и святых. (ll. 668–690)

And before there was earthly paradise, but now Nicholas cleared out that paradise with his careful hand. There people decay alive, are walking coffins, the men are the mob of Judas, the women are slaves. What will I find there? Hypocrisy, desecrated honor, the triumph of impertinent trash and base vengeance.... No, no I do not want to see the sell-outs and the blockheads, I will not show myself to the executioner of the free and holy.

Trubetskaia's political awakening occurs because of the political reversal of fortune that her husband experiences. She demonstrates her sense of duty and desire to share in her husband's fate: "Another obligation, / both higher and holier, / calls me" (ll. 539–541). Throughout the poem, Nekrasov illustrates Trubetskaia's voluntary submission to a difficult fate, emphasizing her willing sacrifice to improve her husband's lot: "I know, terrible will be / my husband's lot. / Let my life / not be more joyful than his!" (ll.575–578). Nekrasov valorizes this sacrifice as the ultimate gesture of spousal devotion. He also portrays Trubetskaia's gesture as political defiance against the tsar: "Having taken an oath in my soul / to fulfill to the end / My duty—I will not bring tears / to the damned prison— / I will save his pride. / I will give him strength! / Scorn for our executioners / and consciousness of our righteousness / will be our faithful support" (ll. 641–649). Exalting the Decembrists' wives' proud forbearance, Nekrasov provides a powerful image of female sacrifice and love that profoundly influenced later writers. Historians at the turn of the century would follow his lead in their work on the Decembrists' wives.[58]

In the second half of Nekrasov's poem, Princess Maria Volkonskaia also undergoes a period of growth and maturation. Rather than experience political enlightenment, Volkonskaia discovers her deeply moral and religious side. Earlier she had allowed others to dictate her actions and had followed her flights of fancy: "Only in my twentieth year did

I discover that life is not a plaything" (ll. 425–426). Nekrasov stresses Volkonskaia's sense of duty as well as the stigma she would feel if she remained:

> Куда ни пойду я,—на лицах людей
> Я свой приговор прочитаю:
> В их шопоте—повесть измены моей,
> В улыбке укор угадаю:
> Что место мое не на пышном балу,
> А в дальней пустине угрюмой,
> Где узник усталый в тюремном углу
> Терзается лютою думой,
> Один...без опоры.... Скорее к нему!
> Там только вздохну свободно.
> Делила с ним радость, делить и тюрьму
> Должна я...Так небу угодно! (ll. 469–481).

Wherever I go, I will read my sentence on the people's faces; the story of my betrayal I will glean in their whisper, their reproach in their smile: that my place is not at the splendid ball but in the far stern wilderness where a tired prisoner in his prison corner falls prey to fierce thoughts, alone without support.... Quickly, to him! Only there will I breathe freely. I shared joy with him, I must share prison also.... So the heavens will it!

Nekrasov depicts Volkonskaia's decision in religious terms: the heavens compel her to follow her husband to Siberia. However, by joining her husband in exile, she takes on an even more difficult choice: she must also leave her child according to the conditions set by Nicholas. Nekrasov's text justifies Volkonskaia's decision by imagining that she wants to avoid her son's reproof:

> Но если останусь я с ним...и потом
> Он тайну узнает и спросит:
> «Зачем не пошла ты за бедным отцом?»...
> И слово укора мне бросит;
> О, лучше в могилу мне заживо лечь,
> Чем мужа лишить утешенья
> И в будущем сына презренье навлечь...
> Нет, нет! Не хочу я презренья! (ll. 497–504)

But if I remain with him . . . and then he learns the secret and asks:
"Why did you not go after my poor father?" . . . And he throws me
a word of reproof; Oh, better for me to lie down in my grave still
living than to deprive my husband of comfort and to incur the
future scorn of my son. . . . No, no! I do not want contempt!

Forced to choose between husband and child, Volkonskaia favors her
husband, entrusting relatives with her son.[59] Volkonskaia rational-
izes her decision by citing spousal duty. In society's eyes, this choice
ennobled the women as the epitome of wifely devotion and sacrifice.

Nekrasov reaches the height of hagiographic technique, portraying
Volkonskaia's love in religious terms. Imagining her husband in prison
attire, she experiences an epiphany:

> И я полюбила его, как Христа . . .
> В своей арестантской одежде.
> Теперь он бессменно стоит передо мной,
> Величием кротким сияя.
> Терновый венец над его головой,
> Во взоре—любовь неземная. (ll. 531–546)

And I loved him like Christ . . . in his prisoner's clothing. Now he
always stands before me, radiating gentle grandeur. A crown of
thorns upon his head, unearthly love in his gaze . . .

Volkonskii becomes a Christ figure inspiring his wife's religious ecstasy.
She envisions her husband literally transformed into a martyr by his
new garb, embellishing it with a crown of thorns, the primary trapping
of martyrdom. His sacrifice for humankind only increases his stature
and her love. This emphasis on martyrdom transforms her sacrifice
from a personal to a sacred one. Volkonskaia asserts: "Our sacrifice is
pure—we are giving up everything for our chosen ones and God"
(l. 1177). Just as the men have become chosen by their "heroic deed,"
the wives' dedication becomes a sacred task. They become pilgrims, or,
to use Decembrist Andrei Rozen's words, "guardian angels."[60]

Exploiting Volkonskaia's reference in her memoirs to the Virgin's
descent into hell,[61] Nekrasov depicts her as an angel descending into
the Siberian salt mine to find her husband. The apocryphal text provides the sacred paradigm of the virgin who crosses from life to death
to redeem sinners. Noticing Volkonskaia's approach, the other prisoners exclaimed: "Is this not an angel of God? / Look, look! . . . We aren't

Figure 3 *Volkonskii's Dream* (1880s), anonymous artist.

in paradise, you know / The cursed mine is more like hell!" (ll.1335–1338). Nekrasov subverts the mine's image as hell for Volkonskaia. Upon seeing her husband, Volkonskaia experiences a holy feeling. She kneels before him to kiss his chains, recalling the biblical parallel of

Mary Magdalene washing Christ's feet. Her respect for his suffering moves the other prisoners to tears and brings the hush of "holy quiet" over the mine. The location is transformed and Volkonskaia, on leaving the mine, calls the world above "hell" and the world she has left "paradise:" "And as if from paradise I descended into hell..." (1. 1459). Nekrasov condenses Volkonskaia's memoir's two scenes—of reunion and of descent—into one, making it standard for later accounts of the Decembrists. The mythic depiction also influenced the visual arts, as seen in the painting *Volkonskii's Dream* (1880s) by an anonymous artist. (See Figure 3.)

Nekrasov changed the poem's original title, from "Decembrist Wives" (*Dekabristki*) to *Russian Women*, signalling that self-sacrifice and spousal devotion were valued as traits potentially existing in all Russian women, though the Decembrists' wives were perceived as their loftiest exemplars. The poem immediately made a strong impression on the reading public, as I. A. Goncharov and A. M. Skabichevskii attested.[62] The sacralization of the wives dominated subsequent literary works through the twentieth century. When in 1919, Princess Sofia Volkonskaia "replicated" the gesture by leaving her child behind in safety to rejoin her husband, Prince Petr Volkonskii, jailed in Petrograd: "Everyone around her, including her husband and his jailers, seems to know how to 'read' her actions" because of the poem's cultural resonance. Volkonskaia attributed her husband's release to Felix Dzherzinskii's knowledge of Nekrasov's poem.[63]

The Myth Breaker: Leo Tolstoy's
Anti-Romantic Tendency

It has long been a commonplace of Russian literary history that Tolstoy's *magnum opus*, *War and Peace* (1863–1869), arose out of his exploration of the Decembrist revolt's origins. Influenced by the impending return of the Decembrists after their amnesty (and subsequently by his personal acquaintance with several Decembrists), Tolstoy conducted research into their history. Tolstoy suggests he began a Decembrist novel in the autumn of 1856, though manuscript analysis disputes this date.[64] He worked intermittently during 1860–1861 and 1862–1863 on the Decembrist theme in contemporary times, abandoned his work in spring 1863 but returned to the topic again from 1877–1884. Writing to Herzen in 1861, Tolstoy discussed what his Decembrist should represent: "[he] must be an enthusiast, a mystic, a Christian, who returns in '56 with his wife, son and daughter, and tries his strict and somewhat idealized view on the new Russia."[65] To explain his shift from the Decembrists to the Napoleonic era, Tolstoy later discussed the relationship between his earlier fictional exploration of the Decembrist theme and *War and Peace*:

> In 1856, I began to write a tale with a certain orientation, the hero of which was to have been a Decembrist returning with his family to Russia. Unwittingly I turned from the present to the year 1825, the epoch of my hero's mistakes and misfortunes, and abandoned what I had begun. But in 1825 my hero was already an adult family man. To understand him I had to go back to his youth, and his youth coincided with Russia's glorious epoch of 1812. Once again I put aside my beginning, and started to write from the period of 1812. (13: 54)

The unfinished novel, eventually entitled *The Decembrists*, was envisioned as a trilogy revolving around the dates 1812, 1825, and 1856 since Tolstoy perceived a symbolic relationship among the three epochs with the Decembrists as their nexus.[66] Tolstoy's prolonged study of the uprising's genesis ultimately led him to the earlier historical eras and resulted instead in his epic novel. Thus, the Decembrists have been credited with inspiring Tolstoy to create a masterwork, though it turned out differently from his original intention. Kathryn Feuer has already discussed the complex evolution from *The Decembrists'* Pierre and Natasha Labazov to Pierre and Natasha Bezukhov of *War and Peace*, which I will not repeat here.[67] Most important, Tolstoy's desire to write a publicistic and politically-oriented novel evolved into the need to examine a historical issue more deeply, leading him to switch from "the novel to the chronicle," as Eikhenbaum suggested.[68] The remaining section of this chapter treats Tolstoy's challenge to the Decembrists' idealization.

In his representation of the returning Decembrist, Labazov, Tolstoy exploits the Decembrists' legendary status for social commentary. He satirizes Muscovite society's reaction to the Decembrists' return by portraying the liberals' mania for the lionized former prisoners. Though initially personae non grata in Russian elite society, Decembrists have become á là mode:

> Three years ago no one thought about the Labazovs and if they remembered them, they did so with that vague feeling of fear with which one speaks about the recently deceased. Now how vividly all their former relations and wonderful qualities were

remembered, and each lady already devised a plan to obtain a monopoly of the Labazovs and entertain other guests with them. (17: 25–26)[69]

Tolstoy underscores societal caprice while drawing attention to the unexpectedness of the Decembrists' reversal of fortune. Allowed to return to Western Russia in 1856 by the newly crowned emperor, the Decembrists experienced a dramatic return of status from state criminals to respected members of high society. Labazov and his family create a stir when they make their re-entry into society by attending mass at the Cathedral of the Assumption:

> "Who is that elderly man, long burned by the sun and not recovered, with prominent, straight, laborer's wrinkles, which are not wrinkles acquired in the English club, with hair and a beard white as snow, with a kind and proud glance and energetic movements? Who was that statuesque woman with stately gait and tired, large and beautiful eyes grown dim? Who is that girl, fresh, shapely and strong, but not fashionable or timid? Are they merchants or Germans or noblemen? They aren't typical noblemen, but important people." So thought those who saw them in the church and for some reason more quickly and eagerly gave them way, than to men in rich epaulettes. (17: 27–28)

Tolstoy depicts the Labazovs' ceremonial reincorporation into society as sensational. Tolstoy demonstrates that the returning exiles are marked as special in the public eye even before it is known that they are Decembrists. Tolstoy draws two contrasts: first, between the simplicity of the Decembrists and the artificiality of "club" society, illustrated in the Labazovs' unstrained and genuine feelings; and second, in Labazov's physical vitality compared to his contemporaries' decrepitude. Using exterior appearance to reflect inner qualities, Tolstoy extols his hero's morally upstanding character and his good health. Labazov unexpectedly meets a toothless and bald general friend, who remarks: "But you're still so fresh.... Evidently, Siberia is better than Petersburg" (17: 32). Tolstoy suggests that the Decembrists profited from their exile, given the moral and physical degeneration of those remaining behind:

> In my incomplete novel *The Decembrist* one of the thoughts was to represent two friends, one who traveled the path of society life, frightened of persecutions which one must not fear and betrayed

his God, and the other, who went to prison, and what happened with them both after 30 years: the one's clarity, vigor, heartfelt reason and joy, and the jadedness, both physical and spiritual of the other, hiding before others his chronic despair and shame beneath trivial distractions, lusts and haughtiness, in which he himself does not believe. (70: 49)

Tolstoy remarked that the surviving Decembrists he met were "vigorous, intelligent and joyful" compared to their peers: "those who spent their lives in service, at dinners and cards, were pathetic ruins, not needed by anyone in any way, with nothing good to mark their lives" (73: 43). For Tolstoy, the Decembrists' suffering strengthened their characters because it led them to adopt the simple life.[70] Tolstoy specifically noted this quality in Volkonskii, who worked with the peasants and kept the accoutrements of peasant labor in his quarters.[71]

Yet Tolstoy does not idealize the Decembrists as his predecessors did, revealing an awareness of his reading public's expectations: "However much I would like to present a Decembrist hero above all weaknesses to my readers, for truth's sake I must confess that Petr Ivanych especially meticulously shaved, combed his hair and gazed at himself in the mirror" (17: 27). He implies that an imperfect Decembrist hero is truer to life and less heroic than Herzen, Ogarev, and Nekrasov's Decembrists. Beyond mocking Labazov's vanity, Tolstoy pokes fun at the other "weaknesses" of his Decembrist and family, depicting Labazov as childlike, Labazov's wife, Natasha, as too proud of her sacrifice, and their son Sergei as petty.

These excerpts manifest Tolstoy's interest in combating the Decembrists' legend rather than denigrating the Decembrists themselves. Yet since he did not complete his narrative, we cannot definitely say how the characters would have evolved. Sofia Tolstaia attributed Tolstoy's inability to complete his novel to feelings of ambivalence though he may not have finished for other reasons. Tolstoy sought access to the Decembrists' court proceedings but was denied by the authorities. M. Tsiavlovskii speculates this fact prompted Tolstoy's decision to cease working on the novel. Though he shelved his novel, he continued to muse on the Decembrists' significance as late as 1905 (a date especially convenient for later political mythmakers): "The peasants' liberation in Russia was achieved not by Alexander II, but by those people who understood serfdom's sin and tried to free themselves of it...people like Novikov, Radishchev, the Decembrists, those people who were prepared to suffer and themselves suffered...out of loyalty to what they considered the truth" (36: 228). By directly attributing serfdom's abolition to the Decembrists' efforts, Tolstoy validates them as the moral progressives of their time. He also valorizes their suffering for their cause, as did Herzen and other political activists.

Once literary critics began the search for Decembrist references in prerevolutionary literature, *War and Peace* became a primary text in the Decembrist myth. Pierre Bezukhov's evolution recapitulates the development of many Decembrists in his temporary fascination with Napoleon and his involvement and subsequent disillusion with freemasonry. In the novel's epilogue Pierre establishes a secret society, evidence to Soviet critics that he belonged to a pre-Decembrist circle. Tolstoy presents Pierre's progressive views of social reform in contrast to Nikolai Rostov's conservative opinions. After criticizing Alexander I's autocracy, Pierre proclaims:

> "Well, everything is on its way to ruin. Thievery in the courts, only discipline, pageantry and settlements in the army—the people suffer; enlightenment is suppressed. Anything that is young and honorable is persecuted! Everyone sees that it must not go on this way. The strain is too great and something certainly will snap,"—Pierre said (as men always say who look at the actions of government since time began). (12: 283)

Pierre hopes to "widen the scope of the society, let the slogan be not just virtue, but independence and action" (12: 284). Pierre's preference reflects the Decembrists' internal divide after 1816 between members who focused on virtue and enlightenment and those who strove for political action. Moreover, Pierre believes that his secret society is not necessarily hostile towards the government:

> It is a society of genuine conservatives. A society of gentlemen in the full meaning of the word. We want to ensure that a Pugachev does not come to slit the throats of my and your children and that Arakcheev does not send me to a military settlement. We come together with the single goal of common good and general security. (12: 284)

Nikolai remains unconvinced, insisting that the society is harmful to the government and people. Since Nikolai knows what is right in his heart, rather than intellectually, Tolstoy implies that Nikolai holds the proper opinion and reveals his own bias: "In his soul, not by reason but by something stronger than reason, he knew of the indubitable truth of his opinions" (12: 285). Nikolai professes his duty to obey the government and to fight against the secret society even if Pierre, his best friend and brother-in-law, belongs. Tolstoy depicts the infectious nature of Pierre's rhetoric by showing the discussion's effect on Pierre's godson, Nikolenka Bolkonskii: "Every word of Pierre's burned into his heart, and without noticing it himself, with his fingers' nervous movements he broke the sealing wax and quill pens at hand on his uncle's table" (12: 285). Nikolenka listened "in a trance." Later that evening, the young boy has a frightening dream which reflects his confused understanding:

> In the dream he saw himself and Pierre in helmets like the ones drawn in Plutarch's volume. He and Uncle Pierre walked at the head of a huge army. The army was composed of white thin lines, filling the air like the cobwebs which float around in autumn and which Desalles called 'le fil de la Vierge.' Ahead was glory, just the same as those threads, but only a bit denser. He and Pierre were carried lightly and joyfully closer and closer to their goal. Suddenly, the threads moving them began to weaken and tangle; it became distressing. And Uncle Nikolai Ilyich stopped before them in a threatening and stern pose... "I loved you, but Arakcheev commanded me, and I will kill the first person who walks forward." Nikolenka looked around at Pierre, but he was no longer there. [Instead of] Pierre was his father—Prince Andrei, and his father did not have shape or form, but it was him.... His father caressed and pitied him. (12: 294)

Nikolenka interprets the dream as his father's approval of their future feat and decides to do whatever his Uncle Pierre says so that his father will be proud of him. In this scene Tolstoy portends Nikolenka's involvement with Pierre in a military revolt.

Citing the epilogue, critics commemorating the Decembrist centennial proclaimed that Pierre represented a proto-Decembrist in his critique of the government, Alexander I and Arakcheev. They asserted that Nikolenka's delight in Pierre's speech foretells enthusiasm for a conspiracy[72] and that Pierre, Denisov, and Nikolai Rostov serve as examples of the era's three different activists: "One of them will become a participant in the rebellion, presenting himself at the same time as 'a helper' to the government, the second will not endure any waiting and duplicity and will use his concealed revolver on a careless general; but the third according to his proclaimed oath, will swiftly cut his way through the crowd of rebels with a squadron of cavalry."[73] This interpretation ignores the apparent irony pervading the novel regarding man's inability to influence history. Critics insist that Tolstoy drew a parallel between Nikolenka Bolkonskii and Herzen's generation, as if proving the historical accuracy of Tolstoy's portrayal.[74] When nineteenth-century works were explored for possible Decembrist links, Tolstoy was validated by *The Decembrists* and by his alleged desire to make Pierre Bezukhov a Decembrist in a sequel to *War and Peace*. Tolstoy's literary works, as well as those of the aforementioned authors, became ideologically useful during the centennial to popularize the Decembrist myth among the masses.

CHAPTER TWO

Literariness and Self-Fashioning in the Decembrists' Memoirs

Memory is the only paradise from which there is no exile.

—Andrei Rozen[1]

The Decembrists' memoirs challenge official representations of the uprising and its participants, especially Korf's account. Though Zavalishin says the Decembrists conceived a collective memoir-writing project while in Chita prison (1828–1829), and created a special commission gathering historical materials,[2] Rozen appears to be the only Decembrist who started writing in 1828. Most Decembrists began their reminiscences after Korf's publication,[3] as the desire to provide a counternarrative to the official version proved a strong impetus. At least 37 Decembrists wrote reminiscences in some form.[4] Decembrists N. V. Basargin, A. P. Beliaev, I. I. Gorbachevskii, I. D. Iakushkin, N. I. Lorer, I. I. Pushchin, M. I. Pushchin, V. I. Shteingel, and S. G. Volkonskii wrote during the 1850s and 1860s; M. A. Bestuzhev began anew in 1869 after having destroyed his memoirs in 1862.[5] Most important, the majority penned their memoirs long after the fact, at a time when they already mulled over the significance of their actions.

Because these memoirs cross boundaries stylistically and thematically, ranging from accounts of military service to family chronicles, they cannot be considered monolithic. Given their large scope and number, I concentrate on memoirs that discuss the eve of the uprising, the events of December 14 and the execution. By focusing on the dominant mood and images carried over into later accounts, I explore how the narratives become mythic and subsequently propagate a sacrosanct image of the Decembrists.

★   ★   ★

Literary critic Lydia Ginzburg points out that the memoirist's task is to "pave the way from the fact to its significance."[6] Ginzburg argues that memoirs "are a kind of plotted structuring of an image of reality and an image of a human being,"[7] and, as aesthetic interpretations of real-life experience[8] necessitate choosing among the most important events of a life to give a particular representation to the reader. Factual exactitude takes a back seat to the memoirist's aims; the manner in which the memoirist chooses to portray himself/herself and the events focused on to flesh out that picture prove significant. The Decembrist memoirists consciously construct their own image to assure proper remembrance. Though the majority explicitly argue that their works are a true representation of what happened, more important than authenticity is the intersection of reality and myth, or mythmaking, in these accounts:

> Inherent in the very essence of the genre is a kind of ferment of "unreliability"....No event of the external world can be known to the memoirist in all the abundance of its participants' thoughts, experiences and motives; he may only speculate about them. Thus, the writer's own point of view reshapes the material, and imagination ineluctably strives to fill in the gaps—to retouch, to render more dynamic, to bring to a conclusion. It is understandable that great artists and thinkers have in their autobiographies and memoirs particularly yielded to these temptations.[9]

The memoirs provided a powerful platform from which the Decembrists could fashion their own self-image. They reshape history by framing their actions differently from the official view. Hence the memoirs function as an important source for subsequent mythmakers.[10]

An awareness of the slanted official accounts came early. Ivan Pushchin, on his way to Siberian exile in 1826, wrote to his sister: "One should not judge decisively about the disastrous day of December 14 according to what was printed for the public. There will be a time, some time or other that will clarify somewhat the event for many who see it now perhaps from a different point of view."[11] Writing with the benefit of hindsight, Rozen expands on this point: "The actions or the actors of December 14 were judged in a variety of ways: some saw them as dreamers, others as madmen. Others abused them and called them apes of the west, others reproached them for excessive ambition. One censured unconditionally; another took pity. There were few who judged dispassionately and those almost secretly. . . . The newspapers at that time did not dare to print the truth."[12] Rozen, Shteingel, Iakushkin, and Trubetskoi explicitly state their memoirs correct spurious official accounts. They had little hope that their works would be published in Russia, but they felt strongly about their mission. Through Herzen and Ogarev's efforts and the endeavors of the Decembrists' descendants and sympathizers, some were published abroad beginning in the 1850s. Two journal editors, P. I. Bartenev of *Russkii arkhiv* and M. I. Semevskii of *Russkaia starina* were instrumental in publishing memoirs in Russia (in the 1870s), though because of censorship they appeared with significant changes.

In any case, the narratives could be read among the Decembrists, their families and sympathizers, and in fact were discussed for the purpose of commentary and critique.[13] Iakushkin tells of their search for a complete version of the events: "In conversations our talk very frequently turned to our common cause and, listening daily to parts of accounts, checking these stories and confirming them with one another, with every day all that related to this affair became more understandable. The meaning of our society, which had existed for nine years despite obstacles its activities encountered, became clear. Also the meaning of December 14 became clearer, and with it all the Commission's actions."[14] Here Iakushkin presents their collective urge to understand the uprising and to derive meaning from their current situation. Though this desire may have been a stay against despair, most likely a greater psychological impulse motivated the memoirists. Lotman has already called attention to the era's psychology as one aspiring to great deeds and perceiving the individual's historical significance. The Decembrists' memoirs reflect a conviction of their importance in the annals of Russian history. Moreover, their memoir-writing attests to their desire to shape their own history and their expectation of an audience, whether in the present or future.[15] The Decembrists as a group provided a counternarrative to the imperial version with the tsar as a sacrificial victim, and they posited their own sacrificial victims, their executed leaders, Pestel, Ryleev, Muraviev-Apostol, Bestuzhev-Riumin, and Kakhovskii.

In contrast to official narratives, the memoirs avoid mentioning the specific events of December 14, as if suppressing the painful memory of psychological crisis. For example, Trubetskoi gives extensive details about the conspirators' plans before the uprising, yet he does not mention his appointment as "dictator" or his inaction during the uprising. He dismisses the revolt: "The events of December 14 and the following days are well known. The solitary cells of Peter-Paul Fortress were insufficient to house all those arrested, taken in the capitol and brought from all ends of the vast Russian empire."[16] By not representing the uprising, he disassociates himself and renders it meaningless. The Decembrist Evgenii Obolenskii also avoids detailed discussion of the uprising:

> I lived through a great deal that memorable day; much remains imprinted in indelible marks on my memory...I will not speak of possibility of success: could any of us be certain of that! Each hoped for an auspicious occasion, for unexpected aid, for that so-called lucky star. However, despite the improbability of success, each felt obligated to the Society to fulfill his word—to fulfill his calling—and with these feelings and the conviction of the necessity of acting, each stood in the ranks. Each person's actions are well-known. On December 15 I was already in Alekseevskii *ravelin* (fortress). After a long, exhausting day I was alone. That was the first joyful feeling I experienced that long torturous day.[17]

Here Obolenskii evokes the participants' strong sense of duty as well as suggesting the ambivalence they felt toward their actions.

Unlike the revolt, which was distinguished by chaos, confusion, and failure, the eve of the uprising provides an emblematic moment of self-definition. The memoirists describe it as the movement's rallying point and a scene of spiritual elation and communion. Ryleev plays the role of the rebellion's leading man and an archetype of inspiration and revolutionary charisma, willing to sacrifice himself for the cause. Many Decembrists portray Ryleev as a typical Romantic hero poised to make a decision that will alter the course of history.[18] All accounts emphasize Ryleev's ardent words and flashing eyes, and his actions inspire his onlookers' exaltation. Ryleev purportedly quoted Hamlet's famous speech "To be or not to be" and noted that the society's members were men of deeds, not words.[19] (For the Decembrists, Hamlet became a heroic figure, who decided after much deliberation to challenge tyranny.) Shteingel remembers that Ryleev's words, "now or never," roused the entire group that night, proclaiming that Ryleev "breathed freedom."[20] M. Bestuzhev reminisces: "How beautiful Ryleev was that night!...his countenance was as pale as the moon, but shone with some kind of supernatural light."[21] His brother, Nikolai, recalls the deliberations about whether to rebel or wait for arrest, recounting his opinion: "Better to be taken on the square than in bed. Better for others to discover what we have died for than for them to be surprised when we suddenly disappear from society and no one will know where or for what we perished." Nikolai notes Ryleev's response: "Our fate is decided! Of course, now all obstacles augment our doubts. However, let us begin. I am certain that we will perish, but the example will remain. Let us sacrifice ourselves for the fatherland's future freedom!"[22] Nikolai's emphasis on Ryleev's "sacrifice" portrays Ryleev as a surrogate victim and the Decembrists' cause as a mission geared toward the general good. Rozen also describes Ryleev's martyr-like disposition on the eve, reporting Ryleev's words: "Though there are few indicators of success, all the same it is necessary, necessary to begin. The beginning and the example will bear fruit."[23] The Decembrists present themselves here as martyrs and models for later revolutionaries, who would go further in the battle for freedom. Rozen remarks: "The majority of secret society members never thought or dreamed of being lawgivers, representatives, administrators; they took on themselves the task of sappers, pioneers, bridge-builders."[24]

In their self-fashioning, the Decembrists exploit imagery used by revolutionaries across cultures. As Turner notes: "Many [Mexican] revolutionaries have indeed walked a *via crucis*—like Christ, men of the people, or men of religion, they have preached a message, achieved initial success, been disgraced or frustrated or physically suffered...have been betrayed by a friend or alleged supporter, executed or assassinated by major political state authorities, and have then experienced a curious resurrection."[25] The Decembrists follow this pattern in their narratives and lives. The Christian motif of suffering figures largely in their memoirs though they suffer because of a political act rather than religious belief. Some Decembrists, however, explain their self-sacrificial leanings in predominantly religious terms, suppressing political motivations. Trubetskoi describes his experiences as if they were ones typical of an initiand during a religious rite of passage:

> Since my infancy, it has been implanted in my heart that divine providence leads man to good no matter how difficult and unhappy the path seems by which he goes...I am convinced that if I had not experienced the vagaries of fate and gone unhindered along the shining path which stood before me, with time I would

have become unworthy of divine mercies and would have lost true human dignity. Now I bless the hand of God, which led me along the thorny path and with it cleansed my heart of its reigning passions, showing me what human dignity and the goal of human life truly consist of, and meanwhile rewarding me even in my earthly existence with family life's incomparable happiness and the unprecedented spiritual benefit of peace of conscience.[26]

Trubetskoi clearly adheres to the behavioral models for self-sacrifice abounding in the Russian Orthodox tradition. Martyrdom in Russia's name frequently elevated mortals to sainthood. The first Russian saints of Orthodox Christianity, Boris and Gleb, died *in imitatio Christi*, by not resisting their throne's usurpation by their rival Sviatopolk in 1015 CE. These *strastoterptsy* (passion-sufferers) became venerated in the popular tradition as intercessors to God across the ages.[27] Trubetskoi implicitly refers to this model of nonresistance as if drawing a parallel between his experience and the passion-sufferer's, not mentioning his participation in the secret society as the source of his suffering. This denial of accountability may be psychological self-justification, but it nonetheless reflects an ingrained reliance upon traditional behavioral patterns. It is no surprise that Trubetskoi points to his high moral stature as a sufferer; he gains peace of conscience in living and suffering for his ideals. In Turner's schema, Trubetskoi and other Decembrists in Siberia undergo a "protracted rite of passage," during which they become marginal or liminal figures because of their reversal of fortune and separation from society. Through this experience, they gain great sacred power despite their degraded status and social isolation.[28]

Though their religious faith supports them once they begin suffering and retroactively explains their self-sacrifice, piety dominates their discourse only after they faced difficulty. Instead, a different urge initially drove them to change their country's government and laws at any cost. In describing their actions the memoirists profess their desire to serve their beloved fatherland. Trubetskoi stresses that the members were prepared for anything: "They had long ago doomed themselves to the Fatherland's service and had foreseen the fear of ignominy and shameful death."[29] In the Decembrists' eyes, service to fatherland necessitated sacrifice and potentially shame. This notion that service to the fatherland stood on a higher plane than loyalty to the tsar was unique to the Decembrists in the history of opposition to Russian monarchs. Regarding this new mode of thinking, Marc Raeff comments: "It was the first time that an influential group in Russian society held a conception of the Russian state as distinct and separate from ruler, people and specific administrative institutions....For the Decembrists the welfare of the people—of the fatherland—was indissolubly tied to the power and the dignity of the Russian state."[30]

Prior to the uprising, they frequently looked to models of antiquity (like Brutus) or leaders of recent revolutionary uprisings (like Riego) for inspiration.[31] Jacques Le Goff explains these historical references as a "legacy of the French revolution," calling it the "religion of the fatherland."[32] Most Decembrist memoirists initially assert that this calling supplants other spiritual beliefs and gives them access to another level of spirituality; in some sense, they acquire prophetic qualities. Many memoirists state that they or Ryleev specifically foretold their fate.

Nikolai Bestuzhev recounts the credo of the self-aware Romantic revolutionary in his "Reminiscence of Ryleev" ("Vospominanie o Ryleeve"). To illustrate Ryleev's prophetic capacity, he cites Ryleev's poem "Nalivaiko's Confession" ("Ispoved' Nalivaiki," 1824) as his epigraph:

> Известно мне: погибель ждет
> Того, кто первый восстает
> На утеснителей народа
> —Но где, скажи, когда была
> Без жертв искуплена свобода?
> Погибну я за край родной:
> Я это чувствую, я знаю...
> И радостно, отец святой,
> Я жребий свой благословляю.

I know that ruin waits for him who first rises against the oppressor of the people—But tell me, where and when has freedom been bought without sacrifices? I will perish for my native land: I feel this, I know....And Holy Father, I happily bless my lot.

Nikolai's brother Mikhail lived at Ryleev's at the time of the poem's completion. Mikhail purportedly asked Ryleev: "Do you know what you have predicted for yourself and all of us? You seem to indicate your destiny in these lines." Nikolai reports Ryleev's response: "Do you think that I doubt my calling for a moment? Believe me every day persuades me of my actions' necessity, of the future ruin with which we must buy our first attempt for Russia's freedom and, at the same time, of the necessity of an example to awaken the sleeping Russians."[33] Nikolai Bestuzhev conflates Ryleev's poetry with his self-creation. The citation of Ryleev's poem and Mikhail Bestuzhev's response became standard fare for later representations of the Decembrists.

By dwelling on Ryleev and other Decembrists' willingness to sacrifice themselves for their country's good, the memoirists emphasize the group's lofty moral cause. Shteingel refers to the participants as *zhertvy* (victims or sacrifices) and *stradal'tsy* (sufferers), religiously charged terms: "At least those condemned to sacrifice tried as they could to perish for the benefit of the fatherland. After suffering, they would die with the comforting hope that posterity would give them this justification."[34] The idea that they should perish for the general good marks them as willing surrogate victims. Decembrist N. P. Tsebrikov writes similarly of his experience: "Having resolved myself to die for the just cause of Russia and knowing that there was no mercy to be expected from Nicholas...I turned over my fate to the will of God."[35] Thus the majority of Decembrist memoirists paint themselves as self-sacrificing and self-aware heroes who, on the eve of the uprising, knew the futility of their deeds, but anyway strove to benefit future generations.

Expanding on Lotman's work, I suggest that the Decembrists' portrayal of their behavior merits as much attention as the behavior itself. They exploit the theatrical nature of their actions as they write. Both Ryleev and Alexander Bestuzhev depicted other surrogate victims in literary works written and published immediately before the uprising. Ryleev's *Meditations* (*Dumy*, 1821–1823) featured heroic national figures from bygone eras and found great popularity among the reading public, especially his poem on the seventeenth-century noblewoman Natalia Dolgorukova who accompanied her exiled husband to Siberia.[36] What occurs is a curious interplay between literature, life, and the subsequent literary representation of life. In the same way that the Decembrists looked to literary and historical models for a blueprint for their behavior, they desired to provide models for later generations of Russian revolutionaries. In writing their memoirs, they look to those past literary and historical models for inspiration. Ginzburg calls this complex act a moment of personality modeling, when an individual "finds realization in the historically regulated forms of collective consciousness."[37]

The Decembrists' self-representation as sacrificial victims greatly colors their portrayal of their leaders' execution. Though not witnesses, most Decembrists reimagine the execution in their memoirs to memorialize their colleagues. This canonization is particularly effective regarding Ryleev. Though he already emerged as a ready sacrifice in depictions of the uprising's eve, Ryleev gains greater moral status after his execution. The leaders' death sentence was legally justified, given the severity of their treason against the state and tsar. State crimes had a precedent of bloody punishment; both Stenka Razin and Emelian Pugachev were quartered for leading rebellions against the autocracy. Yet capital punishment had been de facto abolished by Empress Elizabeth in 1755 and Catherine the Great's 1785 charter exempted nobility from corporal punishment. Because of the relatively indulgent attitude toward the nobility, there was a general feeling in elite society of cultural advancement in punishment practices, despite the fact that the lower classes were still publicly punished by knout and flogging.[38] The notion that Russia was more enlightened was shattered by the Decembrists' execution. I suggest that the nobility's thinking changed for three reasons: (1) the Decembrists' high social status and their proximity to imperial circles; (2) their regicidal intentions were not followed up by action;[39] and (3) the public's inability to see the spectacle. Since the execution was not public it took on even more scandalous shades of illegality.

Michel Foucault points out that executions can be socially useful as a means of control only when onlookers are sufficiently impressed by the spectacle of the event: "Public torture and execution must be spectacular, it must be seen by all almost as its triumph. The very excess of the violence employed is one of the elements of its glory."[40] He focuses on the growing negative feelings toward capital punishment in Europe at the eighteenth century's end "as if the punishment was thought to equal, if not to exceed, in savagery the crime itself, to accustom the spectators to a ferocity from which one wished to divert them, to show them the frequency of crime, to make the executioner resemble a criminal, judges murderers, to reverse roles at the last moment, to make the tortured criminal an object of pity or admiration."[41] Foucault argues that the negative association between crime and punisher provided strong impetus for the nineteenth century's "age of sobriety in punishment": "The great spectacle of physical punishment disappeared; the tortured body was avoided; the theatrical representation of pain was excluded from punishment."[42] Since in monarchical law punishment is a "ceremonial of power;" as Foucault asserts, once the edificatory aspect of the punishment has been withdrawn or undermined, the execution had little value in mobilizing societal support in the tsar's favor. The rite orchestrated by Nicholas would be witnessed only by officials and members of the military who did not need convincing of their loyalty to the state. The problem was that the public's vengeance would not become part of the sovereign's vengeance against those threatening his person and the state.[43]

"Correcting" Foucault, Pieter Spierenburg argues that the shift to private punishment was directly influenced by European state-formation processes and evolving opinions about how undesirable behavior should be treated.[44] Given Europe's changing mentalities and politics, it is no surprise that Western diplomats and educated Russian society viewed the execution for the most part negatively. The disjuncture arose once Russia's level of legal development clashed with its citizens' moral evolution.[45] Therefore, Nicholas's decision to punish the conspirators severely could appeal only to the most zealous and conservative patriots, given the Decembrists' class standing, somewhat ambiguous actions and, in many cases, total disavowal of revolutionary fervor after incarceration and questioning. The Third Section also noted the public support for the Decembrists and negative reactions to the sentence, its attention underscoring concerns about unrest in reaction to the execution. Thus imperial authorities suppressed information about the execution before and after it took place and closely monitored public reaction for at least five days afterward.[46]

None of the imperial family saw the execution, though they were informed about its every aspect; the priest Myslovskii, officers, and guards told the Decembrists about the execution while they were incarcerated in Peter-Paul Fortress.[47] Most Decembrists memorialize the execution to bridge the gap of representation: they did not see the event, but want to preserve it for posterity. Rozen pondered why the execution was not made public: "I don't know to what to attribute the reason for the execution not being performed before our eyes. To delicacy? Or calculated caution? Or oversight? Of course, they didn't want to suppress it, it must serve as an example and a horrible sight: but somehow one thing doesn't fit with the other—with popular spirit and with openness."[48] Not acknowledging the imperial authorities' ambivalence and discomfort regarding the execution, Rozen highlights that the execution contradicted claims of openness in the official manifestos and other proclamations. Tsebrikov comments: "Since the entire execution was very early in the morning and since the public absolutely did not know about it, there were relatively few people in comparison to those who would have been there if the day and hour of this autocratic celebration had been announced."[49] Tsebrikov explicitly notes the execution's ritualistic aspect and echoes that the spectacle should have been public, as appropriate to rites of power.

With the exception of official accounts, a sense of moral outrage permeates many memoirs, which depict the execution as a sacrifice rather than punishment due to criminals. The Decembrists and their

sympathizers referred to the executed men as "our five martyrs."
Tsebrikov describes the preparations:

> At seven o'clock in the same evening of July 12 the clergymen
> came to prepare our Martyrs for death. At eight o'clock shrouds
> and chains were brought to them, ringing out sadly with a clat-
> ter. Then everything fell silent. The weariness, utter exhaustion
> and spiritual agitation of that day compelled all others to be silent
> and this solemn quiet, interrupted only by the major's and the
> adjutant's incessant repetitions not to speak with those sentenced
> to death, was strikingly majestic. The soldiers looking after the
> cells' inhabitants walked on tiptoe not to interrupt the quiet. They
> wept.[50]

Tsebrikov highlights the solemnity of the condemned Decembrists' last
hours. In Tsebrikov's imagination, the leaders' death for the cause sanc-
tifies them.

The punishment made a strong impression on the few spectators who attended. A horrified reaction predominates in accounts of
the Decembrists' sympathizers' and presiding officials. The German
historian, Jean-Henri Schnitzler (1802–1871), who lived in Petersburg
from 1823–1828, calls the execution a "terrifying spectacle." The
writer N. Putiata, a friend of the Decembrists and Pushkin, comments: "Several nights after that I could not sleep peacefully. As soon
as my eyes closed, the gallows and the victims (*zhertvy*) fallen from it
appeared before my eyes." One official claims that ill-fortune befell
several participants: "The spectacle made a strong impression on those
immediately present: the [scaffold's] architect died a month later from
a fever. Police Captain Posnikov suffered from illness for more than
a year and died; he always said that this was the cause of his illness.
Having finished his account, he cried and said: 'Much time has passed
since then, but I cannot recall those criminals without tears.' "[51]

These accounts display the popular superstition that an execution's
participants become tainted by association with the hangmen and
related instruments of death.[52] Hence the official need for cleansing
ceremonies, performed ostensibly to cleanse the site of the uprising's
bloodshed and to congratulate Nicholas for preserving the Russian
state. In his speech to the troops afterward, Nicholas emphasized the
ceremony's significance as "a purifying sacrifice for Russian blood
shed for the faith, tsar and fatherland on this very spot."[53] The services
occurred immediately after the punishment, signifying the episode's

closure. Yet they may stem from a need to neutralize not only the revolt but also the punishment. According to a Third Section document, the tsarist government regained some support only afterward:

> The purifying service, performed with extraordinary piety, has already brought about a happy reversal of minds....All this increased the true patriots' veneration and turned doubters to the just cause's side...but the inveterate chatterboxes, unable to be satisfied with any kind of official government, still repeat, though in a whisper: 'quelle horreur!' etc. Especially the women, of whom the first category are the 120 criminals' wives, sisters, mothers, relatives, friends and their friends' friends.[54]

After the execution, oral legends circulated regarding the Decembrists' last words and greatly influenced those who were not witnesses since they substituted for seeing the actual execution. Foucault discusses this genre as a popular printed form in eighteenth-century France and treats the texts as "two sided-discourses": "In the wake of a ceremony that inadequately channeled the power relations it sought to ritualize, a whole mass of discourses appeared pursuing the same confrontation; the posthumous proclamation of the crimes justified justice, but also glorified the criminal."[55] Something similar resulted with the Decembrists. Most accounts idealize their final moments, bravery, and unquenchable thirst for justice and in some cases, depict a combination of repentance and irreconcilable opposition simultaneously.

Ryleev's last words exist in several variants. A police official, who helped Ryleev remount the scaffold after his noose broke, reports Ryleev uttered, "What misfortune!" when approached.[56] This version does not reappear in other accounts, which highlight Ryleev's fiery, poetic nature. Tsebrikov cites Ryleev's last words in verse: "Ryleev died as a criminal / Let Russia remember him!"[57] Schnitzler relates several versions. The first example illustrates Ryleev's courage while also depicting his remorse: "So they will say that I couldn't get anything right, even dying!" Schnitzler reports that some believed Ryleev (or Muraviev-Apostol) exclaimed: "Damned land, where they don't know how to carry out a conspiracy nor to judge, nor to hang!" He denies the likelihood of a third variation: "I did not expect that they would hang me twice."[58] In her diary, Dowager Empress Maria Fedorovna claims Ryleev said: "Even here it's necessary for me to fight with death."[59] M. Bestuzhev relates the account circulating among aristocratic circles, mythologizing Ryleev as tyranny's opponent. Ryleev supposedly exclaimed: "'You, general, probably came to see us die. Delight your tsar that his wish is fulfilled. You see—we are dying in torment." To Governor-General Golenishchev-Kutuzov's order to hang them again quickly, Ryleev purportedly countered: "Base *oprichnik* (terrorist) of the tyrant! Give the executioner your aiguillettes so that we don't have to die a third time."[60] The multiple versions demonstrate the ambiguity of what happened. They allow for the manipulation of Ryleev's image and illustrate the power of the condemned Decembrists' last words as a testament to the living. In using a particular version, each memoirist shapes the desired portrait as passive martyr or active rebel at the end.

The memoirs have been tremendously productive in creating the Decembrists' image as brave, honorable men, unafraid of death and fighting out against despotism to the very last breath. In combination with the fact of the execution, the legends surrounding their last words worked to transform these convicted criminals into martyrs. Foucault discusses examples in French history where a criminal became revered after his death as a saint with his memory and grave honored.[61] A similar hagiographic process occurred with the executed Decembrists in the frequent references to Christ and martyrdom recurring in accounts of the execution.

Among Decembrists, the tendency was to deify the five who were hanged, especially Ryleev. Rozen stated: "I entered [Ryleev's cell] as if into a holy place; I prayed for him, for his wife, for his daughter Nastenka. Here he wrote his last letter known to everyone. I drank the water remaining in his tin cup."[62] Rozen behaves like a devotee at Ryleev's altar. His symbolically loaded gesture—drinking the unfinished water from Ryleev's cup—acknowledges Ryleev's sainthood and demonstrates communion with the sacralized poet. Rozen further propagates the Decembrists' saintly image, discussing the esteem for Muraviev-Apostol: "His fiery spirit, his firm and purest faith long before the fateful minute nourished in [the priest] Myslovskii such deep respect. He often told people: 'When I enter Sergei Ivanovich's cell, a blessed feeling comes over me, as on approaching the altar during divine service.'"[63] Frequent comparisons between Muraviev-Apostol and Christ further highlight the sacrificial image. (Though the second half of Muraviev's name might contribute to this perception, no contemporaries mention it.) An official witness notes that as he approached the scaffold Muraviev-Apostol commented: "What a shameful death! For us it doesn't matter, but it's a shame that the stain will lie on our children. Well, there's nothing to be done; Christ suffered also, having been less guilty than us. We have a clean conscience, and God will not desert us."[64] Here Muraviev-Apostol feels shame only because he will be hanged, a dishonorable death, as opposed to execution by firing squad. The memoirist reports that Muraviev-Apostol compares himself and his comrades to Christ, revealing that he perceived his punishment as a sacrifice. Tsebrikov states that on the way to the scaffold Muraviev-Apostol said to the priest "You are leading five bandits to Golgotha."[65] By referring to Golgotha ("the place of the skull"), Muraviev recalls Christ's crucifixion site.[66] Tsebrikov's version glorifies the Decembrists while also suggesting that they were aware of their crimes and their salvation. Yet Tsebrikov downplays the Decembrists' sense of wrongdoing in his frequent references to the executed men as *mucheniki* (martyrs), as does Rozen, Gorbachevskii and Shteingel. N. Bestuzhev calls Ryleev a "martyr of truth."[67]

Again the Decembrists' mythmaking recapitulates a commonly exploited cross-cultural martyrology. Along with Cherniavsky's discussion of Russian cultural myths, Turner's work applies: "The Christ myth here is the model, not in a cognitive and bloodless way, but in an existential and bloody way....To be bloodily killed by the establishment, after betrayal by a traitor to one's own cause...and after proclaiming a message that includes support for the impoverished and exploited—are the ingredients of a career that, following an archetypal myth, becomes itself a myth generative of patterns of and for individual and corporate processes."[68] These persecuted, executed, and misunderstood leaders serve as compelling mythic symbols across cultures and generations, speaking to basic human emotions.

As their memoirs and correspondence makes clear, the exiled Decembrists used their time in Siberia to discuss the execution and exchange information they received from various sources.[69] It became an important topic of debate for the survivors. Especially in later years, they felt the imperative of preserving their version of events. Remarking on his memoirs' publication abroad in 1870, Rozen cited the corrective nature of his work: "I firmly defend the memory of my departed friends."[70]

★   ★   ★

The Decembrists' memoirs explore the critical moments of their history for self-definition and self-presentation to future generations. The Decembrists perceived themselves as ardent patriots and represented their executed colleagues as sacrificial victims and martyrs who knowingly dedicated their lives to their cause. They also portrayed themselves as a brotherhood in support of each other. Aware of their identity and cohesiveness as a group, M. Bestuzhev cited their imprisonment together in Petrovskii zavod as important to their survival:

> If we had been spread out among the prisons, as the law said... then not even ten years would have passed before we all would have perished most likely... or, finally, gone mad from boredom and suffering. The confinement united us, gave us each other's support, and finally, through our guardian angels, the women, joined us to that world from which we would forever be torn away by political death, connected us to our relatives, gave us a desire to live in order not to grieve those who loved us and were beloved by us, and, finally, gave us the material means to exist and provided moral nourishment for our spiritual life. The fortress gave us a political existence beyond the limits of political death.[71]

The Decembrists' ability to obtain emotional, spiritual, and even financial support from each other enabled them to endure their difficulties. Their closeness also allowed them to exchange information, discuss their past actions and enrich their accounts by adding to each other's narratives, as seen in the commentaries made by many Decembrists on their comrades' memoirs.

The Decembrists were aware that their deeds could be idealized. Yet few resist the tendency to mythologize. Iakushkin's memoirs provide a notable exception: "It came to me now, that I was playing the role of Don Quixote, going out with a bared sword against a lion, which having seen him [Quixote] yawned, turned and calmly lay down to sleep. Now I remembered my family with whom I made reunion impossible, perhaps because of empty vanity."[72] This reference to Don Quixote is especially meaningful for two reasons. First, Don Quixote stands for the hopeless idealist who tilts at windmills. Second, Don Quixote distinguishes himself as a literary persona because of his inability to differentiate between reality and literature. He uses the chivalric tales to decipher reality, though they always lead him astray. Iakushkin's reference implicitly confirms the Decembrists' own exploitation of literature for dual purposes: as a device to structure their reality (their deeds) as well as a model for their self-representations (their words). Contemporaries also noticed the Decembrists' resemblance to Don Quixote because of their eccentricity and apparent folly.[73] In his reminiscences, Iakushkin later remarks to Nikita Muraviev: "If we return to freedom, we will have to take care that people do not look on us better than we deserve."[74] Their doubts, however, are momentary and few. In the last analysis, the Decembrists represent themselves collectively and individually as martyrs for a lofty cause. The sacrificial image they created permeates later portrayals and offered a model to future generations. The Decembrists' self-mythologized image inspired the revolutionary activists Herzen, Ogarev, and Georgii Plekhanov, among others, who drew upon it in their writings, further disseminating it among the Russian and European public.

CHAPTER THREE

The Image in Flux in the Early Twentieth Century

"The Decembrist uprising's anniversary [December 14, 1917]. They, too, almost one hundred years ago, were here in these cells [in Peter-Paul Fortress].... They died believing in their cause....
—A. I. Shingarev[1]

Prerevolutionary Commemorations

Although the Decembrist uprising was celebrated before the 1917 Russian revolution(s), the practice became legally sanctioned and officially established only after 1917. Prior to this time, celebrations took place only in secret or abroad. Incarcerated Decembrists commemorated December 14 with a celebratory dinner; they also sang "Whatever the wind blows" ("Chto ni vetr shumit"), M. Bestuzhev's composition in honor of the "solemn, holy day."[2] As early as the 1830s, Polish radicals commemorated the Decembrist revolt at home and abroad.[3] The first Russian affirmation outside Decembrist circles dates to 1855 (also the year of Nicholas' death), to a literary evening dedicated to the 30th anniversary, organized by Ivan Sergeevich Turgenev.[4]

Only in the twentieth century did celebrations of the Decembrists' political significance echo back to Russia. In Geneva in 1900 the Decembrist uprising was commemorated by the leading Social Democrat, Georgii Plekhanov. He began by attributing great significance to the Decembrist movement, placing it in the context of world history: "Sympathetic remembrance about it makes the hearts of all those Russians—and perhaps not only of Russians alone, but of those people not interested in supporting autocracy and not indifferent to those institutions that turn its Philistines into citizens, that is, those which secure the benefit of political freedom for their country—to beat with great force."[5] Unlike others, Plekhanov discussed the Decembrists' predecessors and posited Alexander Radishchev as the first staunch Russian revolutionary from the intelligentsia, a position that the Decembrists later assumed in the Russian revolutionary martyrology. Plekhanov cited Herzen and Pushkin as well as Iakushkin, N. Bestuzhev, and Ryleev to demonstrate the Decembrists' civic motives and their centrality in the Russian revolutionary movement. Emphasizing the Decembrists' sacrificial role, Plekhanov claims the Decembrists as the forefathers of the Social Democrats: "Seventy-five years have passed since this time and our unfortunate country witnessed many other executions, many other sacrifices were carried out for the cause of Russian freedom! But the names of Pavel Pestel, Kondratii Ryleev, Sergei Muraviev-Apostol, Petr Kakhovskii, and Mikhail Bestuzhev-Riumin will remain in the memory of all freedom-loving Russian people, as the names of the first of our numerous martyrs" (29–30). Plekhanov highlights the enduring appeal of martyrs to the revolutionary movement. Though he discusses the reason for their failure (no popular support), he insists that they should be exalted: "Namely because we esteem these people as our forefathers and want to continue their cause, we do not have the right to close our eyes to those circumstances that hindered their *immediate success*" (30, author's emphasis).

Plekhanov suggests that his contemporaries have much to learn from their predecessors. In closing he confirms that Social Democrats have found the proper program of action allowing them to defeat tsarism and obtain political freedom while also avenging "these victims who have fallen and who fall beneath its blows"(30). Subsequent enthusiasts and detractors of the Decembrists return to these motifs of self-sacrifice, suffering for the people's cause, and lack of the masses' support.

The Social Democrats' newspaper, *The Spark* (*Iskra*), edited by Vladimir Ilyich Lenin, not coincidentally carried an epigraph from the Decembrist poet Odoevskii, "The flame will flare up from the spark" (*Iz iskry vozgoritsia plamia*). It publicized literary evenings dedicated to the Decembrists in the years immediately prior to 1905 and discussed the revolt for agitational purposes in leaflets and other materials.[6] Published abroad in Leipzig beginning in December 1900, *Iskra* was the central ideological organ of the new organization that would eventually become the Bolsheviks.[7] Even before playing the central role in the Bolshevik faction's formation, Lenin considered the position of various Russian revolutionary groups within the tradition. Lenin and his friends in jest called themselves "Decembrists" upon their arrest by the tsarist police in December 1895.[8] Lenin was also acquainted with the eldest son of Annenkov while living in Samara from 1889–1893.[9] That these facts became important in scholarly materials on "Lenin and the Decembrists" signifies Lenin's participation in the Decembrists' mythologization and prefigures their role in Soviet mythology.

The Revolution of 1905 and Its Aftermath

If the first period of *glasnost* regarding the Decembrists was after their amnesty in 1856, then a second wave resulted after the 1905 Revolution. Though this period was not distinguished by commemorative events, significant changes made the Decembrists more widely known in Russia. With the relaxation of censorship decreed by the Fundamental Laws of 1906, information about the Decembrists reached a wide reading public. Moreover, the perception of the Decembrists changed as a result of the actual experience of revolution, as the historian N. P. Pavlov-Silvanskii (1869–1908) noted in 1906: "We [now] understand the psychology of the people of those epochs. What we formerly saw as a story, almost a fairytale, now we clearly experience as the vivid picture of life."[10] Along with Pavlov-Silvanskii, the historians P. E. Shchegolev (1877–1931), V. I. Semevskii (1848–1916), and M. V. Dovnar-Zapolskii (1867–1934) were inspired by the experience of the 1905 revolution to dig deeper into the history of the Russian revolutionary movement. They produced individual analyses of the Decembrists' leaders, edited journals and collections of memoirs, and authored groundbreaking surveys of the oppositional movement.[11]

The Decembrists' memoirs were especially popular at this historical moment. In 1905–1906, Iakushkin's memoirs alone went through four editions in different publishing houses and Maria Volkonskaia's went through two editions.[12] Beginning in 1906, a series entitled "The Decembrists' Library" (*Biblioteka dekabristov*) was published by the Russian Fellowship (*Russkoe Tovarishchestvo*); it included selections from Volkonskaia's, Obolenskii's, and Basargin's memoirs and Fonvizin's and Muraviev's articles and constitutional projects. Official documents also became available through greater access to archives and publication. The increased proliferation of printed sources for historians and writers in addition to the earlier oral tradition fed the reading public's interest in the Decembrists and signaled the growing politicization of Russian society during this period.

The developing Decembrist cult was reflected in the popularity of their portraits. In 1906, Ryleev and Pestel were included with Balmashev, Sazonov, and Lieutenant Schmidt on a postcard with the following inscription: "Glory to the fighters for the people's cause, / Glory to the heroes of our native land, / Glory to those who gave both soul and body / For eternal freedom and holy truth!"[13] Postcards with photographs of major and minor participants and sketches of relevant Siberian sites were also issued at this time. Another attestation to the Decembrists' popularity was the publicity received by M. Zenzinov, a private collector and publisher of Decembrist materials.[14] Born and raised in Nerchinsk, Siberia "where legends of the fettered prisoners always lived and breathed," Zenzinov created a Decembrist museum in his home, but hoped to place his collection in a museum in Moscow.[15] Zenzinov's project made the news in 1911 on the Decembrist uprising's anniversary.

The most influential representation of the prerevolutionary period was Lenin's article "In Memory of Herzen" (1912), written in honor of the centennial of Herzen's birth. Lenin adumbrates his version of the Russian revolutionary pantheon beginning with the Decembrists, who "roused Herzen." Lenin elaborates the Decembrists' distinguished role in Russian history:

> Honoring Herzen, we clearly see three generations, three classes active in the Russian revolution. First, the nobility and landown-ers, the Decembrists and Herzen. The circle of these revolutionar-ies was very narrow. They were terribly distant from the people. But their cause did not disappear. The Decembrists roused Herzen. Herzen deployed revolutionary agitation. The revolutionary *razno-chintsy* [intellectuals of varying backgrounds] took over, broadened, strengthened and tempered it, beginning with Chernyshevsky and ending with the heroes of the People's Will. The circle of fighters became wider, their tie to the people closer. "Young navigators of the future storm," Herzen called them. But this was not the real storm.[16]

Seeking viable historical models for Russian revolutionary action, Lenin privileges the Decembrists and endows them with great mythic value as originators of the Russian revolutionary movement.

But why would Lenin choose the Decembrists as the progenitors? Plekhanov posited Radishchev as his martyrology's starting point, yet Lenin ignores Radishchev and the popular heroes Pugachev and Razin, instead tracing the line from the Decembrists to Herzen to the People's Will. When Lenin penned his article, he was working out the educated elite's role in revolutionary movements, which later turned into a discussion about the vanguard leading the masses. He points to the Decembrists, the era's most progressive thinkers, as important models for the group that later became the Bolsheviks, most of whom had origins in the intelligentsia rather than the working class. Only after the Bolshevik revolution in October 1917, led by a revolutionary vanguard purportedly for the workers and peasants' benefit, did Lenin and others begin to think about the relationship of the Bolsheviks and their predecessors to the common people.

The 1917 Revolutions and the Civil War (1919–1922)

After the February 1917 Revolution, the Decembrists could be consistently portrayed in a positive light in the Russian press. References were made to the link between the February Revolution and the Decembrists' aborted coup. The writer Dmitrii Merezhkovskii dedicated *Firstlings of Freedom (Perventsy Svobody*, 1917) to Alexander Kerensky as the Decembrists' spiritual descendent: "We must not think that the revolution began in our February days and ended in March. It has not finished—there is still so much ahead. And the revolution itself began almost 100 years ago in 1825."[17] Merezhkovskii saw both events as positive manifestations of democracy. His sympathetic assessment lasted until the October Revolution, after which he began to view the Decembrists differently. His disapprobation of the Bolsheviks tainted his later portrayal of the Decembrists in his novel, *December 14* (1918).

On March 18, 1917 on the initiative of a group of writers and artists, the Society for the Remembrance of the Decembrists (*Obshchestvo pamiati dekabristov*, hereafter OPD) was formed, with the practical goals of discovering "the truth" about the movement, erecting a Decembrist monument and locating the Decembrists' graves.[18] An article in the newspaper *The Day* (*Den'*) announced its establishment and emphasized the Decembrists' historical importance:

> The Decembrists' cause and their names must never be forgotten. Especially now, on the first free Russian day—we must reverently

perceive the importance of their feat and all the depth of their intention. The Decembrists' heroism is precious also because many of them, the more sagacious ones, rose with weapons in hand without any hope for victory. They bravely and justly believed that their martyr-like death would lay the first indestructible stone of Russian freedom.[19]

The society wanted to allow the "light of history" to illuminate the Decembrists' ideals, which were not well known to the public. The article closes with the imperative: "Bring the Decembrists' holy relics to the society, impart reminiscences, letters, portraits, send donations for the publication of works and construction of a worthy monument, become a member and organize local divisions of the society! Respect for the memory of the past is respect for oneself and for the entire great people's cause."[20] The use of the religiously charged term "holy relics" signals OPD's view that the Decembrists were saints, albeit revolutionary ones, who achieved their status through martyr-like death. The closing line neutralizes the religious image by equating the past, the individual, and revolutionary cause.

The society's founding members included Maxim Gorky, Ilia Repin, Vera Figner, Vera Zasulich, and other revolutionaries, journalists, academics, authors, and artists; the advisory council was composed of Figner, Repin, the academicians Shchegolev, N. A. Kotliarevskii, E. A. Liatskii, and V. V. Sviatlovskii. They organized different commissions—artistic, musical, publishing—within the group and planned to commemorate the Decembrist uprising annually.[21] Few of OPD's concrete goals were accomplished until 1925. Though this may have resulted from a desire to coordinate publications and monuments with the centennial, it was most likely due to the Civil War's financial constraints. OPD vanished leaving little more than a few documents in its wake. Some original members, however, continued their study of the Decembrists. Figner and Shchegolev published articles on the Decembrists through 1925 and reappeared as honored elders in the centennial's commissions.

After the 1917 October Revolution, the Decembrists' historical significance was publicized more widely. In accordance with Lenin's plan of monumental propaganda, Ryleev and Pestel were included in a list of people to whom monuments should be dedicated. Richard Stites believes that the Decembrists and other regicides and assassins were added to the list to suggest that the extermination of the tsar and his family had historical precedents.[22] In honor of the 92nd anniversary in December 1917, a slew of laudatory articles and poems by workers and peasants as well as acclaimed poets Zinaida Gippius and Osip Mandelstam appeared in Petrograd newspapers. Georgii Ivanov's "Decembrists" links the Decembrists with the Bolsheviks' success:

> Слава мученикам свободы,
> Слава первым, поднявшим знамя,
>
> Знамя то широко веет
> Над Россией освобожденной:
> Светло-алое знамя чести.
> Пропоем же вечную память
> Тем кто нашу свободу начал,
> Кто своею горячею кровью
> Оросил снега вековые—
> Декабристам.

Glory to freedom's martyrs, Glory to the first ones who raised the banner, waving over Russian liberation: The bright scarlet banner of honor. We will sing "eternal memory" to those who began our freedom, who watered age-old snows with their hot blood—The Decembrists.[23]

Commemorating the anniversary, "The Decembrists: An Artistic Album" (*Dekabristy: Khudozhestvennyi al'bom*) also repeats the established rhetoric, calling the Decembrists "martyrs for freedom."[24] It illustrates the Decembrists' wide popularity at the time as it was sold to raise money for war veterans and included portraits of the Decembrists, biographies and memoir accounts.

Since the Civil War period was one of social and political unrest and instability, the Bolsheviks needed to shore up support and legitimize their claim as a ruling entity. The Museum of the Revolution in Petrograd, established in 1919 on the initiative of Gorky, Figner, and Shchegolev (the most visible former members of OPD),[25] also made the connection between the Bolsheviks and Decembrists. G. E. Zinoviev explicitly linked the museum's opening with the Decembrist uprising's anniversary in his keynote speech: "In Petrograd as in a living book, one may read the history of our revolution. We have tied the opening of our Museum of Revolution with the celebration of the Decembrists' memory...Petrograd was the place where the first members of the contemporary intelligentsia tried to raise the banner of the republic 95 years ago. Then the first great martyrs, the

Decembrists, came out of the ranks of the military intelligentsia, and Petrograd stood at the crucible of freedom."[26] Zinoviev mentions the Decembrists for two reasons: to provide the Bolsheviks a valid revolutionary genealogy and to sanctify and preserve Petrograd as a literal museum-city of the revolution: "Many of the buildings, squares and streets of Petrograd and other cities are the most valuable historical revolutionary monuments."[27] Stites notes that museums established during the Civil War period played an important part in preserving prerevolutionary culture and art during a time of iconoclasm and looting, and maintained a conservative attitude toward the vestiges and symbols of the past. Incidentally and ironically, the new Museum of Revolution was housed in the Winter Palace. Despite the fact that the Decembrists did not take the Winter Palace in 1825, they occupied it literally in 1919. The ruling elite and scholars cultivated a growing consciousness of the Decembrists in the rarefied circles of Soviet society and restored the Decembrists to their rightful place in Russian history.

On a basic level the Decembrists' image also reached the masses, infiltrating revolutionary festivals held during the Civil War period. Scholars Mona Ozouf, Richard Stites, James von Geldern, and Katerina Clark have already discussed the propaganda function of revolutionary festivals in generating support for a ruling group and educating the masses in a new regime's values and objectives.[28] Von Geldern highlights that celebrations serve as a "powerful tool for social manipulation."[29] The Bolsheviks, who "joined the tradition of fledgling regimes using festivals to propagate legitimizing genealogies,"[30] followed a tradition already well-established by Russian and Western monarchs. As early as the first quarter of the sixteenth-century Russian tsars created a legend of origins going back to Emperor Augustus to legitimate their claim to the throne.[31] Just as the monarchy's legitimating myths changed over time according to the challenges faced by the ruler, so would legitimating myths necessarily change according to circumstances faced by a non-monarchical power.

The Bolsheviks thus faced a new challenge. Von Geldern sums up the situation: "The revolutions of 1917 shook Russian political culture to the foundation and discredited the alternative that appeared. A hoary tradition of discourse on political power and legitimacy, revolving around religion, bloodlines and fealty was effaced; the democratic language spawned by the February Revolution was discredited by hunger, disorder, and continuing war; the Marxist idiom remained incomprehensible and alien to most of the population."[32] Because of the Bolsheviks' inability to point to their divine right to rule Russia, they needed to find a different heritage to establish their claim and maintain power. Thus they turned to a mythological tradition of famous revolutionaries, from which they could selectively co-opt their ancestors.

Revolutionary festivals could instill in the masses a feeling of solidarity with the Bolsheviks and propagate the favored legitimating genealogy. At this point ideologists turned to Lenin's revolutionary pantheon as the source of their "myth of destiny," in which they defined the Bolsheviks' ancestors[33]: "They understood their historical mission through a mythic frame through which their movement was a lone island in an ocean of bourgeoisie, linked with similar islands by symbolic bridges across time and space. When they narrated history in the mythic frame, the Bolsheviks did not follow the tsars or the Provisional government, they merely occupied the time after; they followed the French Revolution, the Paris Commune and other great rebellions."[34] How could the Bolsheviks combine such disparate elements as the Decembrists whom they considered *dvorianskie revolutionery* (noblemen or gentry revolutionaries) with the Paris Commune? The Bolsheviks co-opted the Decembrists as the most progressive actors of early nineteenth-century Russia and included them in their legitimating genealogy. It helped that some Decembrists subscribed to regicide to gain their ends. Yet by conflating the Decembrist uprising with the French Revolution and other great events of world history, the Bolsheviks gave the uprising a much grander if bizarre status on the world stage. The juxtaposition of a failed revolt, during which few shots were fired, with some of history's bloodiest and cataclysmic revolutions, jars the imagination. Given its scope, it does not belong in their ranks. But precisely this new historical conception explains the Bolsheviks' ability to sponsor mass dramas in which the Bolsheviks themselves were associated "with Spartacus, the French Revolution, the Cossack rebels Razin and Emelian Pugachev, the Paris Commune and even the Decembrists."[35]

In the winter of 1919–1920 in Petersburg Proletkult staged an improvisational cycle depicting populist Russian revolutionary movements, which featured the Decembrists. The organizers positioned them after the eighteenth-century peasant uprisings and before the 1905 revolution.[36] Despite Lenin's earlier claims of the distance between the Decembrists and the people, when it suited ideological purposes, the Decembrists *were* the people. Here the Decembrist revolt—instigated by noblemen and officers afraid of involving the masses in their coup—became through some creative maneuvering a bourgeois, even "a people's," uprising.

Obviously, an officially established assessment of the Decembrists had not yet been set by the Soviet regime. Despite variations in emphasis, the Decembrists were consistently referred to by the Bolsheviks as important models and historical precursors. These early festivals should be seen as steps in determining the Bolshevik revolutionary myth:

> Embedded in this myth was the first text in the genealogy of the Russian Revolution—subsequently elaborated in the historiography of the 1920s. It was a startling picture which obliterated the old regime's virtues, heroes, and values and substituted a stark two-line family tree: a Russian line of peasant rebellion, intellectual radicalism, Populism, the first storm of 1905, War and the revolutionary year 1917—all seeming to point inexorably toward October; and a European line of slave revolts, the French Revolution, the Paris Commune, and three generations of the socialist family—the grandparents (the utopian socialists), the parents (Marx and Engels), and the children (the Bolsheviks). This mythic history announced Russian solidarity with the world proletariat and invited it to join its "history" to that of a victorious revolution... together the revolutionary myth unveiled in the monumental shows of 1918 and theatricalized in the Petrograd spectacles of 1919–1920 constituted a fanciful text that wove cultural, psychological, and historical episodes and dramas far removed in time and space from October 1917 into a mythic textbook.[37]

The Decembrists' heroism, sacrifice, courage, and nobility of spirit allowed them to become a part of the revolutionary myth despite their class origins and failure. Another important element comes into play here. Clark discusses the 1924 revision of the Revolution's official genealogy, which drastically reduced its scope from ancient Greece through the present to a century's events in Russia alone and reflects the altered party attitude ("Socialism in One Country") as well as growing Russo-centrism in some intelligentsia circles: "By the mid-1920s, the 1825/1905/1917 genealogy assumed official status.... The emphasis in cultural policy was no longer on iconoclasm but on creating new and enduring icons."[38] Although initially the Bolsheviks included Western and Russian revolutionaries in their martyrology, they eventually staked their claim on an all-Russian lineage. Party ideologues believed that the all-Russian pantheon was most comprehensible and appealing to the masses and thereby more effective in achieving their goals.

As the next chapter demonstrates, the Decembrists emerged among the preeminent Soviet cultural icons.

Dmitrii Merezhkovskii's *December 14*

Given all the attention after 1917, it is not surprising that authors thinking about the revolution's cosmic implications turned their gaze on the Decembrists. Though initially favoring the autocracy's overthrow, Merezhkovskii re-assessed his view after the violence of the October revolution and onset of Civil War. His novel *December 14* (*Chetyrnadtsatoe dekabria*, 1918) focuses on Prince Valerian Mikhailovich Golitsyn (1803–1859), a minor player in the Decembrist uprising. Merezhkovskii presents Golitsyn as a study in two extremes: religious devotion and political Jacobinism. His entire novel is a *bildungsroman*, in which these extremes reconcile. From its beginning, Merezhkovskii gets at the heart of Golitsyn's (and his own) religious questions: can there be freedom with God and/or a revolution with God? On the eve of the uprising, Golitsyn and Ryleev ponder this very topic: "Golitsyn, does God exist? Just simply tell me—does he?'" "'He does, Ryleev,'" Golitsyn answered and smiled. "'Yes, look how simply you said so,'"—Ryleev also smiled. "'Well, I don't know, maybe He exists. But what's that to you? Surely you want freedom?'" "'Is there no freedom with God?'" "'No. With God, there's slavery.'" "'There was slavery, but there will be freedom.'" "'Will there? And when will that be?'"[39] Merezhkovskii uses the Decembrist insurrection to examine religious issues within the framework of political action.

Merezhkovskii depicts similar conversations between Golitsyn and his close friend, Prince Evgenii Obolenskii, who shares Golitsyn's religious devotion and desire for revolutionary action. Portraying the profound effect of a duel during which Obolenskii murdered his opponent, Merezhkovskii employs the religiously-charged word *podvig* (feat): "He had to go somewhere, and first he entered the Masonic lodge, and from there straight to the Northern Secret Society. And soon he felt that here he would find something he was looking for—his expiatory feat" (44). Merezhkovskii suggests that a strong psychological need for suffering predisposed some Decembrists to their self-sacrificial actions.

Merezhkovskii further explores the link between religion, sacrifice, and revolution. In a conversation about the necessity of violence during revolution, on the eve of the revolt, Obolenskii pontificates: "You know that we are going to crucifixion together, all together. There

is nothing greater on earth than this torment" (47). Responding to
Golitsyn's incomprehension, Obolenskii concludes: "All the same it is
necessary to begin. Let us be weak—we will become strong. Let us be
base—we will become pure. And let us do nothing—others will do it.
'Let there be one king on heaven and on earth, Jesus Christ,'—all of
Russia will say this sometime—and it will happen. The Lord will not
abandon Russia. If only with Him, if only with Him—and it will be
such a revolution as the world has never seen!" (48).

Merezhkovskii's novel synthesizes several earlier texts. He includes
memorable scenes from varied Decembrists' memoirs in his portrayal.
Like the memoirists, he emphasizes the Decembrists' exalted feelings
on the eve of the uprising. Merezhkovskii depicts the heated discussions on the best plan for the revolt, but diminishes the scene's grandeur
and inspiration by revealing the conspirators' doubts. Merezhkovskii
conveys Golitsyn's ambivalence: "'Nothing will happen,' Golitsyn
thought. 'But maybe it will? Madmen, lunatics, plotters, but maybe also
prophets? Maybe all of this is not the fulfillment, but the harbinger?
The flash but not the lightning? But where there is a flash, there will
also be lightning'" (69).

Unlike Decembrist memoirists, Merezhkovskii deflates the moment
by injecting the absurd. In his depiction, Pushchin and Kiukhelbeker
stand in a corner discussing natural philosophy while their co-
conspirators argue about their course of action. When Pushchin
questions whether Kiukhelbeker's philosophy will allow him to participate in the revolt, the latter answers: 'My absolute is completely
in agreement. There must be an eternal battle existing between good
and evil. Knowledge and virtue are one and the same. Knowledge
is life and life is knowledge. To act well, one needs to think well!'
Kiukhlia exclaimed and, awkward, absurd, ugly, but entirely illuminated by an internal light, was almost beautiful at that moment" (72).
Merezhkovskii highlights the insurgents' eccentricity and oddness to
reinforce the distance between them and the people. This strategy is
especially apparent in Merezhkovskii's portrayal of the revolt, when the
conspirators reject the surrounding crowd's assistance.

Merezhkovskii emphasizes the Decembrists' child-like aspects during
the revolt as well. While waiting on the deserted square for the conspirators and their troops, Pushchin muses that Ryleev must be late because he
overslept. Golitsyn disdainfully remarks: "Oh, let us not oversleep Russian
freedom" (80). When the troops arrive, the rebels act like children, or
as if intoxicated: "The Secret Society members' embraced, kissed three
times as if giving Easter salutations. All the faces suddenly changed, were

made new. They recognized and didn't recognize each other, as if they met in the other world. They spoke hurriedly, incoherently interrupting each other, as if feverish or drunk" (84). They experience a sacred intoxication. Merezhkovskii gives their deed a religious overlay by describing their greeting as at Eastertime, the most sacred Orthodox holiday.

Moreover, Merezhkovskii depicts the Decembrists as if they were playing, and unaware of the import of their actions: "It was like a game of giants: big, terrifying like death, and funny, innocent like a childish prank" (85). Kakhovskii stands at a distance from the other conspirators, "with a pouting lower lip and pitiful eyes, like a sick child's or a dog's." When Ryleev appears on the square, the other conspirators call him by his diminutive, Ryleiushka, and tease him, further underscoring their childish behavior. The Decembrists' giddiness segues into indecision as they wait on the square for their appointed dictator Trubetskoi. Kakhovskii asks Golitsyn if he knows how to play at give-away (109),[40] comparing the game of draughts with their situation on the square and trivializing their stand against autocracy.

Merezhkovskii's account of the conspirators' questioning also diminishes their heroism, by emphasizing the Decembrists' child-like trust in Nicholas, their sensitivity and their desire to appear as noblemen and benefactors even under the most compromising circumstances. Merezhkovskii depicts the tsar's deception of the impressionable Odoevskii, who betrays his comrades. Nicholas is a cold manipulator and Odoevskii a naive pawn: "I first thought: it's necessary to save people. But now I think, from whom? From an angel? You know, I myself see now the tsar is an angel, not a man" (174). Odoevskii seems hypersensitive, hysterical, and deluded.

In Merezhkovskii's fictionalization, the question of God's role in the revolution occupies many Decembrists' minds during and after the revolt. At times Obolenskii acts like a religious fanatic, continually referring to the path of Christian suffering that lies before the rebels. As the cannons fire, Golitsyn recalls Obolenskii's words: "God is with us! No, Kakhovskii was wrong; there will be revolution in Russia, one which the world hasn't seen before!" (113). At the violence's climax, Golitsyn has a revelation. First, it seems to him that the conspirators are shooting at the Bronze Horseman, the symbol of Russian autocracy and might. Then, he sees the tsar as a "beast" (*zver'*) and suddenly "knew what he had to do: to kill the Beast" (117). This depiction exceeds the violence with which Evgenii menaces the statue in Pushkin's *Bronze Horseman*; instead of merely threatening, Golitsyn needs to kill the tsar as the Antichrist's incarnated representation.

Merezhkovskii poses the question of revolution and anathema by embedding another literary text within his primary narrative. He serves as the ghostwriter for Sergei Muraviev-Apostol's "Reminiscences," where he combines actual snippets of Shteingel's and Matvei Muraviev-Apostol's memoirs, among others, to create a fictional account of Sergei's childhood, the southern uprising and his religious and philosophical views. Collapsing apocalyptic, religious, and historical motifs, Merezhkovskii has Muraviev-Apostol reproach himself for his inability to articulate his "truth": "Alas, my end has come and I have not illuminated the world with any kind of light. But it still seems to me that I had a great thought, an all-illuminating great light; only I could not manage to tell people about it. Knowing the truth and not being able to say it is the most terrible of all human torments" (219). Muraviev-Apostol castigates himself for his resemblance to Don Quixote, his inability to do something with his great idea, and his incapacity to save Russia by giving her "his testament—freedom with God" (219; 221). (Like Golitsyn, Muraviev-Apostol strove for "freedom with God.") Merezhkovskii recounts Muraviev-Apostol's terrifying dream of traversing Russia as "conqueror" with rebel troops and bandit gangs: "Everywhere—freedom without God, evildoings and unquenchable fratricide. And over all of Russia like a black fire is the bloody sun, the bloody chalice of the Devil. And all of Russia is a bandit gang, drunken riff-raff that follows me and cries: 'Hurrah, Pugachev-Muraviev! Hurrah, Jesus Christ!...No, Chaadaev was wrong: Russia is not a clean sheet of paper—on it is already written: The Kingdom of the Beast.' The tsar-beast is frightening, but perhaps the beast-people are even more frightening" (234). Merezhkovskii clearly suggests that Muraviev-Apostol profanes the sacred idea of God's apostle by bringing revolution rather than "the truth" to Russia, instead acting as a failed apostle or Judas. Moreover, Merezhkovskii reveals his true motive: by alluding to contemporary events through the prism of past history, he foretells the worst aspects of the people's revolution as evil unleashed by the Bolsheviks.

Invoking earlier rebels against autocracy, Merezhkovskii refers to Pugachev in his depiction of the revolt. At the beginning, the crowd calls Nicholas a "Pugachev, a Pretender" (106). Afterward, Merezhkovskii says that Nicholas had proved himself "not a pretender, but an autocrat" (120). He transfers the appellation to the conspirators, who have turned into Pugachevs, in at least one rebel's eyes. As Muraviev-Apostol sees it, the Pugachev forces are aligned with the devil, whereas he desires a revolution with God: "And who knows, if I agreed to be the ataman of that bandit gang, to be a new Pugachev, maybe they would not have betrayed me; from everywhere devils would have come down to help me. We would have marched on Kiev, on Moscow, on Petersburg and very likely would have shaken the Russian kingdom" (229). Pugachev later becomes a proto-Bolshevik in early Soviet literature, but here Merezhkovskii depicts him as an unscrupulous, "bloodthirsty villain-hero"[41] and establishes the connection between Pugachev and both the Decembrists and Nicholas. He blends demonic forces with banditry and bloody overthrow, portraying the type of revolution the Decembrists hoped to avoid. He elides one revolt with the next, to its ultimate successor, the October revolution. For Merezhkovskii the Pugachev revolt, the Decembrist uprising and the October revolution are one and the same; each revolution has tragic results for Russia. By association Merezhkovskii indicates his complete disavowal of revolution and lack of support for the Soviet regime.

Given its attention to religious questions and its negative assessment of the *narod-zver'* (people-beast), Merezhkovskii's novel should have been ignored during the centennial. Merezhkovskii was already persona non grata after his 1919 flight to the west. Yet his novel was selectively pilfered by centennial organizers for canonic moments: the eve of the uprising, Trubetskoi and Ryleev's questioning, and the leaders' execution were included in centennial anthologies. Since these scenes followed memoir accounts closely though not faithfully, they could be separated from the novel's more imaginative sections.

Merezhkovskii initially gave a positive assessment of revolution though his view changed after the October revolution. Like his fictionalized Decembrists, Merezhkovskii feared a godless revolution of the masses. In Merezhkovskii's eyes, the Bolshevik revolution appeared to be just that. For Merezhkovskii, the historical novel allowed a veiled critique of current issues. Merezhkovskii questioned Bolshevik practices, refracting them through a historical prism. Deconstructing the Bolsheviks' glowing appraisal of the Decembrists as their forefathers, Merezhkovskii cuts them down to size and in so doing, denigrates the Bolsheviks and their vision. The perspective on revolution as an elemental force with providential overtones is not unique to Merezhkovskii—recall Alexander Blok's *The Twelve* (*Dvenadtsat'*, 1918)—but Merezhkovskii characterizes the Decembrist revolt's participants as knowing but childlike rather than as the ignorant agents of destruction in Blok's poem. Though both writers initially welcomed a change of ruling order in 1917, they quickly shared a growing distrust of the new government and its leaders.

The combination of veneration, and, in Merezhkovskii's case, the demonization of the Decembrists reflects the political and social instability in early twentieth-century Russian society. Concerns with how to establish and firmly maintain power occupied the thoughts of a number of political groups, ranging from the monarchy in the prerevolutionary period to the Bolsheviks before and after 1917. A variety of individuals reflected upon the Decembrists' political and symbolic legacy to come to terms with their own revolution and to determine how the past influences the present. Marxist-Leninist historians of all generations repeatedly refer to Lenin's maxim to affirm the Decembrists' status as progenitors of the revolutionary pantheon and to prefigure the Bolshevik success in 1917. The changes in Decembrist anniversary celebrations illustrate how the Bolsheviks viewed the Decembrists' legacy before 1925. These commemorations set the stage for a discussion of the Decembrist centennial's special import in rewriting history. It was only fitting that the Decembrists should be remembered after the Bolshevik Revolution of October 1917. However, the question remained as to how, where, when, and to what extent the Decembrists' memory should be celebrated. The polemics that ensued during the Decembrists' centennial illuminate the regime's struggle to establish its legitimacy by selecting its own set of coherent symbols and traditions from a sea of possible signifiers.

CHAPTER FOUR

The Battle over Representation during the Centennial

The best monument to the Decembrists is the USSR itself.
—Comrade Cherniak[1]

The Decembrist centennial coincided with the 1905 revolution's twentieth anniversary, making 1925 a pivotal year for commemorations. Capitalizing on the Decembrists' and 1905 martyrs' heroic deeds, the Bolsheviks emphasized their own legitimacy as the last in the long line of Russian revolutionaries. The ritualistic repetition of the recently established genealogy 1825/1905/1917 asserted the regime's stability despite Lenin's death in 1924. Once the beginning and end points of 1825 and 1917 had been put forth, locating and confining the pre-communist chaos, the appearance of order could be maintained, while behind the scenes the struggle for power within Party leadership raged. It was in the leadership's best interests, then, to remind the masses of the Decembrists in all accessible media.

The Decembrists' inclusion in the Bolshevik revolutionary genealogy was initially contested. Questions immediately arose during the centennial's organizational meetings whether the Decembrists should be appropriated as predecessors. The intricate process of selecting some revolutionary figures (the Decembrists, Herzen and the People's Will) and excluding the others (the Socialist Revolutionaries and, for the most part, the Social Democrats) indicates the Decembrist myth's durability and malleability and demonstrates a conscious manipulation of their image for political purposes. This choice was ultimately determined by two sometimes conflicting factors: the shape of the myth before the 1920s and the ideological demands of the early 1920s.

The Polemics

Plans for the centennial began in 1919 when a special commission was established to organize the celebration.[2] Although at first it focused on the publication of archival and biographical materials, it also sought to increase the number of publications for the masses. "The history of the Decembrist movement must be popularized widely," urged the scholar S. Shtraikh, who authored the first articles detailing anniversary plans, and later played a leading role in the Decembrists' centennial.

In 1923, debates commenced concerning the centennial. M. S. Olminskii, an Old Bolshevik and head of the Commission for the Collection and Study of Materials on the History of the October Revolution and the Party (*Istpart*, 1920–1928), sparked the polemics with his article "Two anniversaries: 1905 and 1825." Olminskii noted the overemphasis on the Decembrist centenary compared to the twentieth anniversary of 1905. He opined that the history of the Decembrists was already "chewed over and reiterated" and bemoaned the fact that "the names of the Decembrists who suffered on the gallows, in penal servitude and exile were surrounded by legend." As he saw it, the 1905 revolution had "wrecked the legends of the *batiushka tsar'* and with them the legends about the Decembrists." Olminskii was dismayed that many good communists had forgotten about 1905 in favor of those defunct legends.[3] Olminskii reminded his readers that the Decembrists were afraid of a popular or military uprising and that many recanted their beliefs during their interrogation and trial. Olminskii concluded: "It is understandable that the 100th anniversary will unite the White Guard, Russian and abroad, but what business is it for the Society of Former Political Prisoners? And to whom did the Petersburg comrades establish a monument, to the noblemen betrayers or to the forgotten and unhappy soldiers made fools by them?"[4]

Olminskii's article caused a furor. The editors of *Worker's Moscow* (*Rabochaia Moskva*) published it with the disclaimer that they did not necessarily agree with the author and encouraged people to respond to the article. Several articles appeared in *Worker's Moscow*, *The News* (*Izvestiia*) and *Young Guard* (*Molodaia gvardiia*). One response, "Is It Worth Celebrating the One Hundred Year Jubilee of the Decembrist Uprising?," chastised Olminskii for his "moments of true personal error, which, unfortunately, are capable of planting in young comrades' minds an incorrect representation of the role of the 1825 Decembrist uprising and of its actors."[5] The anonymous author cited Plekhanov and Zinoviev:

> We are prepared, furthermore, to bare our heads before the Decembrists, the earliest generation of bourgeois revolutionaries, who also went into battle against tsarism. These people, representing in the literal sense of the word the cream of the aristocracy, the nobility and the military, separated themselves from their class, broke with their families, gave up their privileges and entered into battle with the autocracy. Even though "they did not have a socialist program, and they were only bourgeois revolutionaries"—our generation does not reject this legacy. We say that this is a glorious past and we bow low before the first representatives of revolutionary populism, those who perished for the people in those days when the *working class was just being born, when there was no proletariat and there could not be a proletarian class party* (author's emphasis).[6]

The anonymous author repeats Zinoviev's assessment that the Decembrists were "bourgeois" (not "gentry") revolutionaries and calls the Decembrists representatives of revolutionary populism *despite* awareness of their class origins. The Decembrists' reconceptualization as populists was the first step in the complex process of remaking their image to conform to Bolshevik requirements. To accept the Decembrists' legacy, the Party must prove that the inheritance was meaningful.

In *Worker's Moscow* P. Kramarov asserted that the Decembrists "with full rights may lay claim as the most progressive people of that time."[7] Noting that earlier no doubts had arisen regarding the jubilee's celebration, Kramarov stated that the Decembrists could not be judged from a contemporary (working-class) standpoint as Plekhanov and others suggested. Kramarov concludes by calling the Decembrists "pioneers of mass political penal servitude." For Kramarov, the Decembrists' significance lay more in their Siberian experience than their revolutionary action. These articles demonstrate the intellectual and political somersaults the ideologues performed to reconcile the contradictory class labels of populism and nobility. As in 1919, when the dissonance did not hinder the Decembrists' inclusion in Proletkult's mass festival dramatizing Russian *populist* revolutionary movements, ultimately it was not a stumbling block in 1923.

The historian Mikhail Pokrovskii (1868–1932) provided the definitive response to the controversy. Pokrovskii utilized all his tactical skill in casting the upcoming anniversary in a politically beneficial light. Initially disparaging jubilees as a "bourgeois custom" and therefore "extraordinarily individualistic," he continues:

> We are obliged to remember our first proletarian revolution [of 1905] each December, regardless of whether it is the 20th, the 18th or the 23rd anniversary, because we should on this occasion remember it, dedicate articles to it, speak about it, organize evenings of reminiscences, etc. . . . As far as the Decembrists are concerned no one is suggesting that they be remembered every December, but marking their centennial is necessary all the same.[8]

Pokrovskii reassesses the Decembrists, providing another corrective to Olminskii's appraisal. He points to the little-known program of the United Slavs as reason alone to celebrate the jubilee.[9] By including the information about the United Slavs in the Decembrist movement's history, he hoped to fill a gap. To bolster the Bolshevik claim to the Decembrists' legacy, he asserts: "we all come from the agrarian program of Pestel."[10] Pokrovskii then cites Herzen, Lenin, and Plekhanov to support the commemoration. He closes his article with the challenge:

> And let White Guardists of all stripes, of whom Comrade Olminskii is afraid, also celebrate their memory. We will tell them: the Decembrists were the revolutionary avant-garde, and you are the counterrevolution's avant-garde, and for that reason only we have the right to consider the Decembrists our forefathers and raise a monument to them.[11]

Evidently, the polemics boiled down to a battle over lineage. Who could claim to be the Decembrists' legitimate heirs? The Bolsheviks wanted to assert their birthright, so to speak, over claims of other political groups at home and abroad.[12] By calling the Decembrists the revolutionary avant-garde of their time, Pokrovskii makes explicit the connection between the Decembrists and Bolsheviks as contemporary avant-gardes. Pokrovskii relies on Herzen and Plekhanov to reshape the Decembrists' image to conform to Bolshevik demands, but his references also reinforce the myth's original intelligentsia orientation.

After his vehement assertion of birthright, Pokrovskii won. The polemics affirmed the celebration's importance and preparations pervaded all institutions of cultural and intellectual life. For the Bolsheviks' rhetoric to be meaningful and powerful, they had to stake their claim as the Decembrists' heirs. They included rituals in their commemoration symbolically underlining their kinship. Thus references to the common points of their programs figure prominently in the centennial. Ritualized repetitions of the Decembrists' desire to overthrow the autocracy, to achieve their goal through regicide, and to enact a radical agrarian program abound in literature discussing the movement. Yet the common points had to be evaluated in the appropriate class context to explain the Decembrists' failure and to assert that only the Bolsheviks—as opposed to other revolutionary parties—could have succeeded. The legitimating genealogy demonstrated the Bolsheviks' organic evolution out of the Russian revolutionary movement. The 1825/1905/1917 schema represented a Marxian dialectic of thesis + antithesis = synthesis. In other words, take the Decembrists (the intelligentsia), mix in some peasants and workers (the 1905 revolt) and, in 1917, you get the Bolsheviks.

Attention to burial rituals and ancestral graves also indicates kinship, hence the commemorations' emphasis on the Decembrists' remains. Attempts were made to find the Decembrists' bones and bury them properly. The centennial of the Decembrists' execution was yet another opportunity to redress the wrongs of the tsarist regime and reaffirm their kinship with the Bolsheviks by finally attending to the executed leaders' burial. The notion of proper burial, as Katherine Verdery suggests, evokes some of humankind's strongest feelings and provides a vehicle for political symbolism. Verdery notes that in many cultures, the belief exists that proper treatment of ancestors enables them to become protective spirits and orders relations between the living and the beneficent dead: "Kinship notions are powerful organizers of feeling in all human communities; other social forms (such as national ideologies) that harness kinship idioms benefit from their power."[13] Verdery elaborates further on their interdependence: "National ideologies are saturated with kinship metaphors....Many national ideologies present their nations as large, mostly patrilineal kinship (descent) groups that celebrate founders, great politicians, and cultural figures as not just heroes but veritable 'progenitors,' forefathers—that is, as ancestors."[14] These concepts also apply to the case of a political group establishing a set of legitimating ancestors. Especially relevant here is the reburial and thus reclamation of the dead as protective or beneficent ancestors.

Verdery argues that in times which require "cosmic reordering"—after revolution or some break with the past—corpses lend themselves particularly well to political manipulation (especially in societies where victimhood and suffering are part of national ideologies) because of their evocation of the awe arising when one considers "cosmic" concerns.[15] Verdery's discussion focuses on the 1990s in the former socialist world, but her points are also apt regarding the concerns of 1917–1925. After the October revolution, as the Soviet state took shape, the need to make meaning of the new cosmic order was especially urgent because of White Guard and wartime challenges. These cosmic questions re-emerged in 1925, since Lenin's death in 1924 evoked concerns of the meaning of life and death and the manner in which the Soviet state should deal with his body.[16] His death raised anew the question of political legitimacy since Lenin had been the Bolshevik party's "main source of legitimacy even during his illness, when party leaders invoked his spirit to authorize policy."[17] Lenin's dictum validated the Decembrists as the Bolsheviks' forebears. The commemorations highlighted the order of succession that Lenin established in his revolutionary genealogy. Thus the Bolsheviks engineered the political, symbolic, and literal return of the Decembrists to their rightful place within the cosmic order to maintain their own legitimacy.[18]

The Organization

The All-Union Society of Former Political Prisoners and Exiles (*Vsesoiuznoe obshchestvo byvshykh politicheskikh katorzhan i ssyl'no-poselentsev*, hereafter VOBPKS) played the centennial's central organizing role, in 1923 forming the "Commission for the Celebration of the 100th Jubilee of the Decembrist Uprising."[19] Composed of 13 members, its primary purpose was to decide the practical questions connected with the celebration. In its first year, the committee focused on publications, making available a wealth of new archival materials. The committee discussed two other arenas of activity: the restoration and maintenance of the Decembrists' graves throughout the union, and the arrangement of a public lecture series for the mass audience.[20] VOBPKS's sponsorship of the jubilee made the intelligentsia orientation clear from its initial stages. Delegates from Moscow, Petrograd, and Chita were invited to take part in organizing the commemoration.

As discussions proceeded, the preparations grew more complex. Various sub-commissions were established: the Decembrist commission of the Central Archive (*Tsentrarkhiv*), to publish documents relating to the uprising, trial, and exile and a special committee for the jubilee's preparation within VOBPKS. The latter committee included the elder revolutionary Vera Figner and distinguished historian Pavel Shchegolev. A permanent subcommittee on the study of the Decembrist movement, headed by Figner, was also created within VOBPKS. This group's main goal, tied to the founding goals of the larger society, became research on the Decembrists' experience during penal servitude and exile.[21] Its stated aims were to publish archival documents and a series of popular brochures and pamphlets on their Siberian period. Finally, the planning commission discussed establishing a Decembrist monument and museum in Chita. Those activities would parallel the quest for the executed Decembrists' graves (ongoing since 1917) and the placement of a Decembrist monument in Leningrad. By marking the locus of Decembrist activity in Siberia, the center could ensure the involvement of the union's outlying regions. The valorization of the Decembrists' exile also linked them with subsequent revolutionaries, since many were also sent to Siberia for punishment.

The organizers must have hoped to elicit greater support among the intelligentsia for the jubilee by including figures from the scholarly and revolutionary communities, such as the historians Shchegolev and Shtraikh, and Figner, one of the most visible and venerated of elder revolutionaries. The intelligentsia assisted the official Soviet cooptation of the myth by providing the scholarly resources to determine which aspects of the Decembrist movement served Soviet purposes. The official appeal to the two communities also was an attempt to unite them in support of the government. The inclusion of an elite revolt into the legitimating genealogy of a state established ostensibly by and for the workers and peasants alludes to the necessity of the learned elites' support. It also suggests the tension between the three groups (government, scholars, and elder revolutionaries) and their visions. The Decembrists' incorporation makes explicit the connection between the groups as vanguards of their eras, of course with the qualification that the Decembrists lacked popular support, unlike the Bolsheviks. The refashioning of the Decembrists' image gives another example of elite manipulation of historical narratives for political advantage. But as Thomas Sherlock argues, more than merely "cultural tools" to support power, "the myths have survived as powerful normative and symbolic frameworks for both elite and mass politics."[22]

Despite the intelligentsia's dominance of the organizational process, attempts were made to appeal to a popular audience. VOBPKS sponsored the publication of an "Inexpensive Library" (*Deshevaia biblioteka*) of short brochures on the Decembrists including at least eight titles, ranging from "Who Were the Decembrists?" to "Nicholas I and the Decembrists" to "The Chernigov Troop Uprising."[23] In 1925, Shtraikh, also a member of VOBPKS, took stock of the nineteenth-century sources on the Decembrists in a presentation to organizers of centennial "Decembrist evenings." His lecture was subsequently published as a separate brochure, which became a primer for organizing centennial materials and was distributed union-wide.[24] Explaining how the Decembrists should be presented to the masses, Shtraikh takes the first step in forming a Soviet canon of Decembrist texts. He details the jubilee's polemics and recommends approaches for speakers and organizers of anniversary events. Discussing the anniversary's broad scope, Shtraikh lists the local commissions involved and stresses the importance of workers' and Red Army clubs in disseminating information about the movement. Shtraikh proposes that lectures (illustrated by diapositives with portraits and pictures of Siberia) should be given in clubs union-wide. He recognized the theater's utility in disseminating the Decembrists' image, suggesting the "brightest moments of the history of the Decembrist uprising, their trial and life in Siberia" should be staged for the populace.[25] Shtraikh acknowledged the Siberian period's appeal to a still religious population in its aspect of redemptive suffering.

Shtraikh places Pokrovskii as his first authority, then adds Plekhanov's address, "December 14, 1825," despite its hagiographic slant. Shtraikh expects the Decembrist centenary to assist not only in the masses' enlightenment regarding the Decembrists' true role but also to illuminate the tsar's true character. Shtraikh outlines the correct historical perspective on Nicholas, setting two parallel processes into play. As the Decembrists become more glorified, the tsar becomes more discredited. The tsar's confirmed moral bankruptcy reinforces the autocratic system's breakdown and further legitimates the Soviet government in the populace's eyes.

VOBPKS' journal, *Hard Labor and Exile* (*Katorga i ssylka*), disseminated information on the jubilee preparations. It announced publishing activities, plans for public lectures, and dedications of "Decembrist corners" in museums. These "Decembrist corners" echo "Lenin corners," shrines for worshipping the hallowed leader, and were secular versions of the Orthodox placement of an icon for veneration in a domicile's northwest corner.[26] In the first issue of 1925, a longer discussion of the Decembrists appeared addressing the centenary's meaning and significance.[27] Reflecting the disparity between Pokrovskii's official (Marxist-Leninist) view and the competing intelligentsia assessment, this article posits the French Revolution as the starting point for the development of Russian political consciousness. Prior Russian popular uprisings are not discussed. Whereas Pokrovskii highlighted the Decembrists' earlier cult status among the prerevolutionary intelligentsia, and corrected the view by foregrounding the movement's "Russian" aspects, the anonymous author shows the movement's universality. The revolt's character and plan is simplified and somewhat misrepresented: "The goals and tasks of the Decembrists' conspiracy consisted in the freedom of all the people from the autocratic system's political and economic yoke and in wide social reforms on a democratic foundation."[28] The article presents, in short form, the same canonical moments from other commentators: Herzen's comment about the cannons' thunder rousing all of Russia, Pushkin's epistle to Siberia and Odoevskii's response to Pushkin. It stresses the importance of publishing activities: "The best way of honoring the Decembrists' memory is to familiarize today's reader with their ideas, their personalities, with their heroic feat (*podvig*). Therefore, the first stage of the jubilee celebration is to publish their works, their political and social programs, their own memoirs and letters and also to conduct research on all aspects of their lives and activity (183)." The article details forthcoming publications of new and archival materials.

The planning committee's meeting minutes (November 23, 1925), provide more information on the celebration. Initially comprised of representatives of VOBPKS and the Central Archive, the committee expanded its membership to include The Lenin Library (Rumiantsev Museum), the Museum of Revolution of the USSR, the Historical Museum in Moscow, and the Society of Lovers of the Russian Word. The planners also personally invited the scholars A. M. Zaionchkovskii, E. E. Iakushkin (grandson of Iakushkin) and S. I. Mitskevich, a member of the Society of Old Bolsheviks, to participate. Two new sections were created: the literary section and the lecture-excursion section. The latter group sought to organize a series of instructive lectures and excursions (i.e., mandatory field trips) for educators and Red Army schools and used Shtraikh's aforementioned brochure. The lecture commission would provide speakers not only to Moscow but also to the provinces. The VOBPKS presidium decided to commemorate the Decembrists at its second All-Union meeting on December 20 at the Bolshoi Theater. Government representatives, member of the diplomatic corps and other institutions were also invited. Another meeting

was set for January 12, 1926 dedicated to the Chernigov troop uprising, the Southern Society's revolt. It would include lectures and an
artistic performance. The Museum of Revolution's exhibition on the
Decembrists would coincide with VOPBKS' all-union meeting. The
organizational committee requested 50,000 rubles from the state to
pay for various aspects of the celebration, including the publication
and dissemination of informational materials, museum exhibitions, the
commemorative meeting, and lecturers' fees.[29]

Attempting to control the Decembrists' image, VOBPKS created
an information bureau related specifically to the centennial's organization. The bureau was charged with providing a central point for
disseminating substantive information about centennial activities and
addressing any institutional or private inquiries about the Decembrist
movement.[30] The ties of the information bureau with the Soviet press
ensured minimal uniformity in the Decembrists' presentation and
allowed it to provide articles for mass publication.

I have found evidence contradicting Clark's assertion that the
Decembrist centennial was less publicized than the 1905 anniversary.[31]
Official rituals may have featured 1905 more prominently than 1825, but
the intellectuals' involvement assured that the Decembrists' centennial
was commemorated widely in journalism, prose, scholarly publications,
theater, and opera. All the important journals celebrated the uprising;
museums mounted exhibitions; poems and articles were dedicated to
the Decembrists in union-wide and local newspapers; workers' clubs
and schools organized performances. Events and articles continued
into January 1926 to commemorate the Southern Society's revolt. The
public was reminded of the Decembrists yet again in July 1926 during
the execution's centennial. The three anniversaries constituted seven
months of celebrations, with the execution's centennial emerging as an
equally important component for its political symbolism.

The Decembrist Jubilee: The Affirmation of the New Genealogy

The Decembrist jubilee occurred in Moscow, confirming it again as
the center of Soviet life, culture, and government.[32] A few smaller
scale events took place in Leningrad.[33] The most important aspect of
the Leningrad commemoration was the renaming of Senate Square
(*Senatskaia ploshchad'*), the site of the revolt, as Decembrists' Square
(*Ploshchad' dekabristov*), which allowed the Decembrists a prominent
place in Leningrad's landscape.[34]

The main event, the second annual meeting of VOPBKS, occurred on December 26 in Moscow's Bolshoi Theater and celebrated the Decembrist centenary and twentieth anniversary of the first Russian revolution of 1905. Leon Trotsky opened the meeting with a speech entitled, "The Year 1905," depicting 1905 as the rehearsal for 1917. After Trotsky's remarks, the orchestra played a burial march and the audience rose to honor the Decembrists. Felix Kon and Vera Figner then spoke about the Decembrists. Kon's presentation, "The Decembrists in Penal Servitude and Exile," emphasized their suffering and sacrifice was a model for later revolutionaries, concluding: "Not a single drop of blood, not a single drop of suffering, fell in vain."[35] Figner discussed the Decembrists' contribution as the progenitors of the Russian revolutionary movement,[36] closing with the promise "to braid a wreath of honor and glory for our grandfathers, the Decembrists."[37] Following Lenin's statements on the Decembrists, Figner highlighted their generational significance. A reporter from *Worker's Moscow* spoke of the touching effect of Figner's speech and portrayed the evening in sympathetic terms. However, an account in *The Worker's Newspaper* (*Rabochaia gazeta*) viewed things differently: "Too many gray-haired heads. This is not like our usual meetings. But this is an unusual meeting. This is a meeting of the veterans of the revolution, those who were in the tsarist camps for a collective total of more than 12,000 years."[38] This commentator respects the sacrifice of the elder revolutionaries, but implies that their views diverge from contemporary concerns.

Delegates from Khabarovsk, Chita, Verkhneudinsk, Omsk, Iakutiia, and other cities attended the meeting; various party, professional, and Komsomol organizations sent telegrams and letters with greetings.[39] The widely-attended meeting was supposed to give even-handed treatment of the Decembrists and 1905 Revolution. However, it appears that Trotsky (a high-level party functionary with little prior contact with the society) was meant to give the correct ideological spin and provide the centerpiece speech. Was this an attempt to railroad the meeting and shift the emphasis to 1905? Or was it merely a way of commemorating both revolutions at once and saving time and expense? Certainly the privileging of the Decembrist uprising by two speakers (appointed by VOBPKS) indicates the society's, and intelligentsia's, disposition to favor 1825 over 1905.

In any case, the commemorative evenings following VOBPKS's meetings drowned out talk of 1905. Not only did the events and publications honoring Decembrists outnumber those celebrating 1905,[40] but the luminaries connected with the Decembrists outshined those associated with 1905. This dominance reflects the intelligentsia's privileging of the noblemen revolutionaries over the peasants and workers of 1905 to counteract Marxist-Leninist rhetoric. The Decembrists' descendants remaining in Soviet Russia were trotted out for the celebration, bolstering intelligentsia attendance and interest: Iakushkin's grandson, Kornilovich's descendants, I. N. Shumov and Grim-Grzhimailo, Brigen's grandson,[41] and A. M. Muraviev's granddaughter, Natalia Vachnadze.[42] The descendants were a valuable resource; Vachnadze lent family portraits and other memorabilia to the Decembrists' exhibition in Moscow. Most important, they were a living link to the past glory of the Decembrists' feat.

Though the vibrancy of the Decembrists' legacy was emphasized, death references surfaced (as in the burial march played during the All-union meeting). On December 27, famed director Konstantin Stanislavskii made opening remarks at the Moscow Art Theater's commemoration. Stanislavskii called the event a "civil requiem" (*grazhdanskaia panikhida*):

> to recall these days and summon onto the stage shadows, pale though they may be, of these images and those people who one hundred years ago sacrificed their lives for us who came many years later.
>
> Let these pale shadows help the assembled more strongly and closely pay attention to those memorable days and their heroes. Let their written words, which will ring out today from our troupe's artists, help the listeners and spectators better understand the thoughts and feelings with which the Decembrists lived.[43]

For Stanislavskii, the Decembrists' legacy was their written testament, now accessible to his contemporaries through publication and dramatization. After the speeches, scenes from a stage adaptation of "The Decembrists" were performed and excerpts from contemporary documents (such as Pestel's *Russkaia Pravda*, and poetry by Pushkin, Ogarev, Ryleev, and Nekrasov) were read by the actress Olga Knipper-Chekhova and others. Later that evening, N. Venkstern's play *In 1825* (*V 1825 godu*) premiered at the Moscow Art Theater's second stage (*MKhAT II*). The play, panned by the critics for its improper, non-Marxist orientation, recapitulated the Decembrists' image from Merezhkovskii's novel.[44]

The Leningrad commemoration took place at the Academic Theater of Opera and Ballet on December 29. Comrade Praskovia Kudelli, head of *Istpart*'s Leningrad division, provided another perspective on the Decembrist uprising. She called the revolt an "exclusively noble bourgeois (*dvorniansko-burzhuaznoe*) uprising," echoing terminology developed expressly for the Decembrists' incorporation into the Bolsheviks' legitimating genealogy. If the Decembrists could be an example of both gentry and bourgeois sentiment, then the transition to Marxism-Leninism in Russia did not occur prematurely. As Marx saw it, bourgeois capitalism had to precede socialism. Once the Decembrists were designated "noble-bourgeois" they bridged the gap between the two developmental phases of feudalism and socialism. Discussing why the revolt could not have succeeded, she emphasized that the uprising's roots were the French revolution, the Napoleonic campaign and the western orientation of noble officers and soldiers. In the end, however, Kudelli dismisses these foreign influences and the class difference between the Decembrists and Soviet citizens: "Their banner was not ours, but all the same, it is necessary to admit that they, not sparing themselves, threw themselves into the cause and perished: December 14 was the first blow to autocracy and today we offer them a tribute of grateful honor."[45] The speech was followed by two pieces by Beethoven, the overture to "Leonora" and the Ninth Symphony, and by two acts from Iurii Shaporin's incomplete opera *The Decembrists*, on the romance between Pauline Gueble and the Decembrist Ivan Annenkov.[46]

Although most newspaper articles do not discuss audience responses to the events, evidence suggests that the masses found the celebrations utterly tedious. One article lamented the poor attendance at the dedication of the "Decembrists' corner," at Pushkin House on December 27: "In the comfortable, bright, and warm home of the greatest poet, in that dear temple of grateful memory, there are so many holy relics, priceless unique manuscripts and portraits and so distressingly few pilgrims."[47] The religious terminology illustrates the Decembrists' continued veneration, despite the authorities' attempts to shatter their legendary status. The audience was comprised of the intelligentsia, scholars who studied the Decembrists, and Decembrists' descendants, including Decembrist Bodisko's daughter, Zavalishin's and A. Muraviev's grandsons, and Muraviev's and Ivashev's granddaughters. In addition to the Pushkin House exhibition, exhibitions opened at the Museum of Revolution in Moscow (December 26),[48] the Tolstoy Museum in Moscow and the State Library in Moscow (December 29). The last exhibition tracked visitor attendance. It had 1,198 visitors mostly from excursions over the course of one month, averaging a paltry 40 visitors per day.[49] Outside the capitals, the Tomsk regional museum dedicated a "Batenkov" corner, imitating the creation of Lenin and now "Decembrists'" corners in many institutions.[50] If the State Library's exhibition was the only one included on workers' and school excursions then this record is a sure sign that the public's interest had flagged, or at least, that the scholars' choice of media did not appeal to them.[51] It may well have been that the public had its fill of "relics" (living and otherwise) and meetings. Clark suggests that the masses' lack of interest in the year's revolutionary commemorations (not to mention in "highbrow culture" in general) resulted from the craze for American adventure films, especially those with Douglas Fairbanks.[52] The Decembrists and 1905 martyrs faced stiff competition indeed.

The celebrations continued in January 1926 in the capital and the provinces. To commemorate the Chernigov troops' uprising, the celebration in Kiev occurred on January 9 at the Ukrainian Academy of Sciences. The academician Hrushevskii spoke about the Decembrists' influence on the Ukrainian national movement. Subsequent speakers discussed the contemporary Ukrainian intelligentsia's involvement in the uprising. V. V. Miiakovskii touched on the legends and songs about the Decembrists arising in Ukraine immediately after the uprising, remarking that "[a] special halo surrounded the name Ryleev," and claimed Ryleev as a Ukrainian patriot. That evening workers' clubs hosted discussions and Kiev's Museum of Revolution featured an exhibition with items of local interest. In another example of the definition of communist space, territory was claimed by the centennial celebrants. Streets were renamed for Decembrists in Kiev and Vasilkov; monuments and memorial plaques were placed in Trilesy (where the local school was renamed in the Decembrists' honor), in Kamenka (at the Davydov estate) and the village Lintsy was renamed Pestelevo. Volkonskii's and Poggio's graves, located on the Volkonskii estate, Voronki, were repaired for the jubilee.[53] These rituals affirm kinship through their figurative genealogy and attention to burial rites, repeating patterns set forth by the capital cities' celebrations.

Newspapers and journals also memorialized the centennial. Most published material, except for items of local interest, was rehashed and borrowed from union newspapers. It was not uncommon for the same article to appear in at least four different newspapers, though not always under the same title or on the same date. Articles appeared from December 23 to January 5. Taking center stage, Pokrovskii's "December 14, 1825" graced the pages of *Pravda* on December 30, 1925, then *Izvestiia* and *Leningrad Truth* (*Leningradskaia pravda*) on January 1, 1926. Regional and local newspapers, *Worker's Path* (*Rabochii put'*, Omsk), *The Hammer* (*Molot*, Rostov on the Don), *Kiev Proletarian*

(*Kievskii proletarii*), *Red Banner* (*Krasnoe znamia*, Tomsk), to name a few, carried similar treatments of the revolt. It appears that all newspapers were obligated to commemorate the Decembrists and to include items of local interest, no matter how mundane.[54] Given his prominence in the Communist establishment—by 1925 he was the head of the Communist Academy, the Society of Marxist Historians and the Institute of Red Professors, to name a few of his official duties—Pokrovskii represents the official Soviet evaluation of the Decembrists at this stage.[55] In addition to "December 14, 1825," his other articles were featured in *Pravda* and *Rabochaia gazeta*, papers with large readerships.[56] In the jubilee articles, Pokrovskii takes an iconoclastic stance, undermining the intelligentsia's treatment of the Decembrists as "holy relics."[57] He vehemently insists that until recently Marxist historical and class analysis of the Decembrists was regarded as sacrilege. Pokrovskii protests too much here, recalling Olminskii's iconoclasm only two years earlier during their polemics on the centennial. Though Pokrovskii and another author discuss the "legend of the Decembrists" to provide a Marxist-Leninist appraisal and educate the masses about the movement's class orientation, most others invoke the highly idealized portrayals of the past, often echoing their hagiographic tone.[58] Even articles that give "class-based" analyses of the Decembrists frequently close in praise of the martyrs: "The red banner of the revolution, stained with the blood of many generations, was transferred from hand to hand. In 1917 it was firmly planted above Peter-Paul Fortress, where one hundred years ago our forefathers suffered."[59] This emphasis and valorization of the Decembrists' martyrdom suggests again that the majority of commemorative articles came from intellectuals rather than party ideologues. These hagiographic articles were most commonly reproduced in local newspapers, easily outnumbering reprints of Pokrovskii's article though his had pride of place in the union-wide publications.[60]

Despite varied authorship, the jubilee articles follow a set pattern. Early on they cite Lenin, Plekhanov, Zinoviev, and/or Herzen. Following Lenin's dictum of the three generations of Russian revolutionaries, they locate the Decembrists' significance as the first organized revolutionary uprising against the autocracy as an institution, thus distinguishing them from peasant uprisings and palace coups. The articles emphasize Lenin's conclusion that the Decembrists did not succeed because they were distant from the masses. They analyze the ideological and economic differences between the Northern and Southern Societies and the United Slavs. Many close with a quotation from Pushkin, Odoevskii or Ryleev for emotional impact. They feature remarkably similar iconography, consisting most often of the frontispiece to Herzen's *Poliarnaia zvezda* (with the profiles of the five executed leaders) (see fig. 3) or portraits of Ryleev, Pestel, and/or Muraviev-Apostol. The articles differ in emphasis according to the writer's purpose. For example, jubilee publications feature Bestuzhev-Riumin and Kakhovskii less frequently, since they did not articulate political programs nor did they play a major role in planning the revolts. However, when authors emphasized their prominence, it was because he espoused regicide, and they wanted to underline the historical continuity between the Decembrists' thought and the Bolsheviks' execution of the imperial family.

The July 1926 Centennial of the Decembrists' Execution

The commemorations of the execution took place in Leningrad, indicating the importance of its physical location. The desire to correct the past by locating the bodies of the executed Decembrists and properly burying them casts the Bolsheviks as the Decembrists' heirs. In finally laying the five leaders to rest, the Bolsheviks endeavored "to attend to the ancestors properly so they will fructify the enterprise of their descendants."[61] The Moscow authorities may have relinquished control to Leningraders because the celebration honored only five men instead of the Decembrists' common experience. There may also have been an effort, conscious or not, to avoid associations with Orthodoxy, where rituals associated with death have greater symbolic meaning than those accompanying other events.[62] However, it seems that this commemoration became more significant to the public specifically because of these associations.

At the time of the centennial, the Decembrists' gravesite remained undiscovered. When in June 1917 an Italian construction company found five graves while laying water pipes on Golodai Island, the Decembrists' purported burial place, OPD assumed that the bones they found belonged to the Decembrist leaders. Before 1925 they were not subject to any scientific analysis. After medical analysis and research by *Istpart* in 1925, the conclusion was reached that they were not the executed men. The definitive statement was publicized in July 1925 in *Evening Moscow* (*Vecherniaia Moskva*); but in any case, the Vasiliev Island regional committee of *Istpart* still wanted to place a Decembrist memorial there.[63] Though lacking the burial site and remains, the planners decided to situate the Decembrists' monument on Golodai Island (later renamed for the Decembrists) near the shore as the most likely burial site, and to continue searching for the "graves dear to us" (*dorogie nam mogily*).[64]

Details of the Decembrists' memorial appeared in *Leningradskaia pravda* in March 1926. An article reported the monument would be on Golodai Island, a red granite obelisk with a "pantheon-museum" at its base, in which leaders' bones would be placed. An electric light in the form of a large red star would be at the top; on the pedestal a bas-relief picturing the executed men. The monument's unveiling was scheduled for July 13/26, 1926.[65] In an ironic twist, the obelisk had been taken from an 1873 memorial dedicated to Alexander I by the builder of the Putilov factory. (Lenin's decree on monuments allowed for re-use of monuments to prerevolutionary heroes and tsars rather than their outright destruction, so recycling was a common practice.[66]) The memorial to the newly claimed heroes of the Soviet regime would be constructed literally from monuments of the past. Alexander I's obelisk would consecrate the hallowed ground of the revolutionaries who originally sought to assassinate him. But the monument would have its Soviet imprint and re-casting as well: it would be electrified (one of Lenin's most pressing campaigns after the revolution was the electrification of the entire union) and would have the red star, a prominent symbol of Soviet power, at its peak. Here the Bolsheviks reclaim the past and incorporate it into a new revolutionary history, memorializing the Decembrists' names and figuratively laying to rest their remains. The monument thus literalized two metaphors about the Decembrists: first their foundational status in Soviet revolutionary genealogy and second, their role in supporting Soviet power, as their bones were literally to lie in the monument's base, beneath the electrified red star.

As the July centennial approached, newspaper articles and poems stressing the Decembrists' martyrdom bombarded the public.[67] "Freedom's Martyrs" by A. Olenin serves as a representative text, repeating many legends, including Ryleev's mythic claim: "We will die, but we will die with glory."[68] Olenin provides short descriptions of the leaders and focuses on their reactions to their death sentence, transcribing their apocryphal last words. The article cites Herzen, Odoevskii, and Plekhanov and closes with Pushkin's epistle to Siberia. The July commemorations ranged from lectures and memorial evenings at several clubs to a large open-air ceremony at the Decembrists' memorial site. The placing of the monument's base provided the central occasion for ceremony and speeches. The tribunal and area for the demonstration would be decorated by slogans and flags done by artists and members of fine arts circles of Leningrad's Vasiliev Island district. Libraries and booksellers would set up displays and stalls selling appropriate materials. After the monument's placement, two factory choirs would perform revolutionary songs and in the evening, a movie would be shown outdoors. From the description of the planned activities, the day was to be like an open-air fair.[69]

The newspaper accounts of the ceremonies depict a solemn festival instead. Tens of thousands of Leningrad workers' delegations from factories and plants, some with orchestras, and delegations from other institutions and organizations, came to the deserted island, creating "a forest of banners and posters" on the site. Representatives from *Istpart*, the Museum of the Revolution, VOBPKS, Veterans of the Revolution, the Academy of Sciences and the large Leningrad factories attended. The relatives of the executed Decembrists—Bestuzhev's granddaughters, Kakhovskii's nephews, and Ryleev's great grandson—also attended the commemoration. Several delegates made speeches. The first, comrade Zhigarev, from the Vasiliev Island regional committee, spoke in the loftiest terms of the "glorious revolutionaries": "Today's gathering proves that the working class honors those who gave their lives for freedom. Our young generation will always remember the names of the executed Decembrists. Eternal memory and eternal glory to the Decembrist fighters."[70] Zhigarev lauded the Decembrists' martyrdom using the vocabulary of the Orthodox burial mass, promising *vechnaia pamiat'* (eternal memory). Comrade Iaunzen (representing VOBPKS) continued the hagiographic tone stating that "the history of political imprisonment began with the Decembrists. The Decembrists began it, we ended it and we are certain that it will not be repeated." A member of the Academy of Sciences, the academician Krachkovskii gave his perspective: "The imperial government, burying the Decembrists' corpses, knew that it was burying freedom's first shoots (*rostki*). However, it did not know and could not foresee what magnificent shoots they would grow." In his mythogenic rhetoric, Krachkovskii conceptualizes the genealogical line from the Decembrists to the Bolsheviks as an organic process. These various explanations for the Decembrists' significance highlight their multivocality as a symbol; they could be something to everyone. Comrade Cherniak, the Communist Party Provincial committee's representative, summed up in appropriate ideological terms: "The best monument to the Decembrists is the USSR itself."[71] The Decembrists' importance was magnified to its largest incarnation and its predestined, logical conclusion: according to the genealogy, the USSR ultimately resulted from their uprising. These mythic statements clearly suggest that the speakers were conducting a massive propaganda campaign. After the speeches, the celebrants read a telegram sent by A. Lunacharskii. At the moment of the monument's placement, the Philharmonic Orchestra played a march by Chopin and a memorial plaque was placed on the site of the future monument (erected in 1939[72]), marked by a large red flag.[73] The commemoration concluded with a sports competition, mimicking the ancient Greek tradition of funerary games honoring dead heroes. The day's events, colorful yet solemn, must have inspired the crowd with a sense of the heroes' greatness: banners and posters, a solemn yet festive march, lofty speeches and games all told of the Decembrists' significance.

Dekabristiana

Much like the precedents set by Western and tsarist celebrations, the Decembrist jubilee provided an occasion to produce popular, marketable objects. The consumer goods represented the canonic moments of the Decembrists' history. Unlike the rampant commercialism of the 1899 Pushkin celebration—which generated kitschy products including Pushkin pens, stationery, tobacco, rolling papers, cigarettes, matches, candy, liqueur, vases, cups, perfume[74]—and the jubilees of the British monarchy,[75] the objects were limited in scope, mainly commemorative stamps and porcelains.[76]

In the jubilee's honor, three different stamps were issued for 3, 7, and 14 kopecks. The scenes, taken from paintings in the Museum of Revolution, portrayed the Decembrist exiles (3 k.), the uprising on Senate Square (7 k.) and the executed leaders' profiles (14 k.). The last image was already very familiar to the public not only because it was the frontispiece to Herzen's journal, *Poliarnaia zvezda*, but also because of its mass reproduction during the anniversary year. The prices assigned to the stamps reflect the hierarchy of the canonic moments and further emphasize the Decembrists' martyr status. F. G. Chuchin asks:

Is it possible for philatelists not to mark the hundredth jubilee of the first and last bourgeois revolution in Russia at the time when the entire free worker-peasant Soviet Republic from small to great has decided to celebrate it? No, of course not. . . .

Many of us old revolutionaries truly recall with pride these heroic images at the dawn of our revolutionary activity, which inspired us in the battle with tsarist autocracy by their personal courage and example, despite their difference in social origins, final goals and ideals of revolutionary struggle.[77]

Calling the Decembrist revolt a "bourgeois revolution," Chuchin echoes the rhetoric of Kudelli's speech during the memorial ceremonies, in which she casts the Decembrists as "noblemen-bourgeois." He also exhorts his contemporaries to keep their memory alive: "As they look at the stamps in honor of the 100-year jubilee, let our readers also recall and clearly imagine these genuine revolutionaries of the young Russian bourgeoisie, who perished with honor in the name of their revolutionary ideals of freedom, despite their aristocratic, noble origins. Let the memory of them live in our hearts and in the hearts of the entire country's young collectors."[78]

The State Porcelain Factory produced several objects for the jubilee, including a vase with a picture of the revolt on the Senate Square and a plate with the profiles of the five martyrs and the inscription: "But you have not perished in vain, what you have sown will rise up."[79] Porcelain manufacture, a familiar part of bourgeois prerevolutionary commemorations, replaced past subjects with more appropriate ones for the new revolutionary regime, yet another refashioning of an old form into a revolutionary medium. The drive to educate the masses about the Decembrists penetrated all realms of popular culture during the centennial.

The Formation of a Decembrist Canon

In the 1920s, during the period of reassessment of Russian history and literature by the Bolsheviks, the Decembrists' image was refashioned for propagandistic purposes. Though a few articles had been written on Pushkin and the Decembrists, no survey had been conducted of the Decembrists' image in Russian literature prior to Shtraikh's seminal brochure *On the Decembrist Jubilee*, which recommended appropriate literary representations for the Bolsheviks' ideological purposes and shaped the myth's literary canon as it developed in the 1920s. In Shtraikh's ranking, Tolstoy takes first place for his fragment on the Decembrists and his epilogue to *War and Peace*. Merezhkovskii comes next for *December 14*, which Shtraikh claims "artistically represents the period according to precise documentary facts."[80] After briefly discussing Decembrists' memoirs, Shtraikh cites Herzen's axiom about the cannon's thunder to affirm the uprising's significance, asserting: "It is not coincidental that all following generations of Russian political and revolutionary activists considered the Decembrists their spiritual fathers (*dukhovnye otsy*). By their self-sacrifice (*samopozhertvovanie*) and their conscious martyrdom (*soznatel'noe muchenichestvo*) the Decembrists laid the beginnings for the Russian revolutionary movement" (15).

Shtraikh emphasizes the importance of the Decembrists' Siberian experience, highlighting the wives' centrality to the myth. He foregrounds their role by quoting Odoevskii's and Nekrasov's poetry. He treats literature as history without differentiation. Although he provides factual material about the Decembrists' wives, he does not question the artistic works' historical accuracy. Shtraikh closes with citations from Odoevskii's response to Pushkin, Zinoviev's *The History of the Russian Communist Party* and Pushkin's epistle to Siberia.[81] Pushkin "prophetically" has the last word in Shtraikh's text, "foreseeing" the Russian revolutionary movement's success nearly 100 years after the Decembrist revolt. A dual validating principle goes into action; the Decembrists make Pushkin politically correct and Pushkin makes them historically significant by choosing them as a subject for his art, and reveals his prophetic capabilities by "predicting" the Bolsheviks' success.

Shtraikh collects and prepares the validating texts for popular distribution and consumption. Though he benefited from surveying the 1923 polemics, which provided historical sources on the Decembrist movement, he had less guidance in his literary survey. He expands the established canon by including works of Tolstoy, Merezhkovskii, and V. G. Korolenko's "The Legend of the Tsar and the Decembrist," ("*Legenda tsaria i dekabrista*," 1911). Shtraikh's survey of the literary representations broke ground for his contemporaries and for later eulogizers of the Decembrists. With the exception of the Korolenko text, the majority have since become a true Soviet canon. Authors of jubilee literature on the Decembrists continually return to these works to maintain the Decembrists' significance. Shtraikh also sounded the call for more work on the Decembrists and Pushkin, resulting in the rise of a veritable industry of scholarship focused on the Decembrists' influence on various writers.[82] This call would later be satirized as "jubilee-ology," a branch of scholarship remarkable for its formulaic nature and superficiality.[83]

If Shtraikh's brochure is a "short course" in the Soviet canon of the Decembrists, then his version can be juxtaposed to those of N. Brodskii,

S. Gessen, and Figner (in a more limited discussion of the Decembrists' wives), who also desired to define the Soviet myth's form.[84] Brodskii's treatment of the Decembrists is by far the most exhaustive. He provides canonic readings of works normally omitted because of a negative view or unsubstantiated references to the Decembrists. Brodskii details the critical legends related to Pushkin's "Decembrist" works and leanings, from "André Chénier" to the similarities between Lenskii and Kiukhelbeker in *Eugene Onegin*. He confirms the interpretation of Chatskii as a Decembrist (first posited by Herzen)[85] and continues with a long list of well-known and obscure works.[86] He frequently criticizes the authors he cites for their lack of historical accuracy and for their reliance upon official versions of history. All the same, he acknowledges that these writers "complete the circle of a hundred year tradition" of honoring the Decembrists as the first freedom-fighters and people's champions against the autocracy.[87] The sheer volume of works depicting the Decembrists openly or alluding to them illustrates how large they loomed in the nineteenth- and twentieth-century cultural imagination.

Gessen reevaluates the literature on the Decembrists, providing a happy medium between Shtraikh's short course and Brodskii's lengthy list. Gessen cites as primary texts Pushkin's chapter 10 of *Eugene Onegin*; Tolstoy's *Decembrists*; Nekrasov's *Russian Women* and "Grandfather"; Danilevskii's unfinished historical novel *1825*; Gnedich's play *Decembrist*; Merezhkovskii's novels (*Alexander I* and *December 14*); and Nikolai Lerner's play, *Nicholas I*. Gessen suggests that literary works limited to depicting the Decembrists fail because "not one of the authors who turned to the Decembrists' history was capable of wholly grasping the meaning and significance of December 14. The only one who perhaps could have been capable was Pushkin, of course, but the circumstance that he was their contemporary and, if we may express it thus, their foster brother, deprived him of the opportunity to crown his brilliant poetic intention."[88] Though Gessen's reasoning smacks of smugness, it demonstrates a significant phenomenon in Soviet criticism. Pushkin's evaluation transcends all others, signaling his deification in the Soviet literary pantheon. Gessen's preference for the text Pushkin never created also testifies to Pushkin's validating role in the Decembrist myth.

Unlike other works, Figner's 1925 article on Decembrists' wives takes an openly iconoclastic stance. Though not the first to criticize Nekrasov's portrayal, Figner still challenged the wives' mythic images in both literature and history:[89]

Nekrasov's poem *Russian Women*, resurrecting the images of Princesses Trubetskaia and Volkonskaia, appeared in an era when Russian women made great gains. In the 1860s, under the influence of new conditions arising as a result of the peasants' liberation and associated reforms, woman asserted her identity in the domain of family relations, demanded the right to independent labor, to higher education and participation in social activity. Her spiritual growth in this decade was so great, that entering the 1870s, she immediately became the men's comrade in the revolutionary struggle for socialism and freedom, joined secret groups, circles and societies, and participated in peaceful propaganda as well as organized military activities. How distant this is from the relationship of Ryleev and his wife![90]

Figner shows that the wives performed their "moral feat" out of love rather than political consciousness. Conditioned by the valorization of suffering and sacrifice in Russian Orthodoxy, certain members of the intelligentsia and Russian revolutionaries of the mid- and late-nineteenth century transformed this urge into their ascetic values and recapitulated the Decembrists' self-sacrifice in their terrorist acts against the Russian government.[91] While eradicating Russian orthodoxy's hold on the new Soviet man, the new regime preserved models of revolutionary sacrifice beneficial to their own purposes.

Figner also raises contemporary concerns: the question of spontaneousness versus consciousness and the women's equal role in the revolutionary movement:

Yes, life has changed, it overcame the terror before Siberia with other, even more frightful terrors. Yes, it raised the demands on individuals and led woman alongside man to the scaffold and beneath the bullet. But spiritual beauty still remains in the distance of time and the women's enchanting image in the second quarter of the last century shines even now in the undying splendor of earlier days. Their deprivations, losses and moral suffering unite them with us, the women of the latest revolutionary generations. But for them the arrest and punishment brought upon the Decembrists were shocks ripping the earth out from beneath their feet. Their upbringing, their way of life, habits, milieu—all rebelled against the threatening future revealed before them. But the women of our last half century consciously met their fate. They thoughtfully prepared themselves and possessed great good, taking part in the great movement, to see through to its glorious future. That gave them strength and gave them moral gratification and spiritual peace. The Decembrists' wives did not have this.[92]

Ultimately even she falls under the sway of their influence:

> Didn't they reveal before our progressive writers the qualities they called "the valor of the Russian woman?" And after them wasn't the Russian woman obligated to introduce these qualities to our much-suffering revolutionary movement? When you read the Decembrists' touching memoirs, or in the quiet of the evening hours peruse the personal narratives of Volkonskaia and Annenkova, are you not filled with gratitude to these women?... Will we not admit them, in all sincerity, as our precursors, our leading lights, illuminating the expanse of our revolutionary movement?[93]

Figner alludes to her subtext in her conclusion. Ostensibly, she asserts how different the wives were from her contemporaries: they lacked political consciousness, they were not the men's equals, and they sacrificed out of love and duty rather than revolutionary zeal. These deeds, almost as good as her generation's sacrifices, were not politically motivated. Yet, Figner also seems to be nostalgic for a different time, one without the "passionate, cruel and great tribulations" of the last decades. Figner offers these women's memoirs as distraction from current worries. Hilde Hoogenboom argues: "The Bolshevik revolution forced her to think of the role of the individual activist and revolutionary organizations in history," and speculates that Figner conducted a veiled polemic with the Bolsheviks, asserting her former organization's (the People's Will, the terrorist arm of the Populists) right to claim the Decembrists as heirs.[94] In any case, Figner posits the Decembrists' wives as the precursors for her (and in general, women's) involvement in the revolutionary movement because of their self-sacrifice, even after her previous claims to their differences and generational gap. Figner follows a strategy similar to the one used during the centennial's polemics. Figner subverts her original iconoclasm and affirms the "unattainable ideal" that the wives provided.

Figner grapples with the mythic legacy left to revolutionaries and reflects that the Decembrists had to be regarded in sociocultural terms, beyond the confines of Marxist-Leninist history. The polemics in the Russian press questioned the legendary status of the Decembrists. However, in the end, the Bolsheviks asserted their claim to the Decembrists as their forefathers, displacing all other possible heirs (Kadets, SRs, and the White Guard). Despite attempts to shatter the myths, the earlier images of the Decembrists as passion-sufferers (*strastoterptsy*) remained, though with a new twist. Emphasis shifted to literary representations of programs and ideas in which the Decembrists were read as proto-Bolsheviks and the mechanics of legitimization began. We need only recall the ritualistic citation of Herzen's remark about the Decembrists awakening an entire generation to see the tremendous impact Russian literature had in the formation and canonization of the Decembrist myth. Though the Decembrists lost their "artistic" currency when the revolutionary activist was no longer oppressed but ascendant, they gained great scholarly and mythic currency.

★ ★ ★

During the Decembrist centennial, two opposing schools of thought came to resolution regarding the legacy of prerevolutionary Russian history. Stites asserts, "One of the major features of Soviet culture and the Soviet way of life and one of the secrets of its survival is its ability to retain certain key elements of the deep Russian past, modified and harnessed to the use of the regime."[95] The authorities worked out their relationship to specific historical movements and moments; the struggle between the iconoclasts and the anti-iconoclasts within the government and its fledgling institutions was decided in favor of selective preservation of the past and its symbols: "The state decidedly opposed the sweeping away of past culture as a prerequisite to building the new society. While willing to efface Romanov symbols, it nurtured a striking eclecticism that began to emerge in the 1920s and was fully established in the 1930s."[96] The Decembrists' fate manifests this eclecticism. By renaming the Decembrists (as *dvorianskie revoliutsionery*) and placing them as the first phase of nineteenth-century revolutionary movements, Lenin found the Decembrists a prominent place in the Soviet revolutionary pantheon. Once the Party decided it was in its best interests to exploit the myth for legitimating purposes, ideologues were well-armed in the struggle for the Decembrists' legacy. The centennial confirmed the Decembrists' status through its rituals of speechifying and publishing, which, despite other variations continuously, ritualistically repeated Lenin's maxim that the Decembrists were forefathers of the Russian revolutionary tradition.

CHAPTER FIVE

Centennial Representations in Fiction and Film

If not for my childhood, I wouldn't understand history. If not for the revolution, I would not understand literature.

—Iurii Tynianov[1]

Tynianov's New Mythology of the Decembrists

Iurii Tynianov (1894–1943) spent most of his career challenging accepted conventions of Russian literary criticism and history, beginning with his work as a graduate student in S. A. Vengerov's graduate seminar and ending with his historical novels. Tynianov's novel *Kiukhlia* (1925), based on the life and art of the Decembrist poet Vilhelm Kiukhelbeker and titled after Kiukhelbeker's nickname, was commissioned by Kornei Chukovskii at Kubuch publishers as a popular brochure for young readers in honor of the Decembrist centennial. One of the few literary works produced for the centennial, it diverged significantly from a children's story by the time it was finished. Only one other novel written for the centennial, *Severnoe siianie* (*Aurora borealis*, 1926) by Maria Marich (1893–1961), had staying power and was reprinted 20 times into the 1960s.[2] (Soviet print runs did not necessarily indicate popularity but instead reflected what the authorities considered an ideologically useful work and what the public should be reading. Hence the huge print runs of Lenin and Stalin's collected works, for example, compared to the dearth of volumes of Akhmatova and Tsvetaeva). *Aurora borealis* did not match *Kiukhlia*'s literary quality or provide a new perspective. Chukovskii attests to *Kiukhlia*'s uniqueness, calling it "remarkable" for its recreation of the epoch, elegance of its overall composition and psychological richness, and affirmed its acclaim: "Immediately after its appearance in print *Kiukhlia* became the most beloved book of both old and young Soviet citizens, from twelve to eighty years of age. It has become clear that it is really a universal book—both for the highly qualified and the so-called mass reader, for the academician and for the fourth-grade schoolgirl."[3] Given its popularity, the novel serves as a barometer of the Decembrists' appeal to Soviet readers of the 1920s. Though built upon earlier representations, *Kiukhlia* ultimately created a new mythology of the Decembrists.

Unlike the authorities, who debated the efficacy of claiming the Decembrists as forefathers, the intelligentsia quickly seized the opportunity. Clark suggests that Tynianov and other members of the intelligentsia explored the allegorical potential of 1825 in the official genealogy to grapple with their own concerns: "Eighteen twenty-five emerges in their works not just as a revolutionary high point, but more as a nodal point leading to the 1830s and 1840s, that is, to Nikolaevan Russia, which became a particular obsession of intellectuals around this time as an exemplum, generally presented in the grotesque mode, of stagnation, bureaucratism, obtuseness, and provincialism."[4] Boris Gasparov sees a mythological fusion of the eras of the early nineteenth and early twentieth century in modernist writing; the idea of "the age's turning point" (*perelom veka*) penetrated texts produced in the 1920s and early 1930s by authors including Pasternak and Tynianov.[5] As these associations were very much in the air at the time, Tynianov's depiction of the split in Russian society caused by the Decembrist revolt may be viewed as a historical parallel to the societal rift created by the Russian revolution.

Scholarly consensus regards Tynianov's novels as an intrinsic part of his theoretical and critical work, whether one contends that Tynianov merely extended his scholarly research into fiction or that he specifically used fiction to criticize the current regime. Tynianov explains his shift from literary theory to the novel: "My fiction arose, for the most part, from dissatisfaction with literary history which glided from one common point to another and unclearly represented people, currents and the development of Russian literature.... The need to become more closely acquainted with them and to understand them more deeply—that's what fiction was to me."[6] Andrew Wachtel observes that Tynianov blurs the boundaries between history, literature, and the genre of biography to get to a more profound understanding of the past.[7] Tynianov's dissatisfaction with the increasingly "unscientific" methodology of literary criticism led him instead to the creation of the "scientific novel" (*nauchnyi roman*), in Angela Brintlinger's words, "a hybrid genre."[8] Tynianov discerned a metaphor for the postrevolutionary mood in Soviet Russia in the cultural milieu of the 1820s–1830s with its suppression of public debate and liberal causes after the Decembrist uprising. Whether Tynianov looked to the experiences of revolution and its aftermath 100 years earlier to extrapolate potential courses of action in his own time is still open for debate. His representation of the loss of the cream of society after the failed revolt and the subsequent degradation of Russian society anticipates the growing persecution and subsequent destruction of the non-Bolshevik intelligentsia during the late 1920s–1930s.[9]

However, the implicit parallels between the postrevolutionary situations were lost on the critics. *Kiukhlia* was lauded for its "brilliant and delicate portrayal" of Kiukhelbeker and his contemporaries: "One reads the tale about the Decembrist with engrossing interest: page after page it unfolds the events of those amazing years in the history of Russian society and Russian spiritual culture, which comprised the year 1825."[10] Despite the praise, the work was also criticized as a "one-sided elucidation" of the Decembrist uprising that did not give an "objective picture of the uprising or revelation of its reasons and its essence." Another contemporary reviewer cited the book's limitations: "the somewhat idealistic 'aestheticized' presentation of the Decembrist uprising to the reader," the emphasis on the uprising as the basis for the biography of Kiukhelbeker rather than as an "independent social fact" and the supposition that the novel was not written for a mass reader.[11]

The problems the critics cite actually strengthen the representation of the uprising, which diverges from the typical portrayal and occupies the space between fiction and history. Instead of elaborating the rebels' positions and authorities' actions, Tynianov focuses on the revolt's primal nature. He depicts the protagonists' inner thoughts, dwelling on the uprising's psychological implications. Tynianov thus moves away from the frameworks imposed by the historical determinism of Marxist-Leninism and the Romantic conception of great men as the makers of history.

In its psychological orientation, Tynianov's novel is a thoroughly modern work. Much like Claude Levi-Strauss's notion that any historical episode can be viewed as "a multitude of individual psychic moments,"[12] Tynianov highlights the fragmentary nature of historical interpretation, instead providing a highly poetic, lyrical depiction. Tynianov alternates scenes of the revolutionaries' panicked action with vignettes of the imperial forces. To illustrate the revolt's emotional and psychological impact, he zooms in on the minds of Kiukhelbeker and Nicholas. Throughout Tynianov interweaves lyrical passages on Petersburg and its integral role in the uprising. Thus Tynianov continually refocuses his artistic lens, shifting from individual psychology to scenes of panoramic scope. Early in his treatment of the uprising, Tynianov claims that the city of Petersburg exerted an inexorable force in the story. He does so by employing the familiar trope of the contrast between Petersburg and Moscow:

> Petersburg was never afraid of emptiness. Moscow grew building by building which naturally interlocked one with another and became overgrown with little houses. Thus arose Muscovite streets. Moscow's squares cannot always be distinguished from the streets, from which they differ only in width and not in spirit of expanse. The tiny crooked Muscovite streams are also like the streets. The fundamental unit of Moscow is the building, therefore in Moscow there are many dead-ends and alleys.
>
> In Petersburg there are no dead-ends at all, and each alley strives to be a boulevard. In it one isn't really sure if certain streets are boulevards or alleys... The squares were created before the streets. For that reason they stand on their own, completely independent of the buildings and the streets which form them. The unit of Petersburg is the square.[13]

The architectural variations of Moscow and Petersburg allude to a larger spiritual contrast in Moscow's need for crowding and Petersburg's need for expanse. Tynianov explores this contrast by comparing the two cities' revolutionary uprisings: "Petersburg's revolutions took place on the squares: the Decembrists' of 1825 and February's of 1917 occurred on two squares. And in December 1825 and October 1917 the Neva participated in the uprisings. In December the insurgents fled on the ice. In October the cruiser Aurora threatened the palace from the Neva. For Petersburg the union between river and square is natural. Every war in it inevitably must turn into a war of squares" (231). For Tynianov, the variation in the cities' architecture and design indicate not only their essential differences, but also influences the types of revolution occurring in each location, which ultimately shapes the course of history and distinguishes the revolt that will succeed. Tynianov implies that the events of 1825 and 1917 never would have taken place in Moscow, given its overall layout and design. Only in Petersburg, a place with no central point (like Moscow's Kremlin) could such revolutions occur. Since Petersburg's power base is decentralized with the Senate and Winter Palace as important architectural monuments symbolic as loci of power, the rebels of 1825 have to make a choice between them, as in 1917, when the storming of the Winter Palace became the central symbolic moment of revolutionary success. During the Decembrist revolt, the rebels decide not to take the building, contrary to their best interests and Nicholas's expectations: "Nicholas's heart beats resoundingly beneath his thin uniform. They've taken the palace, it's over. Thus pass a few minutes. The crowd of grenadiers reappears at the gates and come closer. The small bowlegged officer is ahead of them all. Nicholas sees the first ranks, makes out the gray stubble on the unshaven cheeks of the old soldiers, unbuttoned ammunition, and now sees clearly the red, inspired face of the small officer. He understands nothing. Where are they going? Why did they abandon the palace?" (253). The troops give up an important strategic position in their struggle, instead joining the rebelling Moscow division on Petrovskaia square. (Nicholas himself directs them to their comrades.) Thus, the rebels' choice to occupy exterior space by staging their revolution on the city's squares rather than taking possession of interior space dooms the revolt to failure.

Since Petrovskaia square figures largely in the uprising, Tynianov dwells on its physical presence, dominated by Falconet's large statue of Peter the Great commissioned by Catherine II. He details the history of the construction of St. Isaac's cathedral on the edge of the square to illustrate the rivalry between Catherine II and her son (and successor) Paul I in architectural terms. Though Catherine stopped work on the massive marble structure, Paul resumed its construction (though in brick, rather than in marble). This denigration of material signifies symbolically the moral fall from Catherine's to Paul's era. Paul's successor and son, Alexander I, decided to rebuild the cathedral entirely since he did not like its appearance. Tynianov relates the verses which criticized the changes, highlighting the Russian tsars' caprices:

> Сей храм—двум царствам столь приличный,
> Основа—мрамор, верх—кирпичный.
>
> Сей храм—трех царств изображенье:
> Гранит, кирпич и разрушенье.

> This church, so fitting for two reigns,
> The base is marble, the top brick.
>
> This church is the image of three reigns:
> Granite, brick, and destruction.

He closes: "So Petrovskaia square, representing the autocracy's might, lay next to St. Isaac's square, signifying its weakness" (232). Tynianov effectively sets the scene for the uprising's ensuing drama among the symbols of both tsarist might and weakness. He extends the parallel to the revolt itself; the rebellion points out the cracks in the imperial edifice, but alone cannot cause that structure to crumble. Tynianov compels the reader to view the architecture as a text narrating Russian autocracy's high and low points. The physical surroundings of the squares, streets, and buildings convey messages and provide the uprising's context. Thus Tynianov portrays the revolt as an event which must be understood within the semiotic system of Petersburg's architecture, further illustrating the interpenetration of history and culture. Tynianov privileges the impersonal, inanimate elements over the individual's impact on historical events; this choice subverts the centrality of men as historical actors. For Tynianov, it was not the men who fought on the squares in a battle for authority, but rather, "the uprising of December 14 was a war of squares" (232). Emphasizing the tyranny of Petersburg's geographical organization as a historical factor, Tynianov evokes Andrei Belyi's *Petersburg,* the quintessential text that synthesized the nineteenth-century myth of Petersburg as a city of spectral hallucinations with the representation of the city as a center for revolutionary activity in the early twentieth century.[14]

Adding to the earlier tradition of Petersburg as a city of illusion, Tynianov infuses his portrayal with a supernatural element. He creates a sense of uncertainty on two levels. First he gives a sense of the instability and changeability of Petersburg architecture. Second, he draws attention to the city's emptiness and quietness, conveying a sense of foreboding: "What does this peacefulness and quiet mean?"(233). Tynianov thus conditions the reader to expect an important event to take place.

Tynianov's representation of the revolt also recalls the metaphorical picture that Pushkin gives of Evgenii's rebellion as the little man caught in a clash between the elements in *The Bronze Horseman*. Wachtel also discusses the allusion: "Tynianov not only marks an overt parallel between his age and the first decades of the nineteenth century, he also draws a parallel between himself and Pushkin as writers describing 'rebellions' in Petersburg in literary form."[15] Like Pushkin, who exploits the flood as a metaphor for rebellion against authority, Tynianov pits man against the elements in his depiction. The climactic scene of the novel artistically and psychologically stresses the revolt's elemental nature within an architectural context:

> The entire day was an exhausting oscillation of squares, which stood, like cups on a scale until the rude push of Nicholas's artillery brought them out of balance. The squares, not the streets, decided and there were no heroes on this day. Ryleev, who could have been a hero, understood the vacillation of the squares better than anyone and went somewhere unknown in an incomprehensible sadness...
>
> They couldn't halt the threatening, dazed condition of the squares, which were carefully weighed.
>
> The old autocracy was weighed, the beaten brick of Paul. If only Petrovskaia square—where the wind carried the scalding sand of the noble intelligentsia—had merged with Admiralty square—with the young clay of the masses, they would have prevailed.
>
> The brick prevailed and pretended to be granite. (233)

Tynianov represents the uprising as a confrontation between elemental forces, but not those of nature such as air, fire, wind, and water. Rather, he transforms the struggle into one of cultural forces, between the civilized, oppressive building blocks of granite and brick (the autocracy), triumphing over sand (the intelligentsia). The actors (Ryleev, Trubetskoi et al.) play at most a secondary role. The city and its components dominate: the squares, brick and granite. The wars are played out between these elements and alliances are made between squares and the Neva. Tynianov asserts that man cannot change the course of events: "Nowadays the frosty, ice-covered squares decide, and not the will of individual people" (249). By emphasizing the architecture's role in the military struggle between tsarist forces and insurgents, Tynianov further downplays the individual's historical role. Tynianov's method of shifting the narrative focus from humans to inanimate objects fits into the context of Russian and European modernist experimentation and distinguishes his depiction of the Decembrist revolt.

Tynianov adds another layer to his picture of human helplessness by emphasizing the internal confusion that the protagonists' experience. On the morning of the uprising, Kiukhlia behaves as if his will is not his own: "From the very morning a light and free madness entered into Vilhelm. His head was heavy, his legs light and empty and each muscle was the part of some whole, the center of which was outside Vilhelm. He moved as if under the control of some terrible and sweet power and each step, each of his movements which seemed funny and strange to an outside observer, were not his movements. He did not answer for them" (235). This terrible yet sweet power takes control of Kiukhelbeker, driving him to commit acts that seemed foreign to him earlier.

Like other representations of the uprising, Tynianov's tale emphasizes the day's disorder and the conspirators' mad actions. Kiukhelbeker's madness (*bezumie*) further manifests itself as he rushes about, trying to rouse support for the rebel troops, brandishing a pistol in his right hand. Tynianov continually highlights that Kiukhlia's arm is divorced from his brain and acts on its own.[16] This otherworldly force (call it revolution) turns him into a walking zombie, whose stumbling and bumbling later leads to the bungling of an important opportunity. After three failed shots at Grand Prince Michael, Kiukhelbeker encounters Iakubovich, who also behaves as if he were playacting. Iakubovich, baring his sword, confronts Kiukhelbeker: "'It's a masquerade,' he mumbled. 'I was volunteered to be a truce-bearer'" (260). This bizarre exchange shatters his hallucinatory feeling. Experiencing a sense of detachment similar to Pierre Bezukhov's estrangement on the battlefield in *War and Peace,* Kiukhlia watches the scene on the square:

> How pleasant and how cold. He eats snow again. And the fog clears a bit. He looks around. He sees how some general rushes from the Moscow regiment. Whistles and cries fly after the general. On the gallop, the general takes his plume from his hat and waves it for some reason in the air. Vilhelm wipes his eyes. Everything is clear again, his legs are light, each muscle is part of a whole, the center of which is outside Vilhelm. And the first thing that he again clearly and distinctly sees: the government troops standing opposite, parted on two sides and between them with the gaping maws of the guns, dimly illuminated by the twilight, stands the battery.
> And gray, transparent quiet falls for a moment. (260)

At the very moment when the battery has been set up to quash the rebel troops, Kiukhelbeker feels a sense of peace. The literal fog (from gunfire) and figurative fog (in Kiukhelbeker's mind) begin to clear, yet Kiukhelbeker still cannot derive meaning from what he sees. He does not understand that the general's signals to the artillery will bring on death and ruin for the rebels.

Tynianov heightens the estrangement by portraying the final rout in musical terms, as a battle between "the delicate singing of canister shot" and "the dry conversation of rifles" (263). The symphony falls quiet after a fourth volley; the rebels can no longer fight. At this point, Kiukhelbeker gets swept into the crowd. As if in a slow-motion camera pan, he glances around him and sees with "terrifying, penetrating clarity" the chaos around him: the wounded and dying, the shuddering of the buildings. He hears the crunch of bones under his feet. Kiukhelbeker's perceptive clarity continues up until his capture several weeks after the uprising. Tired of evading the authorities, he succumbs to exhaustion and allows himself to be arrested on arrival in Warsaw.

Tynianov closes his account of the uprising with a lyrical passage describing the evening of December 14. He evokes a hypnotic mood by listing elements which convey the atmosphere: "On the square were fires, smoke, watchmen's calls, cannons with their muzzles turned to all sides, cordon chains, patrols, rows of Cossack spears, the dull shine of the bared broadswords of the Cavalier guards, the red crackling of burning wood beside which the soldiers get warm, and rifles placed into pyramids" (263). His "method of lyrical associations"[17] lulls the reader with its adumbration of the sights. The description continues with another long list, set off by paragraphs made up of the lone word "night" (*noch'*):

> Night.
>
> The walls, shot through, the dislodged window frames along all of Gallernaia street, the whisper and quiet fuss on the first stories of the surrounding homes, the rifle butts beating the bodies, the quiet, swallowed moan of the arrested.
>
> Night. (265)

This lyrical compendium recalls Alexander Blok's famous poem "Night, a street, a lamp, an apothecary" (*Noch', ulitsa, fonar', apteka*, 1907–1916), the paean to St. Petersburg's nightmarish monotony. His syntactical monotony reflects the city's meaninglessness and unchanging quality on a linguistic level. Tynianov intensifies the feeling of numbness with a surreal and detached elaboration of the brutality that took place:

> The walls of the Senate, bespattered with blood in fan-shaped patterns, corpses. Heaps and solitary bodies, black and bloody.

Wagons, covered with burlap, from which blood drips. On the Neva from Isaac's bridge to the Academy of Arts is a quiet bustle: they push corpses through narrow breaks in the ice. Occasionally one hears moans among them—along with the corpses they push the wounded through the narrow holes. Quiet fuss and shuffling: The police disrobe the dead and the wounded, take rings from them, fumble through pockets.

The dead and the wounded will become attached to the ice. In the winter they will cut the ice here, and in the transparent blue ice floes they will find human heads, hands and legs. (265–66)

This image of separated frozen body parts recalls Kiukhlia's seemingly detached arm as he brandished his misfiring pistol. Besides highlighting the scene's gruesomeness and the tsarist police's cruelty toward the victims, the passage reinforces the revolt's strange end. The dead became one with the frozen Neva. The entombed corpses were still among those living in Petersburg, but not alive. In the same way, the conspirators were among the living in Petersburg, but also not quite alive. As Boris Eikhenbaum put it, Kiukhelbeker became "a living corpse: his civil life ended on December."[18] So were many Decembrists, entombed in the bowels of Peter-Paul Fortress until their sentencing and exile. Thus the living and dead Decembrists became an integral part of Petersburg's concrete structure, and the fabric of the Petersburg myth, adding to the city's spectral atmosphere.

Despite the unusual lyrical form Tynianov exploits, he follows convention by portraying Kiukhelbeker as an eccentric (*chudak*), but in so doing transforms the tired cliché into a meaningful motif. He emphasizes Kiukhlia's quixotic side, continually referring to his eccentric nature (*chudachestvo*) and awkwardness (*nelovkost'*). Not only do his enemies remark upon his strangeness, but so do his friends. An acquaintance, Sofia Dmitrievna Ponomareva, tells him that people say he is a duelist and a dangerous man. His good friend Griboedov calls him a "Don Quixote, a nice little dandy" (155). Tynianov depicts Kiukhelbeker's sensitivity when Lycée classmates mock his poetry: Kiukhelbeker becomes so upset, that he tries to drown himself. Pushchin castigates Kiukhelbeker for allowing literary models to influence his behavior: "After all, you aren't Poor Liza" (44). His sensitivity does not decrease as time passes. When Pushkin lampoons Kiukhelbeker in some new verses, Kiukhlia becomes so enraged he challenges Pushkin to a duel.[19] Even more infuriating, Kiukhlia overhears a conversation on the street during which a young man says to his companion: "Today something's made me kiukhelbekerish" (69). Remarking on the irony of Kiukhelbeker's fate, the critic and writer Andrei Sinyavsky joked: "No matter what the poor guy did—went to Senate Square, wrote a tragedy—nothing helped: he was stuck forever with that "kiukhelbekerish.'"[20] Beyond emphasizing Kiukhelbeker's idiosyncratic personality and behavioral eccentricities, Tynianov exaggerates Kiukhlia's physical attributes: his height, his stooped posture, his nearsightedness, his stammer. One character calls him a "freak"(*urod*) in her diary entries. Faddei Bulgarin's police description takes Kiukhelbeker's odd appearance to its artistic and comic height: " 'Kiukhelbeker, Vilhelm Karlovich, collegiate assessor,' Faddei wrote, 'tall, thin, with bulging eyes and brown hair.'... 'His mouth twists during conversation. He has no sideburns, his beard barely shows, and he walks somewhat contortedly.' Faddei remembered the drawling voice of Vilhelm. 'He speaks in a drawl, is passionate, hotheaded and has an unbridled temperament'" (269). As Tynianov depicts him, Kiukhelbeker manifests his oddity outwardly and internally.

Notwithstanding the comic potential available to the author, why would Tynianov choose, of all the possible heroes for his novel, one who was considered a misfit? Because of his alleged lack of literary talent? Or his inability to fit in to his own surroundings and society? One contemporary reviewer notes: "The unsuccessful poet, the Decembrist unable to fulfill the mission given to him, Kiukhlia is surprisingly inept and often funny in all his appearances. Even through the seeming dispassion of the author, at times one imagines his ironic smile at the adventures of his unsuccessful hero."[21] It appears that Tynianov capitalized on the appeal of the foolish character with genuinely good intentions. Tynianov may have chosen Kiukhelbeker to show the Decembrists' inability to fit into society, to hint at the impossibility of their success and to draw the parallel between them and the high-minded intelligentsia who also did not fit into Soviet society. He also may imply that the Decembrists' clash with the ideology of their day resembled his own questioning of Soviet ideology.

Though Kiukhlia's very awkwardness and misfortune endear him to readers, Tynianov bestows heroic qualities on Kiukhelbeker to make him sympathetic. Tynianov portrays him as a young man who early on is aware of society's inequities. He resents the divide that serfdom places between the Russian people and the landowners, he criticizes the tyranny that the noble class exercises regarding the serfs, he always interferes when he sees corporal punishment inflicted, and feels great sympathy for the Greeks striving for freedom from the Turks and wants to help them. More than the external, physical characteristics of *chudachestvo*, Tynianov points to Kiukhelbeker's moral characteristics as heroic, despite his inability to fit in: he will not be servile and cannot act against his convictions.

Several characters notice these traits and their role in Kiukhelbeker's estrangement from society. Pushkin early on remarks on Kiukhlia's rigidity: "I love you like a brother, Kiukhlia, but when I'm no longer here, remember my words, you will never know neither friend nor beloved. You have a difficult character" (62). Kiukhelbeker fails in Europe because of his incendiary lectures on Russian literature; he does not succeed in civil service because of his nervousness and distaste for capital punishment. While in the Caucasus as General Ermolov's secretary, he distinguishes himself by his unusual behavior and his inability to fit in. He complains to Griboedov: "I am prepared for a crime, for vice, but not for meaningless life. Where can one flee?" (145).

Kiukhelbeker finds a sense of belonging and meaning when he meets Ryleev and Bestuzhev. After discussions with them about literature and other lofty topics, he joins them in producing a journal. Only on the revolt's eve is he brought into the secret society that will alter his life: "When Vilhelm left Ryleev's, he felt joy. His heart beat differently, a different snow was beneath his feet...Ryleev accepted him into the society" (219). Kiukhelbeker senses that his induction into the group has changed him. Tynianov casts the event as an initiatory experience for Kiukhlia. Never again will he feel the purpose in life that he does on the day of the revolt. Recalling Kiukhlia's earlier statement that he was prepared for anything but a meaningless life allows evaluation of his subsequent actions. Despite his adherence to a lofty moral code, Kiukhelbeker brings both shame and ignominy on himself. Tynianov suggests that the search for meaning in one's life should not be based on politics or ideology and that Kiukhelbeker is mistaken to take that path.

Tynianov points to another reason for Kiukhelbeker's alienation. Like many sensitive, artistic personalities, Kiukhlia discovers early on that reality does not measure up to his imagination. His disillusionment with life continues when, after his imprisonment ends, his reunion with his brother does not live up to his expectations: "Vilhelm felt a strange feeling. His brother was alien. Stern, busy, taciturn. The meeting wasn't turning out the way Vilhelm dreamed it would" (322). Pushkin's words have become prophetic. At the end of Kiukhlia's life he feels that he is surrounded by people who don't understand him: "Everything was clear: the marriage was for nothing.... The land and the garden with which he couldn't cope were good for nothing. Only his verses remain, and his drama which could have honored even European theater, his translations from Shakespeare and Goethe, whom he was the first to introduce to Russian literature a quarter of a century ago" (326–7). The only consolation that life affords is his art. Yet even that comfort is temporary and perhaps illusory. On rereading his work one day, Kiukhelbeker comes to a terrifying conclusion: "Suddenly something new pricked him: his drama seemed awkward to him, the verses wilted to the extreme, the similes were forced. He jumped up in terror. The last hope was crumbling. Or was he some Trediakovsky of the new times; with good reason all the literary horsemen laughed at him 'til they were about to drop... From that day on began Vilhelm's true torments" (327). At this point, Kiukhelbeker loses all will to live. The destruction of his hopes to be included in the European literary pantheon weighs too heavily upon him, given his other sorry circumstances. This seems to be his greatest tragedy; the loss of faith in his writing's value means for him the loss of life's meaning.

Tynianov's parallel between Kiukhelbeker and Trediakovsky is especially telling here. He makes this connection to establish a particular literary genealogy for Kiukhelbeker. Irina Reyfman remarks that references to Trediakovsky were always symbolically charged. They frequently served in literary polemics either to suggest a writer's lack of literary talent or to note a writer's use of an outdated literary language, style or genre.[22] The perception of Trediakovsky as an antihero resulted because of mythological modes of thinking during the eighteenth century, which were grounded in an awareness of the novelty of the systems of literary language and literature being created. The poet Mikhail Lomonosov attained the status of culture hero and Trediakovsky became the comical antihero. Though Trediakovsky's image as "the fool" was divorced from historical reality, it took hold on the Russian cultural consciousness for centuries despite attempts by writers and critics to correct it. This begs the question: why would Tynianov choose to ally his hero with Trediakovsky, Russian literature's acknowledged fool and bad poet?

Given Tynianov's study of literary culture, he knew the potentially negative associations involved with invoking Trediakovsky and was not the first to exploit the resemblance. In 1813, Pushkin drew the parallel between Trediakovsky and Kiukhelbeker in an epigram condemning Kiukhelbeker's use of archaisms; again in 1814, Pushkin calls Kiukhelbeker "another father of a second *Tilemakhida*" (1:25). Here Pushkin casts Trediakovsky as the exemplar of bad poet and posits Kiukhelbeker as a direct heir to that tradition. Later in the 1830s Pushkin acknowledges that Trediakovsky's image was not tied to historical reality and comes to view Trediakovsky as a martyr to the cause of literature and innovator in his own way.[23] Tynianov emphasizes these two potentialities by associating Kiukhlia with Trediakovsky. Reyfman comments: "For the twentieth-century modernists, it [the image of Trediakovsky the fool] became a symbol of provocative creativity, of revolutionary disregard for tradition, and of contempt for conventional success."[24] Tynianov thus exploits Kiukhlia's creative and subversive potentiality as a fool by drawing the parallel between Kiukhlia and Trediakovsky as martyr-fools.

Tynianov's reevaluation of Kiukhlia reworks another element common to canonical depictions of the Decembrists. Like many authors, Tynianov discusses the Decembrists' relationship with Pushkin, but does so with a twist. Kiukhlia and Pushkin's friendship, developed during their Lycée years, looms large throughout the text. Relating several anecdotes about their close bond, Tynianov exploits their childhood pranks for all their comic potential, as seen in his portrayal of their duel.[25] However, Tynianov's depiction of the relationship serves a greater purpose seen in the light of the Trediakovsky motif. Since Tynianov posits Kiukhlia as a trickster or fool, his treatment of Kiukhlia and Pushkin's relationship explores the dynamics of mythmaking. Tynianov portrays Kiukhlia's foolish aspects (his allegedly antiquated literary style and his eccentric personality) against the backdrop of Pushkin's literary output and persona. Pushkin figures as the culture hero, a position similar to Lomonosov's in the eighteenth century. Yet neither Pushkin nor Kiukhlia become completely idealized figures in Tynianov's work; he senses the foolish and martyr-like aspects of both characters and emphasizes their resemblance. This awareness heightens the poignancy of their later relationship. As he languishes in solitary confinement, Kiukhelbeker celebrates Pushkin's nameday by imagining they are together: " 'Congratulations, Sasha,' Vilhelm pressed his cheek to Pushkin's. 'My dear, my joy, send me everything that you've written. Imagine, I remember your 'Gypsies' from start to finish.... As you said Sasha, though I go my own way in poetry and consider Derzhavin the greatest poet, your verses are still in my heart' " (303). Recalling Pushkin and his poetry helps Kiukhelbeker survive.

Later in the novel, Tynianov documents the iconic moment when Pushkin coincidentally meets Kiukhlia at Borovichi station on his way to Dinaburg fortress. As the friends embraced, the guards pulled them apart and did not allow them to speak or to say farewell. This scene has become standard fare for all works on Pushkin and the Decembrists.[26] However, Tynianov embellishes his representation to convey more fully Pushkin's sense of tragedy and loss. He imagines Pushkin's reaction to one of Kiukhelbeker's smuggled letters: "Pushkin pressed the messenger's hand for a long time, led him to the doors and then sat in his study over the yellowed page and reread it, bit his nails, frowned and sighed" (312).

The last scene of the novel, at Kiukhlia's death bed, attests to the strength of the poets' bond. Kiukhelbeker, attended by his wife and Pushchin during his last few days, has a final vision of Pushkin as he dies: "He heard some sort of sound, of a nightingale or perhaps a stream. The sound flowed like water. He was lying at the brook, beneath a branch.... 'We have to hurry,' Pushkin said quickly. 'I'm trying'—Vilhelm answered guiltily—'you see. It's time. I'm getting ready. There's not enough time.'...Pushkin kissed him on the lips. He thought he smelled the light scent of camphor. 'Brother,' he told Pushkin with joy, 'brother, I'm trying'" (331–32). Pushkin, Russia's poet-genius and Kiukhelbeker's best friend, guides him to the afterlife. Their reunion was foiled at Borovichi station in 1827, but beyond the grave they come together again. Tynianov handles this scene without ostensible irony, yet the question arises whether this is a genuine hymn to the strength of their bond. Tynianov portrays Kiukhlia at the end as a man who feels like a failure as a poet and as a human being. Can reunion with Pushkin in another realm nullify this sense?

In answer, let us turn to Eikhenbaum and Shklovskii, who commented on the novel's popularity, asserting that Tynianov resurrected Kiukhelbeker from his derided fate. Eikhenbaum claims: "Kiukhelbeker was completely forgotten—both as a poet and as an individual; nonetheless his role in the struggle for new literature was considerable. This role was rather clearly illustrated in [Tynianov's] *Archaists and Pushkin*. But his fate as a consistent Decembrist was not revealed there, though both in the text and notes, flicker details and speculations which depict the tragic face of this great misfortunate."[27] Shklovskii notes that Tynianov reshaped Kiukhelbeker's image, stating that at this point Kiukhelbeker's fame as Pushkin's close Lycée friend eclipsed even that of Delvig.[28] Becoming Kiukhelbeker's champion, Tynianov preserved Kiukhelbeker in the cultural memory alongside Pushkin. He reunited Kiukhelbeker, the modern Trediakovsky, martyr-fool, with the nineteenth-century cultural hero and father of Russian poetry, Pushkin. Whereas Tynianov's criticism seeks to restore Kiukhelbeker to Russian literature's history and to validate his literary output, Tynianov's fiction endeavored to return him to Russian cultural history as a poet, revolutionary and perhaps, as a martyr.

While discussing his choice of topics in literature and literary criticism, Tynianov wrote in his autobiography: "Most of all I did not agree with the established assessments."[29] This struggle against accepted interpretations informs *Kiukhlia*. Clark suggests that Tynianov felt compelled to challenge the seeming one-sidedness of the official revolutionary genealogy because it canonized Pushkin as a "plaster saint."[30] Tynianov also interrogated the facile constructions of the official myth of the Decembrists and took issue with Soviet representations of them as a monolithic group of noblemen revolutionaries, grounded in their own class interests.

Tynianov revivifies the Decembrist myth by switching the focus to the trickster aspect. While the official view emphasized the Decembrists' high seriousness and used this image for self-legitimation, Tynianov sees the myth's subversive potential. He thus restores its original function, as an antiestablishment myth, but transposes it into a new key. The nineteenth-century intelligentsia took the Decembrists very seriously and idealized them for their lofty sacrifices. Tynianov's attention to Kiukhlia's many sides—as an author, a martyr and a fool—creates a wholeness that had previously been missing from both intelligentsia and official Soviet myths. Tynianov's focus on a single Decembrist rather than the group re-establishes their individuality in the face of their interpretation as a cohesive whole. Tynianov thus provides an enriched version of the myth to twentieth-century readers, one which acknowledged the value of individuality and dissent. Tynianov ultimately creates a new image for a new audience: the Soviet *intelligent* who is alienated from the official Soviet view. Tynianov's perspective also influenced his contemporaries, specifically a group of filmmakers who portrayed the Decembrists on celluloid. In later decades, Tynianov's seminal image would be further developed by the Soviet intelligentsia into a remythologization of the Decembrists into dissidents.

Soviet Historical Melodrama: The Decembrists on Film

Though literary representations, whether in memoirs or in belles lettres, were central to the formation of the Decembrist myth in the nineteenth and early twentieth centuries, during the Soviet era other media played an equally important role in shaping the myth and disseminating the Decembrists' image among the masses. Film, theater, and opera all served as more accessible art forms to a poorly educated population and proved important in instructing the masses about the Decembrists' role in Russian and Soviet history.

Just as the 1925 centennial spurred publishers' interest in the Decembrists, film studios also responded, though belatedly, to the call to provide cinematic representations. *The Decembrists* (*Dekabristy*) and *The Union of the Great Deed* (*Soiuz velikogo dela*), known by its Russian acronym *SVD,* went into production late in 1925, and thus were not finished before the centennial. Alexander Ivanovskii, known for the popular success of his films in both pre- and postrevolutionary times, directed *The Decembrists* (1927), a costume drama primarily based on the love story of the Decembrist Ivan Annenkov and Pauline Gueble. Originally Ivanovskii was commissioned to produce two films on the Decembrist movement: *Dekabristy* portraying the Northern Society's uprising on Senate Square and the leaders' execution, and *Russkie zhenshchiny* detailing the Southern Society's story and the Decembrists' exile to Siberia.[31] Ivanovskii seems to have combined the two themes in his final product, so the latter film was never produced. The prohibitive production costs of *The Decembrists* may also have made the studio reconsider a second film. It has been called one of the "most popular, most expensive and most controversial" films of the era.[32] The film generated much publicity because of its outrageous budget—a whopping 340,000 rubles—a sum that would make it the most expensive film made during the silent era.[33] Soviet critics were not pleased that a costume drama with little ideological content could be so popular while other ideologically correct movies (like Sergei Eisenstein's *Battleship Potemkin*) garnered a small audience. Besides a blockbuster budget, *The Decembrists* had a lot of publicity before its opening, which must have generated interest among viewers. Beginning in July 1925, cinephiles could get updates on the film in the weekly newspaper *Kino* (*Cinema*). The production, especially the scenes on location at Senate Square, took such a strong hold on the public imagination that it inspired poetry: "And the noise and sound of voices were great; / Shattering the fetters of time, / Again on Peter's Square / Stand the guard's troops.... Thus are the long-past deeds / Reborn for the screen."[34] Initially scheduled to premier in June 1926, it was not finished until November 1926 for a variety of technical reasons and opened in January 1927, simultaneously premiering at four theaters. The film was indeed a blockbuster; in a survey of the cinema advertisements of Moscow and Leningrad it dominated the screen for three months, an extraordinary feat during an era when the masses favored American films.[35]

Reacting to the popularized story of the Decembrist movement, the directors Grigorii Kozintsev and Leonid Trauberg, and the scholars turned film-scenarists Tynianov and Iulii Oksman collaborated on *SVD* (1927).[36] Tynianov specifically comments on their desire to challenge Ivanovskii's "bourgeois portrayal": "When Oksman and I wrote the scenario for this film we wanted to create a counter-weight to the court dress, the tastelessness and the pomposity shown in *The Decembrists*, and to throw light on the extreme left of the Decembrist movement. The Romanticism of the 1820s in this scenario pleased the FEKS [group] and it was neither the topical nor the historical aspect of the theme that attracted them, but something else—cinematic pathos."[37]

Though both films were called "historical melodramas," at first glance they have little in common other than their subjects. Yet despite many differences, upon closer inspection they fall prey to similar problems. In treating the events leading up to the Decembrist uprising, both lack a clear story line and rely upon the audience's familiarity with the history of the Decembrist movement. Both combine a number of plot lines and sub-plots, losing focus. The films must have been confusing to a viewer unacquainted with the Decembrists' history. At the very least, they would necessarily have been disappointing to the movie-goer who wanted to learn more about the movement, though they satisfied the average audience member's desire for escapism.

The Decembrists (1927), Directed by Alexander Ivanovskii, Sevzapkino

Ivanovskii's film script was written by Pavel Shchegolev, already well-known for his scholarship on the eras of Alexander I and Nicholas I.[38] Shchegolev's involvement, however, did not save the movie from historical inaccuracies. After reading the memoirs of Pauline Gueble and other Decembrists at Shchegolev's recommendation, Ivanovskii decided to focus on the love story. Gueble arrived in Russia in 1823 to work in a fashionable atelier and fell in love with the dashing Guards officer after meeting him at her client's home. She followed her beloved (the father of her illegitimate child) to Siberia despite having to leave their infant daughter with Annenkov's family. They were married in Siberia with Annenkov in shackles and spent 30 years in exile before gaining permission to return to European Russia. Ivanovskii's interest in historical verisimilitude led him to seek out Barbara Annenkova, the great-granddaughter of Ivan and Pauline Annenkov, an actress in Berlin, to persuade her to play the leading role.[39] Despite other contractual obligations, Annenkova agreed to go to Russia to make the film because, "the image of Polina Egorovna Annenkova since earliest childhood—at first through family legend and then through historical literature—captured my imagination."[40] Annenkova thus relived her great-grandmother's experiences and provided a sensitive performance which, in the studio bosses' eyes, lent historical authenticity. Later Ivanovskii acknowledged "the error of basing the scenario on the story of this touching romance as the Decembrist uprising receded into the background."[41] Nevertheless, Ivanovskii tried to make the story ideologically instructive by negatively depicting the despotic landowners and positively portraying Decembrist freedom fighters, but his attempts fall flat. The film struggles with information overload, telling too many stories at once.

The opening alternates from scenes of Ryleev's modest country home to Annenkov's mother's country estate and opulent home in Petersburg. Ivanovskii immediately draws a stark contrast between the enlightened landlord, Ryleev, and Annenkova's despotic estate manager, who attempts to rape a young girl (the fiancée of Ryleev's valet, Nikolka) and beats her elderly peasant father and Nikolka when they interfere. The film's manner is heavy-handed and simplistic; the viewer is expected to feel sympathy for Ryleev, who declaims civic verse, and disgust for the lecherous and corrupt estate manager. When Ryleev confronts Annenkova about her manager's brutalities, she condescendingly dismisses him. (Later Annenkova herself beats a servant-girl in the presence of her son and Pauline Gueble.) After introducing high society mores, the film shows Annenkov and Gueble's budding romance. Interspersed are scenes of Ryleev and Pushchin's battle against the injustices of the court system, secret society meetings and romantic scenes between Prince and Princess Trubetskoi, alternating the love story with events leading to the uprising. Impressive as it is in its cinematic effects—the numerous troops arrayed on Senate Square (filmed on location), the beating of the drums and the shifting focus between Nicholas, the rebels and troops—the action drags. The revolt takes place well after the first hour of the film. In the final minutes, the Decembrists' questioning intercuts with the tsarist troops' disposal of the dead and dying. The contrast is effective and moving, and differs from the slow tempo of the earlier portion of the film. The film closes with the leaders' execution, juxtaposed with spectacular fireworks marking the tsar's ascension to the throne. The final image of five shrouded bodies hanging from the scaffold is stark and striking.

The mise-en-scene indulges the audience's voyeurism: palace interiors, fancy ball dress and luxurious furnishings fill the majority of scenes.

Ivanovskii could not resist filming at least one ball scene, and in fact features two. The violent moments (the rape scene at the beginning and the hanging at the end) also satisfy the public's voyeuristic urges. Even if the audience did not know the Decembrists' history, it could enjoy the film for its opulent scenery, fine costumes, and exciting physical action. It could also marvel at the cast of thousands employed for cinematic effect. According to cinema weeklies, 3,000 people participated in the rebellion scene.[42] Denise Youngblood suggests that the success of historical melodramas have little to do with history: "Although we historians are reluctant to admit it, the public likes history for the *story*, and they like it even more if the story features interesting individuals. Because of the form the politicization of history took in the USSR in the '20s, both 'individuals' and the 'story' were essentially purged from the historical record—but not from historical melodramas."[43] Annenkov and Gueble's affair swayed the public imagination, as evidenced by the movie's box-office success. In fact, it became one of the essential components of the Decembrists' history, recurring in later operatic and cinematic treatments.[44]

SVD (Soiuz velikogo dela, 1927), Directed by Grigorii Kozintsev and Leonid Trauberg, Leningradkino

A member of the older generation of Russian film directors, Cheslav Sabinskii, originally was suggested to direct the film *SVD*, authored by Tynianov and Oksman.[45] The project later passed to Grigorii Kozintsev and Leonid Trauberg, founders and directors of the *Fabrika Ekstsentricheskogo Aktera* (Factory of the Eccentric Actor), known as "FEKS." The FEKS group, founded in 1921, focused on technical innovation and created a new acting style, based on a combination of stylized gesture, physical prowess and the carnivalesque. A typical slogan read: "ART without a capital A, pedestal and fig leaf."[46] Their avant-garde movement, labeled "Eccentrism" sought to unseat pre-revolutionary acting methods and looked to actors such as Charlie Chaplin for inspiration.[47] The cinematographer, Andrei Moskvin, and two leading actors, Sergei Gerasimov and Peter Sobolevskii, already collaborated with FEKS on other movies (such as *Little Brother* [*Bratishka*, 1926] and *The Devil's Wheel* [*Chertovo koleso*, 1926]). Kozintsev and Trauberg's film debuted at the end of August 1927. Following on the heels of the blockbuster success of *The Decembrists* did not hurt its popularity, though its style and aim appeared radically different. Critics appreciated it specifically for its divergence from Ivanovskii's costume drama: "*SVD* is at its core a polar opposite to the *Decembrists*, above all in its approach to history and method of using historical material. FEKS did not make a historical chronicle out of the film, did not drag it out over a long time period, or turn it into a gallery of Nikolaevan uniforms and court rubbish.... From history we obtain not portraits but characteristic features of the radical democratic mood that stirred the Russian nobility in the era of feudal capitalism; not a staging of facts, but a demonstration of the Decembrist movement's typology."[48] *Kino* proclaimed it a "colossal success" since it sold out in the five movie theaters where it played. (Its run continued at the *Partizan* movie house another four weeks.)[49] Though *The Decembrists* became a movie house and archival rarity in Russia and abroad, *SVD* survived, becoming well-known among film aficionados as an example of avant-garde Soviet art film.

Unlike *The Decembrists*, which treats familiar moments in the Decembrists' history, *SVD* concentrates on the January 1826 Chernigov regiment uprising. The film tells of the young officer, Lieutenant Sukhinov, a member of the Southern Society, and the adventurer and provocateur, Medoks, who betrays him and his rebelling comrades to imperial authorities. The final version of the film strays from the facts, seemingly to allow the directors to experiment with a variety of settings and striking cinematic techniques.[50]

SVD opens with a stark visual image of a snowstorm; the contrast of the snow's blinding light and the night's darkness immediately creates a sense of foreboding. A solitary guard post stands at the edge of the road. The guards receive a message from the commander not to let anyone through the cordon across the bridge. Suddenly, a sledge approaches conveying a lone, veiled passenger (Sophia Magarill as Vishnevskaia). Lieutenant Sukhinov (played by Petr Sobolevskii), in charge of the command post, does not let her pass. The desperate passenger breaks free, rushing past him to throw herself off the bridge. The empathetic young lieutenant prevents her calamity and, relenting, lets her by. At that moment, Sukhinov receives the order to arrest the adventurer Medoks (played by Sergei Gerasimov), his former comrade. In the next scene, the desperate woman's riddle becomes clearer. Medoks sits in a tavern playing cards. He wins by cheating and receives from one gentleman in payment a ring with the initials "S.V.D." The gentleman tells him that the initials are his betrothed's. Suddenly, they are interrupted by the lone passenger who was so desperate to continue her journey. (She is the wife of General

Vishnevskii, Sukhinov's commander and leader of the secret society.) Medoks threatens to reveal their past love affair if she does not help him make his way in local society. She attempts to run off with their love letters. At that moment, Sukhinov arrives to arrest Medoks. After Medoks shows him the ring, Sukhinov reluctantly lets him go, since it indicates membership in the same secret society to which Sukhinov belongs. Sukhinov's misapprehension leads to the story's tragic end. Medoks overhears the members planning to overthrow the autocracy upon the death of Alexander I and betrays them to the authorities for financial gain. His betrayal results in the leaders' arrest, but not before their loyal troops free the commanders and begin their march to Petersburg. The uprising occurs spontaneously in the middle of the night and provides the film's most striking footage. Sukhinov barely survives the rebels' rout and joins a traveling circus. After his recovery, he learns that Medoks forged documents to make the local authorities think that the tsar wants the rebels killed while in prison. Wanting to warn his comrades and avenge himself on Medoks, Sukhinov reveals himself to the authorities, who immediately arrest and imprison him. In jail, he tells his friends of Medoks's plot and finds in their cell a cache of weapons, planted to provoke the local authorities to execute them (as they would be accused of attempting escape). Sukhinov convinces them that it is better to die fighting than to sit in prison. He leads the rebels through a hidden passageway from the prison out through a church. The authorities have arrayed troops in the church, waiting for them to escape. When Sukhinov and his comrades emerge, the soldiers shoot them. Though wounded, Sukhinov escapes and dies in the arms of the general's wife.[51]

The story is itself less important than the film's atmosphere. The filmmakers experiment with montage technique and contrasts of light and dark to great effect. They use camera angles to emphasize the smallness of humans against the vastness of the landscape, symbolically emphasizing the individual's struggle against the larger forces of nature and history. The director Kozintsev recalled: "We found in nature itself—cruel frost, infernal darkness of endless night, snow, ice, snowstorms—our distinctive, tragic material."[52] The FEKS group constructed an ice palace in the courtyard of their studio to film the scene where Sukhinov discovers that the unknown woman is actually his commanding officer's wife. They find a quiet corner away from the bustle to converse; the shadows of the ice sculptures loom large, making them look insignificant and vulnerable. The shadows create a sense of foreboding and uncertainty, evoking in the viewer feelings similar to the characters'. It seems as if one cannot believe one's eyes, as if the senses do not reliably portray the truth.

The scene of the uprising is especially remarkable. Set in darkness, the whiteness of the snow contrasts the nighttime sky and the torches of the marching rebel troops. (See Figure 4.) Shots erupt into the darkness; the smoke of the gunfire and the torches blurs the scene. At the beginning of the episode, a young drummer boy joyously leads the rebels into battle. He is mowed down by the gunfire and the camera returns to his small form, dark on the white snow, as he continues to beat the drum while dying. It is a powerful image of the battle's futility and of human bravery.

Though the film was less ideologically tendentious than Ivanovskii's *Decembrists*, Sovkino believed *SVD* could be useful to party agitators in educating the masses and released a brochure with methodological materials on presenting the film to worker and peasant audiences. Recommendations included introductory lectures on the history of the Chernigov uprising, readings (Pushkin's epistle to Siberia and Odoevskii's response among them) and musical numbers. The brochure emphasized that both audiences needed to be told that the Chernigov uprising was a historical fact and not the filmmakers' invention.[53]

Figure 4   Film still from *SVD* (1927), courtesy of BFI.

Unfortunately, no record remains regarding how effective these films were in the masses' inculcation, but they must have drawn repeat viewers to justify their long runs in Moscow and Petersburg cinemas. In an era when American films dominated the screens and proved more popular than native productions, these films held their own.

★   ★   ★

The historical materials of the Decembrist movement elicited a variety of creative responses from authors and filmmakers during and after the centennial. The portrayals ranged from less to more politically engaged and ran the spectrum aesthetically from more traditional or "bourgeois," to stylistically avant-garde and experimental. The artists who created these works were still trying to find an appropriate expressive mode for the new revolutionary society while working according to government commissions with specific political ends. In literature, the most successful and influential work was Tynianov's novel, *Kiukhlia*, one that took risks thematically and stylistically, whereas the artistically more traditional film, *The Decembrists*, won over the contemporary audience though it did not outlast *SVD* in film history.

CHAPTER SIX

Rewriting Russian History: Stalin Era Representations

The Decembrists! That word was pronounced in our home with reverence...Maria Volkonskaia's and Ekaterina Trubetskaia's feat...so struck our childish imagination that for some time we forgot our usual games...and extricated from the shed an old carriage with missing wheels and a tattered leather seat, and, surrounding ourselves with bundles of our favorite toys and dolls...would "go" to Siberia, to the Decembrists. We dreamed of saving them and sharing their proud and bitter lot...

—Lidiia Libedinskaia[1]

In the 1920s, competing interpretations of the Decembrists' legacy could still coexist. The Decembrists' image remained in flux during the 1925 centennial celebration, though attempts were made at a standard interpretation. Some Soviet scholars still spoke of foreign influences upon the Decembrists and followed in the footsteps of prerevolutionary historians, emphasizing the Decembrists' liberal leanings rather than taking a strictly Marxist-Leninist approach. During the Stalin era, Russian history was rewritten to conform to the political demands of an increasingly controlling regime. Limitations were imposed upon all sectors of culture, corresponding to the demands placed upon ideologists for a single, unified genealogy of the Bolsheviks' prerevolutionary precursors. Though this process initially coincided with the cultural revolution in the late 1920s, it came to full fruition by 1937, a pivotal year in the formation of Soviet cultural iconography and historiography. Events taking place on the cultural and political fronts would permanently shape Soviet thinking about the relationship of present to past. For scholars and ideologists, two important moments would be the centennial of Pushkin's death in February 1937 and the publication of the definitive *Short Course on the History of the USSR* (*Kratkii kurs istorii SSSR*) in November 1937. The underlying processes at the foundation of these politicized events were in many ways similar and simultaneous; while, at the urging of ideologists, literary scholars were working on the "transformation of 'the great Russian national poet,' A. S. Pushkin, into an icon of official Soviet literature,"[2] historians were determining the key historical personages upon which to focus in the *Short Course*. It became obvious that the Decembrists' image could not be erased from history, but it could be co-opted and creatively reshaped for new political uses by a regime that sought to devalue rebellion and emphasize conformity. These formative cultural events affirmed the Decembrists' image in Soviet official culture and historiography. The multivocality of the Decembrist myth was suppressed, and instead a growing monolithism took hold. These processes occurred during a time of social and political turmoil, reflecting what was going on throughout the Soviet system: Stalin's Great Purges reached their peak in 1937 and provided the backdrop. In some cases, the purges directly affected the organizers and their "products."[3] In others the purges were reflected in a refracted fashion, in the rhetoric of trials and unmasking of enemies within the anachronistic context of nineteenth-century studies.[4] The Decembrists' image in films, literature, and opera produced during the Stalin era, roughly from the early 1930s until the mid-1950s, follows the ideological shift taking place in Soviet culture. I trace the changes as they occurred, beginning with the journalistic and cinematic materials of the 1937 centennial of Pushkin's death and continuing with the shift in Soviet historiography, to situate an analysis of the quintessential Stalinist representation, Iurii Shaporin's opera, *Dekabristy* (*The Decembrists*, 1953).

The first step toward a standardized approach to the Decembrists occurred with the Pushkin centennial of 1937, whose preparations began several years earlier. Brintlinger asserts that the Soviet regime attempted to stake a claim on Pushkin to assert "its legitimacy on the world political and cultural scene."[5] Teachers and scholars made efforts to popularize Pushkin among the masses. As Karen Petrone suggests, Soviet ideologists purified Pushkin of his noble lineage and foreign influences, neutralizing both his class standing and his maternal grandfather's non-Russian origins by emphasizing Pushkin's ostensible alienation from his family and close ties with his serf nanny, his strong friendships with his Lycée classmates who later became Decembrists and other young radical thinkers. Propagandists thus privileged his early biography and poetry over the events and works of his married life. Accounts played up his "freedom-loving" inspirational poetry, depicting him as a "fervent revolutionary" and discussed how this poetry influenced the Decembrists and their sympathizers. Though these elements obtained in earlier treatments, during this commemoration they gained more prominence and drowned out other facets of the poet's biography and oeuvre. This ideological shift contrasts greatly with tsarist celebrations, where Pushkin's close association with the Decembrists and his poetic rebellion against the autocracy was suppressed.[6]

In jubilee treatments the Decembrists loom large. During the "Pushkin days" leading up to and including February 10, 1937, the official date of Pushkin's death centennial, *Pravda* alone published several articles on Pushkin's bond with the Decembrists, and *Izvestiia* reproduced two paintings of Pushkin among the Decembrists.[7] Historian Militsa Nechkina treated the topic in her article (which she repeated in her speech on February 14 at the Academy of Sciences).[8] Nechkina politicized every aspect of the poet's life to debunk the "legend" of Pushkin's apolitical orientation. Overemphasizing Pushkin's political engagement, she insisted that Pushkin was "an active member of the Green Lamp, the literary branch of the [proto-Decembrist secret society] Union of Welfare."[9] In overstating the Green Lamp's political importance, Nechkina distorted the accepted facts of literary history; yet when compelled to prove Pushkin's involvement, she could not completely ignore the evidence of his marginal participation. So she qualified her statement that Pushkin was not formally accepted in to the secret society by relying upon conventional explanations: that "the Decembrists attempted to preserve the poet from vicissitudes of a secret society member's life and . . . that they doubted that the poet could keep the secret." Moreover, she insisted that on January 11, 1825, Pushchin revealed to Pushkin the secret society's existence, and for this reason "this date is significant in the history of the relationship between Pushkin and the Decembrists." Whereas earlier it was renowned in Pushkin's creative biography as the day Pushchin visited Mikhailovskoe and brought Griboedov's *Woe from Wit*, now the fabricated political meaning subsumed the day's literary significance. Nechkina closed her article by citing the canonical texts justifying a political reading of Pushkin's post–Decembrist poetry, his "Letter to Siberia" and "Arion," which affirmed Pushkin's sympathy after the Decembrists' punishment and exile. This approach rehashes the Decembrists' representation and the canonical texts of Pushkin's political poetry prevalent during the 1925 Decembrist centennial, although Nechkina goes further in aggrandizing the nature of Pushkin's political involvement with the Decembrists. Nechkina's treatment illustrates the tendentious pseudo-historical and pseudo-literary criticism typical of the era, the type of scholarship that Tynianov castigated in his article "Sham Pushkin."[10]

The centennial of Pushkin's death inspired two cinematic treatments, Arkadii Naroditskii's *Youth of the Poet* (*Iunost' poeta,* Lenfilm 1937) with a scenario by Alexander Slonimskii and Moisei Levin's film *Journey to Arzerum* (*Puteshestvie v Arzrum,* Lenfilm, 1937) with a screenplay by Mikhail Bleiman and Ilya Zilbershtein. In both films, Decembrists play prominent roles. Though Lenfilm released them within a day of each other during the "Pushkin days" only the latter, with its overt political message, was shown during the celebration.

Journey to Arzrum affirms Pushkin's continuing political engagement after the Decembrist uprising. The film's central episode consists of Pushkin's reunion with Decembrist friends at their military camp in the Caucasus. He insists that they should tell him what happened during the uprising and execution: "It is necessary to write about them, to write about December 14 and Senate Square." Raevsky agrees, but is more realistic: "Yes, but only through prison bars [can it happen]." Raevsky recites Pushkin's famous epistle, "Deep in Siberian Mines." Pushkin inspires the men with his orations on freedom. This scene demonstrates not only Pushkin's political dedication to Decembrist ideals, but also illustrates his personal devotion to and continued inspiration of the Decembrists. After the conscripted rebels are sent to certain death in a campaign against Turkish forces and perish during their courageous battle, Pushkin castigates their commander, General Paskevich, when he sees their corpses returned from battle.

Lenfilm's promotional brochure propounds the film's proper interpretation. Regarding Pushkin's decision to go to the Caucasus in 1829, it states: "The government understood Pushkin's trip as a political act...Pushkin undertook his journey to meet with his friends. Five whole years had passed since the uprising on Senate Square. Five whole years had passed since the moment that the Decembrists' five leaders were hanged. The government dealt with the remaining rebels in two ways—some were sent to death in Siberia, others were sent to the Caucasus, in those years called a 'warm Siberia'—to a different death."[11] By highlighting Pushkin's determination to reunite with his friends despite the government's wishes, the filmmakers counter earlier representations of Pushkin as apolitical or an imperial apologist, popular during the end of the tsarist era and seemingly in line with Pushkin's oeuvre after his return to Petersburg in 1827. Though reviewers criticized the film for portraying Pushkin as a "secret Decembrist" who "appears in the film as a Decembrist agitator,"[12] these historical inaccuracies did not faze the public or detract from the film's popularity. Instead, the film journal, *Iskusstvo kino* (*Cinema Art*), promised: "*Journey to Arzrum* is the first step in creating the image of the great Russian poet on the silver screen. The Soviet viewer during the jubilee days will warmly greet this film."[13]

The Youth of the Poet draws upon Pushkin's time at the Lycée to illustrate the formative experiences leading to Pushkin's tragic end. The film, according to the meeting minutes of Lenfilm's Directors' Collective in January 1936, should document the first act of Pushkin's political tragedy by stressing the connection between Pushkin and the Decembrists early in life.[14] Lenfilm's promotional brochure includes an essay on Pushkin's Lycée years by the screenwriter and scholar Slonimskii. Slonimskii emphasizes Pushkin's relationship with Pushchin and Kiukhelbeker in discussing the historical material upon which the film was based. The scenario focuses on their close friendship and demonstrates how these young men imbibed the ideals of freedom and brotherhood at the Lycée.[15] In the film, the future Decembrists recognize Pushkin's poetic genius and espousal of freedom, while he acknowledges their worth and devotion to political ideals. In one scene, Pushchin and Kiukhelbeker discuss the importance of freedom in France; in another scene they debate the nature of power. Kiukhlia affirms: "Man arises free from nature's womb and whoever takes away that freedom is a tyrant."[16] The film resonates with the idea of liberty (*vol'nost'*) in all of its permutations: prefiguring the ode "Liberty" (1817) that Pushkin would compose and would subsequently lead to his exile from Petersburg in 1820, as a word-signal (*slovo-signal*) allying and inspiring them. The final words young Pushkin utters in the film are "For liberty" (*Za vol'nost'*),[17] as if predicting his future poetic composition and foretelling his fate to perish for his political—not personal or artistic—ideals. Thus the film utilizes Pushkin's youthful relationship with the Decembrists as the backdrop for Pushkin's emerging political dedication and poetic talent. The film struck a chord with Soviet youth, according to Lidiia Libedinskaia, who saw the film 84 times, and who attended the same school as its young star, Valentin Litovskii.[18]

In both films the Decembrists perform an important symbolic function. In *The Youth of the Poet*, Pushchin and Kiukhelbeker already display devotion to freedom's cause and conduct themselves honorably and loyally, even at their young age. They are completely devoted to Pushkin, defending and encouraging him in his exploits. In *Journey to Arzrum*, Pushkin's reactions to the Decembrists and their tragic fate in the Caucasus show him to be a determined fighter against imperial despotism to contradict any perceptions of antipathy after the uprising. Once again, Pushkin's association with the Decembrists provided the appropriate political and ideological credentials to validate him further in the Soviet literary canon and cultural mythology. Pushkin thus became the ultimate patriot and Russian: loyal to his motherland, committed to fighting against tyranny (in its autocratic form) and for the masses, he sacrificed himself and suffered to better the people's lot. The distilled image of the Decembrists that arose afterward in many ways paralleled the sterilization of Pushkin's image taking place at the time. Like the Pushkin celebration—conceived as an event to co-opt the intelligentsia while also educating Soviet citizens[19]—the Decembrists' official myth also co-opted the intelligentsia in support of the state and helped articulate Soviet national identity.

The Decembrists' image further crystallized in A. V. Shestakov's *Short Course on the History of the USSR*, the monumental project of rewriting Russian history for the Soviet era, published in November 1937. Brandenberger suggests that during the late 1920s and early 1930s, ideologists and scholars sought clarification of the proper interpretation of Soviet history, which after much reworking, debate, and difficulty emerged in Shestakov's work, and became the canonical assessment.[20] *The Short Course* presents the Decembrists and their movement in a simplified fashion, as "gentry revolutionaries" (*dvorianskie revoliutsionery*), the term used by Lenin. Though several individual Decembrists are named, only the slightest distinction is made to differentiate their views. The Northern and Southern Societies' plans for either preserving or executing the tsar and his family and their preferred forms of government are contrasted. Above all, the *Short Course* emphasizes the Decembrists' limitations because of their class standing: "They were few and they were not tied to the people. But the Decembrists were the first to take up arms in the capital against the autocracy in an organized and open fashion. Their cause did not perish. The following generations of revolutionaries continued it."[21] In its conceptualization, the *Short Course* follows Lenin's original parameters, sanctifying the genealogy established in the mid-1920s. Disavowing foreign influences upon the Decembrists, Shestakov suppresses references to the ideas of the French and American revolutions and Enlightenment thinkers. Instead

Shestakov reconfigures the prerevolutionary era and its important actors. Brandenberger comments: "Noticing that the 1825 Decembrists' Revolt presented him with an opportunity to direct attention away from the state and toward 'progressive' social forces, Shestakov then segued in quick succession to Pushkin and Gogol and then to Belinskii, Herzen, and Chernyshevskii.... Deft and subtle, the shift that Shestakov scripted into the events of 1825 was perfectly orchestrated, ultimately allowing the party hierarchy to claim a pedigree that was at once revolutionary *and* statist."[22] Used as a textbook by primary and secondary schools, and in higher education and party discussion circles, it became the exclusive authorized interpretation of historical events.[23] Indicating the appropriate evaluation of the Decembrists, the *Short Course* validated them as a permitted scholarly topic as well as worthy of artistic representation.[24]

The writing and publication of the *Short Course* coincided with the campaign against the historian M. N. Pokrovskii and his school, indicating a major shift in the interpretation of Russian history. Earlier considered the father of Soviet Marxist historiography, Pokrovskii was displaced from his lofty position, and his works and his students were publicly attacked for their incorrect, anti-Leninist approach in January 1936, four years after his death. The denunciation signaled the Stalinist ideological shift from "internationalist materialist historiography...allowing competing russocentric, statist historiographic paradigms to assume a dominant position in the Soviet historical discipline."[25] Pokrovskii's former student, Nechkina, further consolidated the newly accepted approach, by detailing Pokrovskii's incorrect interpretation of the Decembrists in the volume *Against the Historical Conception of M. N. Pokrovskii* (*Protiv istoricheskoi kontseptsii M. N. Pokrovskii*). She asserted that Pokrovskii's conclusions regarding the Decembrists and their historical significance "diverged from the Leninist-Stalinist conceptualization."[26] After a nod to Stalin's estimation of the Decembrists (as a "fact of the *revolutionary* movement[s]"), Nechkina rebukes Pokrovskii by citing Lenin's formulations. Analyzing Pokrovskii's writings before and after the revolution, she takes him to task for several sins: his lack of recognition of the Decembrists' revolutionary orientation as a group; his anachronistic comparisons of elements of the Decembrist movement to more modern movements; his backward glance to court coups as the source of the Decembrists' action; his economic materialist approach, which incorrectly attributed the Decembrists' rise to early nineteenth-century material conditions; his noncompliance to

Lenin's norms, that the Decembrists were "gentry revolutionaries" (*dvorianskie revoliutsionery*), who were limited by their class standing, yet all the same, deserved the title of revolutionaries, and that they not only belonged to, but were also the originators of the period of *dvorianskaia revoliutsionnost'* in Russian revolutionary history. Her final reproach gets to the core of her argument: unlike Lenin, who connected pride in the Decembrists "with national consciousness, revolutionary patriotism and national feeling" Pokrovskii's conception lacked national feeling.[27] Expounding upon Lenin's conceptualization, Nechkina spells out their importance for this new era: the Decembrists comprise an integral part of Soviet revolutionary history *because* they speak to Russian national consciousness. The inconvenient facts of the Decembrists' aristocracy and so-called self-interest (according to certain historians qua Pokrovskii) are suppressed in light of their uprising's "political significance." Despite vociferous denial of his interpretation and apparent disavowal of his historiography, Nechkina still grappled with Pokrovskii's legacy years later. In the *History of the USSR* (1949), which she edited, Nechkina includes a short but thorough summary of the Pokrovskii school's "false conception" of Decembrism. Here she adds a new charge: that Pokrovskii perceived the Decembrists' patriotism, as displayed in the 1812 campaign against Napoleon, as "narrow nationalism" (*uzkii natsionalizm*).[28] Her focus upon patriotism demonstrates another shift, albeit a subtle one, in emphasis, relating to the Decembrists' prominence in Soviet cultural mythology. References to patriotism increased as a result of World War II, in part reflecting the national agenda. Moreover, these manipulations also masked the oppositional aspect of the Decembrists as models for Soviet citizens.

The poet Anna Akhmatova saw the similarities between the Decembrists and the purge victims early in the Stalin era, implying that her endless waiting in lines outside Soviet prisons resembled the burdens undertaken by the Decembrists' wives, and called her contemporary, Nadezhda Mandelshtam a *dekabristka* in her unswerving support for her husband, the poet Osip Mandelshtam, despite persecution by the authorities. However, it took longer for the analogy to come to the minds of those in power. The Decembrists' ambiguous legacy became a point of concern immediately after World War II, when officials recognized the parallels between the returning veterans and the officers who led the Decembrist revolt after returning from abroad during the Napoleonic campaign.[29] An early example of the Soviet intelligentsia's exploration of the anti-mythic capacities inherent in the Decembrists' image can be found in Naum Korzhavin's poem:

Зависть (1944)
Можем строчки нанизывать,
Посложнее, попроще,
Но никто нас не вызовет
На Сенатскую площадь.

И какие бы взгляды вы
Ни старались выплескивать,
Генерал Милорадович
Не узнает Каховского.

Пусть по мелочи биты вы,
Чаще самого частого,
Но не будут выпытывать
Имена соучастников.

Мы не будем увенчаны...
И в кибитках,
                    снегами,
Настоящие женщины
Не поедут за нами.

Envy

We can string together lines
More complexly, more simply,
But no one will summon us
To Senate Square.

And no matter what views you
try to espouse, ,
General Miloradovich
will not recognize Kakhovskii.

Even if you are punished for trifles
More often than most,
Still they will not try to get from you
the names of your comrades.

There'll be no crowns for us...
And in wagons through the snow,
No real women
Will follow us.[30]

Rather than valorizing the Decembrists as patriots, Korzhavin voices the nostalgia felt for the Decembrists' lofty cause and sacrifice. He suggests his generation of poets—and perhaps the intelligentsia—will neither have the opportunity nor the capacity for such deeds. Though the Decembrists' rebellion failed, they remain glorified for their sacrifices. Korzhavin dismisses his own generation's ability to elicit such valorous gestures. Korzhavin's treatment of the lost cause and chances illustrates the intelligentsia's disillusionment with the Soviet system. Geoffrey Hosking claims that the primary experience influencing Korzhavin's work was his arrest and seven-year exile in Siberia and Kazakhstan (1947–1954), though the poem "Envy," written in 1944, suggests Korzhavin's doubts about Soviet authority's underpinnings emerged earlier.[31] These qualms, arising from his (and society's) experiences during and after the war, color his perception and compel him to represent his generation tinged with a sense of disappointment in unfulfilled promises and dreams.

Alexander Solzhenitsyn also recognized the parallel between his postwar experience and the Decembrists', comparing his arrest at the end of the war with that of Kiukhelbeker after the Decembrist uprising. Solzhenitsyn's poem, "The Way of the Enthusiasts" (*Shosse entuziastov*, 1951), includes a pointed reference:

> I am riding like Kiukhelbeker
> To be questioned by hirelings of the tsar,
> My escorts those very same gendarmes—
> Like the poet, I too am right.[32]

For the Decembrists to remain in their prominent position within the Soviet revolutionary pantheon they had to be defanged, so that their image did not contain the potential for rebellion against authority. Instead, their image was manipulated so that they became patriots rather than rebels; their devotion to the fatherland was highlighted instead of their unsettling capacity as opponents against authority. As the emphasis on their patriotism increased, their individuality decreased. The Decembrists were less frequently distinguished as individual actors and more commonly discussed as an undifferentiated whole. The myth became monolithic, nationalistic, and Russified, cleansed of foreign influences (now disavowed). In the end, the Decembrists became fully homegrown patriots.

Iurii Shaporin's opera, *The Decembrists* (1953) provides the best example of the changing approach to the Decembrists. Shaporin (1887–1966) had already completed his training at the St. Petersburg Conservatory before the 1917 revolution. Unlike his contemporary Sergei Prokofiev and his younger colleague Dmitri Shostakovich who were distinguished by their formal experimentation, Shaporin composed in the Russian classical tradition of Rimsky-Korsakov, Tchaikovsky, and Rachmaninoff. Upon completion of the Conservatory, he became involved with the Leningrad dramatic theaters that had just been taken over by the revolutionary government. His duties included conducting and composing incidental music for performances; later he also composed orchestral suites, oratorios, and scores for Dziga Vertov's *Three Songs of Lenin* and Alexander Pudovkin's *Deserter*, among other films. According to Shaporin, Shchegolev approached him at one of Count Alexei Tolstoi's famous Saturday gatherings with the proposition to collaborate on an opera based on the Decembrists in honor of the centennial. In 1925, Shaporin began writing music for a "dramatic poem" (*dramaticheskaia poema*) by Tolstoi (1883–1945) and Shchegolev depicting Pauline Gueble and Ivan Annenkov's romance. Fragments of the work, entitled *Polina Guebl,* premiered at the 1925 celebration. (Despite the ostensible focus on the individual heroine and hero, the play was subtitled: "The Decembrists.") Shaporin labored from the mid-1920s until the opera's premiere on June 23, 1953, at the Bolshoi Theater in Moscow (and on July 4) at the Kirov Theater in Leningrad. Retitled *The Decembrists,* the final libretto was written by Vsevolod Rozhdestvenskii, based on Tolstoi and Shchegolev's original. Long a target of jokes among the musical establishment for its never-ending composition,[33] it was acclaimed by critics and the public alike after its debut. It immediately entered the repertoire and was performed regularly throughout the 1960s.[34] Since the work's gestation period spanned the entire Stalin period, it chronicles the changes the Decembrist myth underwent during that time.

Though some scholars have asserted that ideological problems hindered Shaporin from completing his opera, those differences alone were not the cause of the delay.[35] At issue, it seems, was a basic misunderstanding between the composer and the first librettists regarding the story's focus. Shaporin himself remarked that their intentions were incompatible: "Already at the beginning of my work I began to doubt the expediency of constructing the opera's plot from one episode of the Decembrist Annenkov's life, all the more so because he did not play a decisive role in the movement's fate as a whole. To this day it is unclear to me why Shchegolev chose the Frenchwoman Pauline Gueble and Annenkov as heroes out of the entire Decembrist epic...despite my objections Tolstoi and Shchegolev quickly completed the play."[36] Shaporin completed Pauline and Annenkov's duet and the scene of Annenkov's questioning for the December 28, 1925 performance at the State Academic Theater of Opera and Ballet. A review criticized the music as "lacking in dramatic movement," summing up the crux of the problem: "Simply speaking, there is nothing to sing or to play in Shaporin's opera."[37] However, another critic conceded that it was difficult to judge the opera having seen and heard only two fragments.[38] Some scholars have speculated that Shaporin was simply not ready to compose such a massive work, that he needed to mature as a composer and gain greater experience in the composition of diverse works such as symphonies and oratorio-cantatas.[39] Be that as it may, in the intervening years, while Shaporin held a variety of posts and composed in many different genres, he continued working on the opera, and so it evolved, as a contemporary remarked, from "a gentry 'family chronicle' to a historico-revolutionary epic."[40] In many ways, the opera's shift in focus parallels the complex reshaping of the Decembrist myth according to the requirements of the Stalin era, responding to the new demands upon opera to adhere to the tenets of Socialist Realism in subject and style.

The Gueble-Annenkov affair obviously captured the public's imagination in a way that few stories of the Decembrists did.[41] The story's lasting power needs to be probed: why did it resonate into the twentieth century when it was already well known and re-hashed in a variety of genres in the nineteenth?[42] One reason seems to be purely practical and centers on Shchegolev, who had already researched and treated aspects of the relationship in studies written before the revolution.[43] Though Shchegolev's scholarly interests ranged across varied nineteenth-century revolutionary movements, and he published a number of Decembrist memoirs, it appears that the Decembrists' wives', especially Annenkova's, grand gesture resonated with him, for he examined it through the lens of several genres. Shchegolev published the 1915 edition of Annenkova's memoirs and later used them as the basis for the screenplay he wrote for Ivanovskii's aforementioned film, *The Decembrists* (1927).[44] His collaboration on the dramatic poem (1925–1926) and the subsequent opera libretto emerged from a time when he was already deeply involved in the topic. Yet another obvious reason for the story's popularity lay in its lush romanticism, melodramatic gestures and Gueble's self-sacrifice by following her betrothed to Siberia. These elements inspire operatic treatment, though Soviet opera was striving to take another direction.

As with Soviet literature and other art forms, so with music; after the revolution, artists experimented with new forms to capture the drastically altered reality of post-revolutionary life. A move away from well-established genres (of the thick novel in literature and the opera in music) and toward shorter, avant-garde, fragmentary forms occurred. A variety of stylistic movements co-existed and competed for supremacy. Like Tchaikovsky, Soviet ideologists recognized that opera had the potential "to influence the masses."[45] In the 1920s, producers first grafted new, revolutionary subjects onto already popular operas. For example, Puccini's *Tosca* became known as *The Fight for the Commune*, with its action set in Paris in 1871. Some composers sought new forms by eschewing old operatic traditions, reveling in atonality, random noise, and a lack of coherent narrative as traditionally conveyed through a succession of arias, ensembles and choruses. Prokofiev's 1930 opera *The Nose*, based on Nikolai Gogol's short story, was a primary exemplum of this new trend. It met with harsh reviews because of its difficult music.[46] Beginning in 1932, when Socialist Realism was declared the single appropriate methodological and aesthetic approach in the arts, the Soviet musical establishment had to bring their works into conformity with the official line. This paradigm shift was conservative in nature and signaled not just a "bourgeois-ification" of Soviet culture, but also a return to nineteenth-century aesthetic values by favoring realism, the novel and opera. It also included an admixture of revolutionary heroism. Socialist Realism demanded that works be accessible to the masses and serve an educational function by raising party consciousness, and that they depict reality not as it is, but as it should be. Exactly how these tenets would be translated into music was unclear. Prokofiev once remarked: "The search for a musical language in keeping with the era of socialism is a noble, but not an easy, task set for a composer."[47] In any case, opera, more than other musical forms, lent itself to a socialist realist aesthetic because of its reliance upon an underlying narrative line. Soviet socialist realist opera was to be rooted in the classical traditions and eschew formal experimentation, inspire and display feelings of nationalism, and employ an accessible musical idiom. Stalin declared at the 1935 premiere of Ivan Dzerzhinskii's adaptation of *Quiet Flows the Don* (*Tikhii Don*), Mikhail Sholokhov's acclaimed novel, that the first socialist realist opera had been created. This opera provided a model for composers to emulate in their attempt to create socialist realist opera.[48]

Notwithstanding the challenges of creating socialist realist opera, Shaporin's work was interrupted for a variety of reasons, ranging from changes in his professional appointments to composition of other pieces to quibbles with Tolstoi on the plot line's direction. After the 1925 staging, there was a period of long silence, until *The Decembrists* in "montage form" was broadcast over the radio in the 1937–1938 season.[49] After the radio performance, articles assessed Shaporin's progress on the opera and the problems hindering its completion and achievement of greatness. As one critic put it: "No matter how great the libretto's dramatic structure and how fine its style and language, the composer all the same outstrips the librettist. *The Decembrists*' music provides a picture of the epoch. Its themes create socially and psychologically distinct images and associations more concretely than those created by words."[50] The press voiced the formerly silent struggle between the composer and librettists and their differing visions. This lack of common goal and intention became a repeated refrain in criticism and in Shaporin's private correspondence.[51]

The cultural significance of the opera cannot be exaggerated. It was important to the musical community to produce another successful Soviet opera, and many organizations and individuals felt that Shaporin's opera could potentially fill this gap. *The Decembrists* remained in the forefront of opera news as evident from a special meeting on December 1, 1939 at the Kirov Opera, when attempts were made to resolve Shaporin and Tolstoi's creative disagreements and organizational issues. Though Shaporin made more changes, from this time on the basic outline remained in place. Other questions, related to shifting from the personal lyric drama to "the heroic resonance of the spectacle,"[52] were resolved as well.

Despite variations, certain folk elements remained consistent: the serf girls' song, the satirical and folk piece "Prov brewed beer" ("Prov piva navaril"), the watchman's song ("The watchman's stick," "Kolotushka moia"), the song "Oh you versts" ("Oi, vy versty," originally sung by a coachman, but later taken by Alexander Bestuzhev).[53] In addition to these folk scenes, the Gueble-Annenkov love story remained, though once the decision was made to foreground the Decembrist movement, it should have been excised. Could it be that the composers and ideologists believed the opera had to have romance to be popular? Shaporin's participation in the All-Union Conference on Opera (December 1940) provides a partial answer. Shaporin observed: "The majority of Soviet operas, conceived as national musical dramas in the final analysis turn out to be lyrical melodramas in which the heroes' personal lyrical intrigue prevailed over socio-historical events." Instead, he insisted that Soviet composers must avoid "the falsification of their subjects."[54]

In the expectation that the opera would soon be completed, its premiere was scheduled for the 1940–1941 season at the Kirov.[55]

The interruption of World War II further delayed the opera's debut; during and after the war, Shaporin continued to add to and correct many scenes. Shaporin frequently played various arias and scenes while attending Tolstoi's literary evenings or entertaining friends. These more intimate settings enabled Shaporin to hear the impressions that the music made upon an audience.[56] The writer Konstantin Fedin and the revolutionary N. A. Morozov both testified to the authenticity of Shaporin's understanding and musical rendering of the Decembrists.

In 1951, the opera received two concert performances, which provided another opportunity for the musical establishment (on February 13) and selected academicians (on May 11) to critique the work before its premiere. The first session recommended the addition of the character Pavel Pestel to the dramatic action.[57] The second session made suggestions resulting in the libretto's final revision; hence the decision to change the heroes' names, from Ivan Annenkov and Pauline Gueble to the Decembrist Prince Dmitrii Shchepin-Rostovskii and Elena Orlova, an impoverished landowner's daughter. It is telling that after World War II the committee members would rid the lyric heroes of their foreign associations. In emphasizing the class distinctions between Dmitrii and his beloved (which differed from the true story), the creators also illustrated the Decembrist's socially progressive leanings. As a result, the movement's greater socio-historical context was provided, changing the opera's tone from a "tragic ending" to "historical optimism."[58] This shift in emphasis would be in keeping with the thrust of Socialist Realism, in which the Bolsheviks' predecessors indicated the path to the "radiant future" (*svetloe budushchee*) of communism. As in the past, Shaporin made extensive revisions after these performances.

The opera's final version depicted in broad strokes the Decembrists' milieu, political views, and social conditions. The composer was congratulated for his effective rendering of nationalist spirit and color as well as the typicality of his representation of the Decembrists and the generic diversity of his musical scenes.[59] Though for some critics individual Decembrists were not differentiated enough, one reviewer praised Shaporin's innovative solution, his "expression in music of the Decembrists' unity of feelings and intentions, the commonality uniting their ideas of revolutionary liberation."[60] Shaporin succeeded in creating a "collective" rather than an individual hero. This notion of the Decembrists' collective or group portrait was repeated by the opera critics, for them signifying a positive advance.

In truth, the opera is an imperfect work which foregrounds the tensions between the personal and the social, the individual and the group, and the dramatic versus the static elements inherent in any representation of the Decembrists. Moreover, it adumbrates the problems that artists would have in telling a love story focused on individual heroes during an era when the doctrine of Socialist Realism demanded mass heroes performing monumental deeds. Subsumed by the collective historical portrait, an altered version of the Annenkov–Gueble romance remained as the background to the Decembrists' story. Shchepin-Rostovskii—who participated in the revolt and therefore became Annenkov's substitute in the final version[61]—Alexander Bestuzhev, Trubetskoi, Kakhovskii, Pestel, Ryleev, and Iakubovich—play the central roles. The first act opens on the estate of the wealthy widow Olga Mironovna Shchepina, Dmitrii's mother. She exploits her serf girls and treats them brutally. Her son, railing against serfdom's inequities, he declares his love for his neighbor Elena, a poor noblewoman who is not his social equal. His mother refuses to let him marry her. At the end of the scene, Pestel visits Dmitrii to ask for his assistance in communicating with the Decembrists' Northern Society.

In the second scene, the Decembrists meet clandestinely at a post station tavern, secluded in the nobles' section and protected from the watchful eye of the authorities under the cover of the gathered crowd and gypsy chorus. Trubetskoi, Kakhovskii, and Shchepin discuss their dissatisfactions; at a distance the Decembrist Rostovstev, soon to betray the secret society to the tsar, eavesdrops. The peasant servant, Stesha, entertains the Decembrists with a mournful love song , making the political meeting seem like a drinking party. Suddenly, Bestuzhev arrives with the news of Alexander I's death. The conspirators discuss their plans for social change, criticizing the autocracy and the police. Kakhovskii recites Pushkin's poetry which inspires them to fight for freedom. They decide to go to Petersburg to overthrow the autocracy. Rostovstev rushes to tell the authorities of their plot. Pushkin's famous poem "To Chaadaev" ("K Chaadaevu," 1818) echoes throughout the opera as the Decembrists' leitmotif, first appearing in scene two and recurring musically in each subsequent act. The last lines of the poem—part of Kakhovskii's inspirational aria inciting the Decembrists to action—resound as a memorable refrain:

> Товарищ, верь! Взойдет она,
> Звезда пленительного счастья,
> Россия вспрянет ото сна,

И на обломках самовластья
Напишут наши имена!

Believe, my friend! It will arise, the star of captivating splendor. Russia will spring awake from its sleep, and on the wreckage of the autocracy, our names will be written!

Though Pushkin himself does not appear as a character onstage, these frequently repeated lines—as the Decembrists' credo—makes his presence palpable.

The opera initially grants Shchepin-Rostovskii, Kakhovskii, and Bestuzhev greater roles than Ryleev and Pestel, the de facto leaders of the Northern and Southern societies. Though the initial setting necessitates this portrayal, it deflects attention from the revolt's main players and retards plot development. Instead of having a clear-cut sense of who the central actors are in the Decembrist movement, the audience sees a group of inspired revolutionaries, all of whom (with the exception of the hesitant Trubetskoi and the turncoat Rostovtsev) ardently hope for and urge on positive social change. This imbalance becomes less obvious by scene four, when the Decembrists gather in Petersburg at Ryleev's apartment.

Interpolated between the political discussions of scenes two and four, Stesha and the gypsy chorus (scene two) and the marketplace crowd (scene three) provide local color and demonstrate the commoners' hostility towards the nobility and authorities. As the Decembrists prepare to leave, Stesha and the gypsies sing of a long snowy journey (perhaps to Siberia), foretelling the Decembrists' future lot. The scene also features the chance meeting of Dmitrii and Elena, who pledge their eternal love despite their social differences. Scene four takes place at Ryleev's apartment on the eve of the uprising. The active Decembrists—Ryleev, Bestuzhev, Iakubovich, and Kakhovskii (who in the opera articulates the Decembrists' philosophy)—call for action against the autocracy. Trubetskoi hesitates, worrying that they do not have the necessary support among the troops. Rostovstev appears and attempts to talk them out of their intended action, then reveals that he will betray them to the tsar. After Iakubovich threatens him, he flees. In scene five the audience discovers that Nicholas plans to act on Rostovstev's information about the conspiracy. Nicholas ponders his misfortune to become tsar and to have to shed blood to protect Russia on the very first day of his rule. Scene six begins with the Decembrists and their troops assembled on Senate Square. The charge of the rebel troops takes place on stage, with the tsarist forces and cannons off-stage. The chorus of peasants and onlookers cry out in support of the rebels until the attack begins. Shchepin and Bestuzhev lead their regiments valiantly against the forces, but are repulsed; Shchepin is wounded during the battle.

The last three scenes show the uprising's aftermath in three different venues and among three different social groups. Scene seven depicts the official tsarist perspective, at a masquerade ball attended by the court. The imperial court dances and celebrates as the Decembrists molder in prison. Elena arrives in disguise, to ask Shchepina for assistance in reuniting with Dmitrii and to petition Nicholas for permission to follow Dmitrii to Siberia. Shchepina disowns her son and refuses to help Elena. The tsar attempts to seduce Elena; when unsuccessful, he angrily acquiesces to her request to go to Siberia. Scene eight takes place in the fortress, where Ryleev and Pestel await execution. They meet and embrace one last time before their punishment, affirming their brotherhood and adherence to their lofty cause. The final scene depicts the remaining Decembrists' journey to Siberia. Bestuzhev hears about the leaders' execution from a guard and laments his brave friends' passing. Elena overtakes the convoy and meets Dmitrii again, professing her love and devotion. Repeating Volkonskaia's gesture, Elena kisses Dmitrii's chains as a sign of her admiration and submission to his lot. The scene closes in a dramatically effective but symbolically overloaded manner. The Decembrists' convoy starts on its way at sunrise. Though Kakhovskii and the other leaders have perished, their cause will not die. This time, Bestuzhev reprises the Decembrists' leitmotif, with a musical variation set to Odoevskii's renowned response to Pushkin's epistle:

> Наш скорбный труд не пропадет!
> Из искры возгорится пламя.
> И просвещенный народ
> Сберется под святое знамя.
> Мечи скуем мы из цепей
> И пламя вновь зажжем свободы!
> Она нагрянет на царей,
> И радостно вздохнут народы!

Our grim labor will not be lost! The flame flares from the spark. And our enlightened people will gather beneath the holy banner. We will forge swords from chains and again light the fire of freedom! It will descend on the tsars and the people will sigh joyously!

Shaporin musically underlines the Decembrists' interchangeability here, illustrating their cause's continuation at the dawn of a new era. The people who witness their departure sing out in sympathy, picking up the musical leitmotif's variation:

> Вас, первых вставших на царя,
> Народ помянет добрым словом.
> И жизни светлой, жизни новой
> Взойдет желанная заря.

The people will remember with a good word, you who first rose up against the tsar. And the desired dawn will arise of bright and new life.[62]

The voices of the Decembrists and the chorus have merged into one, symbolizing the future union and eventual success of the *narod* and those who battle against autocracy.

The opera confronts the central problems in treatments of the Decembrists that must conform to socialist realist tenets. The first problem involves the question of dramatic action. In other words, how does one make a static revolt exciting and monumental? Shaporin's decision to focus on the crowd's reaction rather than the "standing revolution" did not satisfy the critics, who generally agreed that the rebellion should have been the opera's climax, but fell short. Deflecting attention away from the Decembrists' inaction, Shaporin highlights their patriotism, their collective desire to bring about a better life for Russian citizenry and their complete dedication to the fight, no matter what the outcome. One contemporary critic remarked, "Shaporin successfully translated the lofty tone of the Decembrists' civic feelings and intentions, the historical optimism of their struggle and instilled in the listeners deep sympathy for the heroes who gave their young lives for the happiness of future generations."[63]

The second issue revolves around another requirement of socialist realist opera, which should dramatize the historical role of the *narod*. How does one write the people into an event in which they played no part? Shaporin resolved this issue by including typical genre scenes featuring the masses: the first scene's serf girl chorus; the market scene's polyphony of voices, ranging from gypsies to carousel riders to the male chorus's drinking song. He also attempted to show the masses' involvement in scene six during the uprising, but beyond the very successful and frequently performed "Soldiers' Chorus" ("Za Dunaem"), there was little he could add without marring historical authenticity or further retarding plot development. Shaporin's solution, to conclude the opera with merged choruses of the Decembrists and *narod*, fulfills the demand as well as could be hoped, and literally and figuratively resolves the tensions between the different social groups.

Grounded in the Russian classical tradition, the opera was a crowd pleaser. The variations on folk themes provide a lovely melodic line and avoid dissonance and atonality. These elements alone would have won over a popular audience, since the opera does not challenge the listener in the same way that music by Shostakovich or Prokofiev can. In this context, Shaporin has been called "a living example of the value of romantic orthodoxy."[64] His music generally received acclaim, was performed throughout his entire career, and, in comparison to other composers he experienced relatively little hardship. More telling is the way scholars and critics located the opera in the socialist realist framework as well as the Russian operatic tradition. The critical literature recasts the Decembrists' representation by denying the opera's tragic aspects and using an unusual phrase to describe it—as "optimistic tragedy."[65] This oxymoronic term, closely related to the critics' needs to emphasize the Decembrist movement's "optimistic spirit," grapples with the Decembrists' ambiguous legacy to make them palatable socialist realist subjects. Indeed, the Decembrists' failure was both a personal and societal tragedy, as the despotic regime reigned into the twentieth century. Nonetheless, in line with the officially sanctioned interpretation, the Decembrists' tragedy presaged the Bolsheviks' future success. Since the Decembrist uprising had to point the audience in that direction, the opera's tragic aspects needed to be suppressed, or whitewashed, suggesting that the Decembrists' banner would lead the masses onward to Soviet successes. In part because of the critics' interpretation, the opera garnered acclaim and became a staple of the Bolshoi Opera's repertoire for more than two decades.

Though Stalin died by the time it was completed in 1953, the opera reflects the Stalinist version of the myth: the valorization of the collective over the individual, the substitution of and preference for a Russian hero and heroine over the historical personages of the Frenchwoman Pauline Gueble and Ivan Annenkov, and the emphasis upon the Decembrists' patriotism over their rebellion against authority. These elements neutralized any unsettling power or subversive model that the Decembrists might suggest to the Soviet public. During the Stalin era, the Decembrist myth ossified in an official variant without open challenge. Any ambivalent references to the Decembrists remained underground, unuttered in official realms, referred to in unpublished literature, such as Akhmatova's *Requiem*, Korzhavin's "Envy," and Solzhenitsyn's "Way of the Enthusiasts." But after the great revelations of Nikita Khrushchev in 1956 about Stalin's and his collaborators' crimes, the generation that grew up in the 1960s began to think differently about the Decembrists and revived their ambiguous legacy as rebels, further influencing their cohort as well as later generations.

CHAPTER SEVEN

The Decembrists and Dissidence: Myth and Anti-Myth from the 1960s–1980s

> Each writes as he hears,
> Each hears as he breathes,
> As he breathes, so he writes...
> Каждый пишет, как он слишит,
> Каждый слишит, как он дышит
> Как он дышит, так и пишет...
> —Bulat Okudzhava, "I am writing a
> historical novel" (1975)[1]

During the Stalin era Decembrist studies became an industry in Soviet scholarship. Scholars continued to propound the official line, as Nechkina, the first among equals of Decembrist historians, affirmed. However, after Khrushchev's revelations at the 1956 Twentieth Party Congress about Stalin's crimes against the Soviet people, chinks began to appear in the edifice of Stalinist culture. Repressed citizens returning from the gulag brought information about what was really happening during the Stalin terror to society at large. As a result, Andrei Sinyavsky suggests that dissidence began in 1956:

> not because the Twentieth Congress opened their eyes, but because it didn't provide a single serious explanation for Stalinism or any serious guarantee that this would not happen again. People were supposed to listen to this news and then go quietly home without giving it any thought, trusting in the Party as before. But many people could no longer blindly believe and not think. Dissidence is thus an intellectual movement first, a process of independent

and courageous reflection on the mysteries of the history and system of the Soviet State.[2]

Though many people did not openly speak about the camps and their horrifying experiences, information seeped out, either through Western publications of former prisoners' memoirs which then made their way back to Russia (*tamizdat*), or through the circulation of unpublished manuscripts clandestinely among select circles (*samizdat*), for example, as with Solzhenitsyn's works. The cognitive dissonance the new information created led to reassessment of the Soviet past, as evidenced by the literature and other cultural products of the Thaw (1956–1963). This brief period enabled new voices and perspectives to emerge. And, in the rare case, a work which detailed the terrible life of the gulag might actually squeeze through the censor and get published in the pages of a prominent journal such as *New World* (*Novyi mir*), like Solzhenitsyn's novella, *One Day in the Life of Ivan Denisovich* in 1962. Other hostile acts perpetrated by the Soviet government, the 1968 invasion of Czechoslovakia among them, led some citizens to question more openly the ruling order's actions and to chip away at those weak points in the hope of affecting positive social and political change. With the crackdown in the political and cultural arenas beginning early in 1963, a period of retrenchment began and continued throughout the 1970s and early 1980s, commonly known as the era of stagnation.

While the Decembrists' official myth formulated during the Stalin era remained dominant, an unofficial perspective re-emerged. This view wrenched the myth out of its stultifying monolithism and re-asserted the Decembrists as individual actors on the historical scene. Their image as tricksters returned after a hiatus of more than four decades. These perspectives, disruptive to the official myth, questioned the foundations of Soviet culture and the system as a whole and remained outside the realm of official discourse.

Beginning in the 1960s and continuing through the 1970s and the 1980s, the literary critic Iurii Lotman (1922–1993) and the popular historian Natan Eidelman (1930–1989) presented the Decembrists from a new conceptual perspective: as psychologically whole individuals within their original historical context rather than in the context of Marxist determinism. Lotman's semiotic conceptualization wrested the Decembrists from Soviet scholarship's rigid framework of historical determinism, enabling new generations of critics to see them in a different light. Two of Lotman's groundbreaking articles deal with the Decembrists' own self-dramatization and have become seminal in

Decembrist studies. In "The Theater and Theatricality as Components of Early Nineteenth-Century Culture," Lotman illustrates the role of theater as an active formant of the era's psychology, documenting the role of art—specifically performance-oriented art—as a model for life:

> Viewing real life as a performance not only offered a person the possibility of choosing his type of individual behavior, but also filled him with the expectation that things were going to happen. Eventfulness, that is, the possibility that unexpected phenomena and turns of events would happen, became the norm. It was precisely the awareness that any political turn of events was possible that shaped the sense of life that young people had in the early nineteenth century. The revolutionary consciousness of the younger generation of the nobility had many sources. Psychologically it was prepared in part by the habit of looking at life "theatrically." It was precisely the model of theatrical behavior that, by turning a person into a character in a play, liberated him from the automatic sway of group behavior and of custom.[3]

Lotman demonstrates that the younger, educated members of the elite perceived that their lives could be meaningful on the world stage and that it was a small step to take their actions out of a recognized pattern to do something unusual and unexpected in the hope of affecting momentous change.

Lotman's second article picks up one of the primary threads of the first and applies the concept to the Decembrists' self-dramatization. In "The Decembrist in Everyday Life," he emphasizes the Decembrist's separation from the rest of society.[4] Lotman highlights the Decembrist's seriousness compared to other high society members and discusses the Decembrist's rejection of dancing, frivolity, and wild behavior (carousing, frequenting brothels, heavy drinking) as something antithetical to his "service life" (that is, his life as a conspirator). Most important, Lotman notes the Decembrist's transfer of literary behavioral models into real life situations, positing that each Decembrist used particular texts as programs for behavior:

> From this point of view, the everyday behavior of the Decembrist appeared theatrical to the contemporary observer, behavior calculated to affect the spectator. It should clearly be understood, however, that "theatricality" of behavior in no way implies insincerity or any other negative characteristics. It is simply the indication

of the fact that the behavior has acquired a certain sense beyond that of real life, that it has become a subject of attention, in which value is attached not to the acts themselves, but to their symbolic meaning.[5]

These behavioral models, drawn from classical literature and history, Russian history and European Romanticism, provided examples of heroic acts which the Decembrist(s) could assimilate and emulate. Lotman explains the Decembrists' less heroic behavior during incarceration as a dearth of appropriate models for their acts and lack of audience to which they could address them. Thus for Lotman, the application of an artistic principle to one's own biography and actions distinguishes the Decembrist: "To the Decembrist, behavior, like art, was not an aim in itself, but a means, an external expression of the lofty spiritual content of the text of life or the text of art."[6] Unlike earlier scholars who plumbed every Decembrist document for proto-Bolshevik ideas, Lotman argues for the consideration of the Decembrists' sociopsychological context and their effect on Russian culture as important as—perhaps more important than—their ideological views. In providing an appropriate interpretive framework for the Decembrists' self-dramatization, Lotman solves the sticky problem of how to view the Decembrists' grandiose and frequently ambivalent gestures which today strike the modern sensibility as melodramatic and overblown. This interpenetration and intersection of life and art explains not only the acts of the Decembrists and their wives but also the fascination that others felt for them. Yet despite his assertion that he would correct previous views on the Decembrists, Lotman eulogizes and idealizes them as much as some of his predecessors:

> The Decembrists brought coherence to the individual's behavior, not by rehabilitating life's prose, but by passing life through the filters of heroic texts and thus simply eliminating whatever was not suitable to be inscribed on the tablets of history. Prosaic responsibility to one's superiors was replaced by responsibility to history and the fear of death by the poetry of honor and liberty. 'We breathe liberty,' declared Ryleev on the square on 14 December. The transferral of liberty from the sphere of ideas and theories into 'breath,' into life, is the essence and the significance of the everyday behavior of the Decembrist.[7]

Lotman provides a new version of the myth in spite of himself. His compelling analysis of the Decembrists' psychology and behavior supplies a different mythological text than the earlier ones of sacrificial heroes or proto-Bolsheviks. Lotman turns the Decembrists into men of action and extricates them from the realm of passive men of ideas, a realm to which the men of the 1860s and more radical activists relegated them.

While Lotman turned his gaze upon the understudied aspects of the Decembrists' behavior, Eidelman went in a different direction, creating for popular history a series of individualized analyses of the Decembrists within their historical epoch. Inspired by Tynianov, he concentrated upon original documents to recreate faithfully a sense of past eras in his historiography as well as in his more fictionalized works.[8] Because of persecution by the KGB in 1957, Eidelman could not pursue a conventional academic career, but instead joined the staff of a small museum outside of Moscow. There he started his work on the nineteenth century, writing about Pushkin, Herzen, and the Decembrists, and soon became a much admired popular historian. Clark summarizes the general situation: "During the Brezhnev years, [however] Soviet cultural production showed an increasing interest in seeking historical precedents in various noncanonical versions of the past. Many intellectuals set themselves up as self-appointed archivists for a particular figure from the past who had been purged or otherwise repressed in the Soviet period and devoted their lives to as much information as possible on their subject, lobbying to publish his or her neglected works, and so forth."[9] Though Eidelman's subjects were not repressed figures during the Soviet era, he fulfilled the preservationist's role by throwing new light on already canonized figures. When questioned about his choice of topics, Eidelman responded: "I studied them—Herzen, Pushkin, the Decembrists—because they helped me live. It was a 'love match.'"[10] With the publication of his book on the Decembrist Mikhail Lunin in 1970, Eidelman created a sensation and established himself as the groundbreaking author of interesting, readable works on the Decembrists. Until his death, Eidelman was considered the most popular living writer of history, valued by his readership for combining "conventionally reliable historical literature" with accessibility and a lively writing style,[11] though more entrenched colleagues did not appreciate his non-canonical approach. Perhaps most important, two aspects distinguish Eidelman's work: a concern for freedom of inquiry and expression and a constant parallel between past and present.[12] These thematic leitmotifs served as the primary sources of his popularity during the era of stagnation, when established scholars toed the official line in their historical writing. It is not surprising then, that "when he wrote about the Decembrists, he evoked thought of modern dissenters" and inspired other artists to explore the relationship between

Figure 5   *The Decembrists. Chernigov Uprising* (1972) by Tatyana Nazarenko. Photograph courtesy of the artist.

past and present, as in Tatyana Nazarenko's painting, *The Decembrists. Chernigov Uprising* (1972).[13] (See figure 5.)

In literature, Naum Korzhavin and Venedikt Erofeev (1938–1990) voiced the unofficial myth of the Decembrists during the 1960s–1970s, and spoke to its fecundity for Soviet artists defining their societal role. Along with them, the poets and bards Alexander Galich (1918–1977) and Bulat Okudzhava (1924–1997) used the Decembrists to evaluate the present in relation to the past Though their approach differed from Korzhavin's and Erofeev's, their work brought to the forefront the inherent ambivalence of the evolving Decembrist myth.

The Historical Context: Conflating the Decembrists and Dissidence

Many works from the 1960s–1980s address the question arising out of the intelligentsia's disillusionment once it learned of Stalin and his cohort's crimes: what happens to the Decembrists' legacy when later generations have become corrupt? The fact that the Decembrist myth could endure such stresses testifies to its multivocality and ability to encapsulate and speak to all kinds of human experiences. Ziolkowski has pointed out that the Decembrists provided a common model for the disenchanted members of Soviet society, as demonstrated by the historical fiction, drama, underground poetry and memoirs produced during the post-Thaw period. Members of the intelligentsia drew the analogy between the Decembrists and purge victims as well as those persecuted after WWII to show parallels between Stalinist and Tsarist Russia.[14] Memoirs especially attest to the Decembrist myth's strong hold upon the intelligentsia while also demonstrating that not all Soviet citizens swallowed the official myth whole. Even at the highest levels, esteem for the Decembrists could be found, as Svetlana Allilueva, Stalin's daughter, writes in her memoirs.[15] The dissident Ludmilla Alexeyeva's personal reminiscences likewise attest that the Decembrists became a model for her generation: "I felt an instinctive bond with the Decembrists. Just a few years earlier, their country had won the war with Napoleon. There was no place for the reactionaries on those battlefields...I could see what brought those young men to Senate Square. It was frustration identical to the frustration I felt while observing *frontoviki* [front-line soldiers] orchestrating "personal cases" against our classmates. Our war was over. Hitler had been defeated. But at peace our rulers needed something more manageable than citizens."[16] Regarding the aims of her generation, she affirms: "The old intelligentsia no longer existed, but we wanted to believe we would be able to recapture its intellectual and spiritual exaltation. Our goal was to lay claim to the values left by the social stratum that had been persecuted by the tsars and destroyed by the revolution."[17] In the truest sense, her cohort sought to reclaim not merely the Decembrists' name, but to imbibe in their essence and traditions. This self-proclamation as the Decembrists' "true heirs" recalls the debates that occurred in the 1920s, shortly after the October revolution, when both the Bolsheviks and the White Guard battled to claim the Decembrists' lineage and legitimacy. However, the situation became more complex in this era. When the acknowledged heirs, the Bolsheviks, and later generations turn out to have become corrupt, how is the Decembrists' legacy valued? Literary representations highlight the struggle between legitimate and illegitimate heirs, positing the legitimate heirs as the morally principled opponents of tyranny versus the illegitimate heirs, the Communists. The question thus becomes one of "dissonance" rather than "continuity."[18] This generation distinguished and asserted itself from its forebears by appealing to the morality of the Decembrists' cause and comparing their deeds.

The guitar poet and bard Alexander Galich takes this analogy to the next level. In "St. Petersburg Romance" ("Peterburgskii romans" 1968), a response to the Soviet invasion of Czechoslovakia on August 21, 1968, Galich challenges his own generation to perform a moral deed as valiant and courageous as the Decembrists': "Dare you go out to the square/At the appointed hour?"[19] Galich echoes Korzhavin's earlier poem "Envy" in questioning his generation's moral complicity. Yet Galich actively queries his cohort, rather than baldly stating that they cannot rise to the challenge. On first hearing Galich's song, Alexeyeva claims: "The hour had struck, announced by the chills that went down our spines. If there had ever been the hour to become a Decembrist, that hour had come."[20] On August 25, 1968, just days after Galich composed his song (August 22), eight dissidents went out onto Red Square in protest of the invasion of Czechoslovakia. Though they may not have known Galich's song, their response to the invasion, the first public protest since the 1920s, indicated a common bond. Vladimir Bukovsky tells of guitar poetry's pervasive influence among Soviet youth, specifically of Okudzhava and Galich's songs: "There wasn't a single false note of official patriotism in those songs, but so much sincerity, so much of our yearning and pain, that the authorities could not tolerate it.... For us, Galich was nothing less than a Homer. Every song of his was an odyssey, a journey through the labyrinths of the soul of Soviet man."[21] Galich's reproach made the authorities take notice; for the first time, he was called in to the Writers' Union and given a stern warning about the song.[22] Readers and critics alike spoke of the profound influence of Galich's songs on generations of Russians, considering him the first to "break the barrier of Aesopian language, to call things openly by their names and ... to give a clear-cut moral credo to his contemporaries."[23]

Alexander Solzhenitsyn also refers to the Decembrists in his work. Though his objective may have been to deflate their official myth he does so for a different end than Galich. Solzhenitsyn does not suggest that his peers are not up to the challenge but that their struggles and persecution were more difficult during the Soviet era, especially during Stalinism. True, he had already drawn the analogy between his experiences after World War II with the Decembrists (discussed in chapter 6). His viewpoint changes to ambivalent at best in his novel *First Circle* (*B kruge pervom*, 1968).[24] To avoid duplication of other scholars' extensive analyses, I cite only one example, where Solzhenitsyn takes on the Decembrists' wives' hallowed image in depicting a conversation between two camp prisoners' wives:

> It was easy to love a man in the nineteenth century! The wives of the Decembrists—do you think they performed some kind of heroic feat? Did personnel sections call them in to fill out security questionnaires? Did they have to hide their marriages as if they were a disease? In order to keep their jobs; so that their five hundred rubles a month wouldn't be taken away from them; so as not to be boycotted in their own apartments; so that when they went to the courtyard to get water people wouldn't hiss at them, calling them 'enemies of the people'? Did their own mothers and sisters bring pressure on them to be reasonable and get a divorce? No, on the contrary! They were followed by a murmur of admiration from the cream of society. They graciously presented to poets the legends of their deeds.[25]

Solzhenitsyn implies that the victims of Soviet repression endured far more onerous sacrifices and fates than the Decembrists. His ambivalence modulates to disdain for the Decembrists and prerevolutionary intelligentsia as his work progresses.[26]

What began in the 1960s as a low rumble exploded in the 1970s. During the mid-1970s, a "second" or unofficial culture emerged, primarily in Leningrad, among disaffected members of the intelligentsia who were unable to find work in their fields and refused to conform to the Soviet system's strictures. This unofficial culture outwardly responded to the Decembrists' rebellious aspect, touting them as forerunners and challenging the official myth. In December 1975, a group of poets and artists decided to celebrate the sesquicentennial of the Decembrist uprising by reading poetry on Senate Square at 11 o'clock in the morning. The group had written to the Leningrad Office of Park and Garden Management for permission. On the morning of December 14, the artists were greeted by a blockade: cars blocked off streets leading to it and police surrounded and cordoned off Senate Square itself. Several people who organized the meeting were detained on their way; the artists Igor Sinyavin and Vadim Filimonov were arrested on the square, but not before Filimonov discarded his placard, inscribed "The Decembrists Were the First Russian Dissidents." The sign floated along the Neva, proclaiming their kinship for all to see. One year later, the authorities again suppressed the group's reading on Senate Square to commemorate the Decembrists. Seven of the fifty people originally planning to attend were immediately detained by the authorities after their arrival on the square.[27]

Bulat Okudzhava's *Poor Avrosimov*

Reevaluation of the Decembrists becomes especially apparent in Bulat Okudzhava's historical fiction. Called a "sign of the times" by one critic,[28] his novels reflect the undercurrents of disaffection in post–Thaw Soviet Union through the author's musings on the Decembrists' status in Russian culture. Okudzhava explained his turn to the past: "Since we were given a distorted version of our history, I developed a serious interest in the true history of Russia. This interest found expression in my novels based on history. It is far more interesting to look into the past because you can study it. It's useless to look into the future."[29] Okudzhava's historical novels consist of narrative lines which twist and turn "like lace . . . in complex patterns, first they disappear then they reappear suddenly on the tale's periphery."[30] More than any author since Tynianov, Okudzhava confronts the ambiguity of the Decembrists' model in his novel *Poor Avrosimov* (*Bednyi Avrosimov*, 1965–1968). *Poor Avrosimov* focuses on the trial of Pavel Pestel, the most prominent Decembrist leader, and reflects Okudzhava's mixed feelings about the Decembrists' deeds. The central character, one Vanya Avrosimov, a young provincial, arrives in St. Petersburg to be a scribe for the investigative commission handling the Decembrists' trial. Avrosimov's aged uncle was one of the first to rush to the defense of the new tsar Nicholas on the fateful day of the Decembrist uprising. As a reward to the uncle for good service, Avrosimov receives the appointment and its concomitant rise in social standing. A limited young man, Avrosimov appears superficial and status conscious. He gets easily distracted from his assignment by daydreams of romance and an idyllic future life in the countryside. Yet as he comes into more frequent contact with Pestel and other Decembrists, he feels their influence. He cannot reconcile the government's treatment of the rebels with their testimony to desiring the best for their homeland. Though initially convinced that Pestel is "evil" and a "criminal," Avrosimov starts questioning everything he hears. He wonders about the true motives of the Investigative commission, and more generally, the nature of imperial power:

> What does insignificant man know about himself? Perhaps only that he is nothing before higher powers....But if this is true, how did he [Pestel] gain the strength to lift his hand against the Sovereign? Against the Deity?...Either the Sovereign is not great, which would be unnatural, or the evildoer is great, which is also unnatural, although it might happen, all because of Satan. But what about God? Well, he would punish. Then why this whole swarm of judges, adjutants, couriers, and all the rest, like Avrosimov himself? Why do they all fulfill divine orders but the others oppose them? What is the truth? Is the Sovereign great? And if he is, how could that criminal have gotten the strength to carry out his dark plans?...Where was the beginning of it all? [Pestel] couldn't simply have been going along and then decided suddenly to murder the Sovereign. Things must have piled up gradually, but where was the beginning? Could he, Avrosimov not have it in himself?[31]

He repeatedly denies sympathy for Pestel, yet he cannot resist the persuasive thinker's dangerous sway. These doubts and fears torment Avrosimov, leading to complete mental and physical breakdown.

Okudzhava explores the Decembrist uprising's devastating effect on the "little men" of history. He explains his focus on Avrosimov rather than Pestel specifically because he wants to create something other than a biography or a history: "It is not the character that is important, but the phenomenon. It grabs me, and that is what I want to analyze."[32] His choice relates to his desire to portray the uniqueness of the era, whose distinguishing feature was the disillusioned officers' reaction on returning to Russia after the Napoleonic campaign: "Music most likely played when they passed through Europe chasing Bonaparte, and their homeland, already reshaped in that European manner, was seen by them from afar. Such was their chagrin when, having returned they found their country the same as it was before; such was their anger and fury at the thought of it all, and already blinded they dashed into their mad undertaking with all their hearts. And who of their opponents desired to give up their accustomed ways?...And the fortress doors opened wide before them" (10). For Okudzhava, the Decembrists' hallmarks were their impetuousness, their inability to reconcile themselves to a homeland less enlightened than Europe, and their mad desire to remake everything by any means necessary. Galina Belaia proclaims: "Okudzhava more than once discussed how, becoming acquainted with the materials about Pestel, he became disenchanted with his hero. 'The fanaticism of this person frightened and alienated me. That kind of heroism did not inspire me. He was not 'my' hero.'"[33] For Okudzhava, Pestel personified the conspiratorial revolutionary's coldness and calculation. Okudzhava thus draws the parallel between Pestel's ruthlessness and willingness to resort to regicide and the strategies that guaranteed the Bolsheviks' success. Whereas in Soviet mythology these similarities valorized the Decembrists and allowed them to serve as proto-Bolsheviks, here they color Okudzhava's perception and make the Decembrists suspect. In the later years of *glasnost*, Okudzhava more than once openly criticized the Bolshevik notion of the ends justifying the means and affirmed Soviet citizens' complicity in crimes against their compatriots during and after the Stalin era.

Anti-Myth and Satire: Venedikt Erofeev's
Moscow to the End of the Line

The author Venedikt Erofeev also challenges the official myth in his novel *Moscow to the End of the Line* (*Moskva-Petushki*, written in 1969, first published in Paris in 1977).[34] He mocks Lenin's historical commonplace that the Decembrists awakened Herzen, who then spurred on revolutionary activism in Russia. Erofeev's Decembrist, first introduced as an "intellectual" (*intelligent*) in a wool overcoat who exclaims "Transcendental" after every vodka shot, enters into conversation with the protagonist, Venya, and his drinking buddies. Venya insists that all Russia's worthwhile people were big drinkers, tracing the line from the Decembrists who "between the Lafitte and Cliquot" (a nod to Pushkin's famous line from the reconstructed chapter X of *Eugene Onegin*) gave "birth to Decembrism" and "finally awakened Herzen." In response, the *intelligent* roars: "Hold it. Go ahead and wake him up, your Herzen.... This Herzen, he was supposed to get off at Khrapunovo, but he's still riding, the dog."[35] Unable to rouse his sleeping fellow traveler, this character has no official role in society. From that point on, the *intelligent* gains the ironic nickname "Decembrist." Erofeev's Decembrist participates in the travelers' philosophical debates on drinking, literature and women, boasting of his sexual prowess. This Decembrist holds no sacred ideals and illustrates the exchange of noble values for coarse vulgarity. The only thing this latter-day Decembrist can do is get drunk and fornicate, just like the rest of the crowd. Erofeev attests to the decay of Soviet society and its formerly best representatives, depicting the collapse of all dreams of a better future. In reflecting upon the new order, Erofeev utilizes the ironic mode to dramatize the distance between past hopes and present-day reality.

Because of its uniqueness and appeal to its audience *Moscow to the End of the Line* became a cult novel and its author became a "major cultural myth of his time."[36] The conflation of the author and the novel's protagonist, called Venya, Venichka, or Erofeichik, all derivatives of the author's name, created a mythic authorial persona and lent a greater personal element to a novel already grounded in autobiographical aspects. The work circulated widely—in hundreds of *samizdat* copies—attesting that an entire generation felt it spoke of their own thwarted hopes and desires and accurately portrayed life's absurdity. The parodied latter-day Decembrist became just another marginalized figure in an alienated group of disillusioned people.

Parody and Irony: Naum Korzhavin's Ballad on the Decembrists

Anatolii Vishevsky points out that the predominance of irony distinguishes Soviet literary culture of the 1970s and stems from disillusionment and despair.[37] Irony pervaded all forms of culture, ranging from prose to comedic monologues to guitar poets' songs. The irony resonated profoundly among the Soviet urban intelligentsia, becoming an integral part of what Vishevsky calls "popular intellectual culture" rather than a "nationwide ideology."[38] Korzhavin likewise employs irony in his poem "In Memory of Herzen: A Ballad of Historic Sleep-Deprivation (A Cruel Romance on A Similarly-titled Work of V. I. Lenin)" (*Pamiati Gertsena: Ballada ob istoricheskom nedosype* [*Zhestokii romans po odnoimennomu proizvedeniiu V. I. Lenina*], 1972). In this poem, Korzhavin parodies the official reputation of Herzen and other Russian revolutionaries in the Soviet pantheon. He also undermines Lenin's genealogical construct by literalizing the metaphor that "the Decembrists roused Herzen":

> Любовь к Добру разбередила сердце им.
> А Герцен спал, не ведая про зло…
> Но декабристы разбудили Герцена.
> Он недоспал. Отсюда все пошло.

И ошалев от их поступка дерзкого,
Он поднял страшный на весь мир трезвон.
Чем разбудил случайно Чернышевского,
Не зная сам, что этим сделал он.

А тот со сна, имея нервы слабые,
Стал к топору Россию призывать,—
Чем потревожил крепкий сон Желябова,
А тот Перовской не дал всласть поспать.

И захотелось тут же с кем-то драться им,
Идти в народ и не страшиться дыб.
Так началась в России конспирация:
Большое дело—долгий недосып.

Был царь убит, но мир не зажил заново.
Желябов пал, уснул несладким сном.
Но перед этим побудил Плеханова,
Чтоб тот пошел совсем другим путём.

Все обойтись могло с течением времени.
В порядок мог втянуться русский быт…
Какая сука разбудила Ленина?
Кому мешало, что ребёнок спит?

На тот вопрос ответа нету точного.
Который год мы ищем зря его…
Три составные части—три источника
Не проясняют здесь нам ничего.

Да он и сам не знал, пожалуй, этого,
Хоть мести в нем запас не иссякал.
Хоть тот вопрос научно он исследовал,—
Лет пятьдесят виновного искал.

То в «Бунде», то в кадетах….Не найдутся ли
Хоть там следы. И в неудаче зол,
Он сразу всем устроил революцию,
Чтоб ни один от кары не ушел.

И с песней шли к Голгофам под знаменами
Отцы за ним,—как сладкое житье…
Пусть нам простятся морды полусонные,
Мы дети тех, кто недоспал свое.

Мы спать хотим....И никуда не деться нам
От жажды сна и жажды всех судить...
Ах, декабристы не будите Герцена!
Нельзя в России никого будить.

Love for the Good agitated their heart.
And Herzen slept, not knowing about evil...
But the Decembrists roused Herzen.
He didn't sleep enough. Everything started because of that.

And, having gone crazy because of their bold act,
He raised a ruckus terrifying to the entire world.[39]
With which he accidentally woke Chernyshevsky,
Not knowing himself what he had done.

And having weak nerves, that one, drowsy,
went to call Russia to the ax,—
which disturbed Zheliabov's deep sleep,
And he didn't let Perovskaia sleep to her heart's content.

And right away they wanted to start a fight with somebody,
To go to the people and not fear the racks.
Thus began conspiracy in Russia:
A big deal—a long lack of sleep.

The tsar was killed, but the world did not begin to live anew.
Zheliabov fell, he slept a bitter sleep.
But before this he woke up Plekhanov,
So that he would take a completely different path.[40]

With time's passage all this would have worked out.
Russian everyday life could be put in order...
What bitch woke up Lenin?
Who did it bother that the child was sleeping?

There is no exact answer to that question.
We have been seeking it in vain for how many years...
Three component parts—three sources
Do not clear up anything for us here.[41]

He himself did not know it, if you please,
Though his reserve of vengeance did not run dry.
Though he studied this question scientifically,—
He sought the guilty for fifty years or so.

First in the Bund, then among the Kadets...perhaps
Traces can be found there? And, angry because of failure,
He immediately made a revolution for everybody,
So that not a single one would escape punishment.

And with a song the fathers followed him
To Golgotha beneath the banners,—as if to the promised land...
Let our half-asleep mugs be forgiven,
We are the children of those who did not sleep their fill.

We want to sleep.... And we have no place to go
From the craving for sleep and the desire to judge everybody...
Oh, Decembrists! Don't rouse Herzen!
In Russia one should not wake up anybody.[42]

Korzhavin demolishes the official version of Russian history, trivializing various revolutionaries' deeds by attributing their actions to sleep deficit. He deflates the sacred genealogy of Soviet revolutionary tradition and challenges the Decembrists' lofty status as the Bolsheviks' forebears. Korzhavin flatly blames the Decembrists for the havoc Lenin later wrought upon Russia and manifests the obvious ambivalence that some Decembrists' "heirs" felt towards their hallowed ancestors and their questionable legacy of revolution, leading to the Soviet system's crimes against its own citizens.

Okudzhava's, Korzhavin's and Erofeev's work all arise from the same impulse to interrogate the canonical tenets of the Decembrist myth, though their results differ. Okudzhava highlights the ambivalence inherent in the Decembrists' deeds and in the myth's official Soviet version. Yet he comes to no definitive conclusions or final judgments, other than the notion that the Decembrists were not "his heroes."[43] Despite their direct challenges to the Decembrist myth, Korzhavin and Erofeev do not effect its total destruction. Instead, their dissenting voices cast them as Decembrist-types themselves. Both writers and members of the intelligentsia, they strive for a lofty cause by challenging established interpretations. In producing their own idiosyncratic literary representations of revolutionary tradition and history, they act as dissenters against the authorized view. While ostensibly satirizing the Decembrists, Korzhavin and Erofeev reinvigorate the myth, raising their voices against the deadened canonical treatment of the Decembrists. In so doing, they allude to their limited spheres of activity and the futility of their attempts to accomplish anything. Alexeyeva remarks that Korzhavin wrote about "us, the generation devoid of a

Senate Square...Korzhavin was not the voice of the dissidents; he spoke for the broader circle of the intelligentsia, people who knew right from wrong but who were unable to act,"[44] much like the implied audience of Galich's "Petersburg Romance." In "In Memory of Herzen," Korzhavin reduces the Decembrists to alarm clocks, unleashing the terrible forces of revolution in Russia and even bringing harm upon later generations. In *Moscow to the End of the Line*, Erofeev's Decembrist cannot effectively act, while the drunken protagonist Venya cannot make it to his destination though he literally reaches his final end. These writers depict a land of diminished expectations in which great sacrifices cannot occur. Yet they transpose the trickster image of the Decembrists onto themselves, highlighting the subversive role played by the intelligentsia of their own day as dissidents, and the revivifying role of artists who question and challenge the mixed legacy of Soviet cultural mythologies.

The Sesquicentennial of the Decembrist Uprising

Despite popular challenges, the official myth remained dominant in Soviet discourse. The 1975 celebration of the Decembrist anniversary followed the general parameters of Soviet jubilees, and repeated many rituals of the 1925 centennial. Volumes of articles were published, scholarly meetings took place from Moscow to Leningrad to Ulyanovsk,[45] museums organized excursions and exhibitions of Decembrist relics, and a new film was released in the Decembrists' honor. All-union and local newspapers and journals featured articles commemorating the Decembrists' hallowed efforts against tsarist tyranny and proclaiming their legacy's continuation to the present. An article in *Pravda*, written by the ubiquitous Nechkina, indicates the level to which the Decembrists' official myth had ossified. "The Decembrists' Cause" opens with a ritual citation of Lenin's article "In memory of Herzen," "Their cause has not been lost" (*Ikh delo ne propalo*). Nechkina repeatedly cites Lenin and Herzen to assert the Decembrists' historical significance as the progenitors of the oppositional movement. Quoting from soldiers' songs and revolutionary hymns, she narrates the iconic moments of the Decembrist uprising and execution, countering their contemporary, the poet F. I. Tiutchev, who insisted that the Decembrist uprising did not leave a trace behind.[46] Nechkina does not allow the Decembrists to speak for themselves, but has Pushkin and Lenin answer for them: " 'Your sorrowful toil will not be in vain!' Pushkin prophetically said to the Decembrists. 'Their cause has not been lost!' Lenin's voice replied from the next century."[47] The Decembrists' own voices have been suppressed, drowned out by Lenin, Herzen, Pushkin and other lesser known writers. The rhetoric remained unchanged; the Decembrists' efforts were sanctified (as a *podvig*), and the continuous link between the glorious past and Soviet present was affirmed.

The Official Myth on Celluloid:
The Star of Enchanted Happiness

As if implicitly responding to the anti-myth's challenges among the intelligentsia, Soviet authorities released a new film during the sesquicentennial. *The Star of Enchanted Happiness* (*Zvezda plenitel'nogo schast'ia*, Mosfilm, 1975), was directed by Vladimir Motyl, well-known for his earlier smash hit *White Sun of the Desert* (*Beloe solntse pustyni*, 1970), and co-written by Oleg Osetinskii and Mark Zakharov. The film's release coincided not only with the anniversary but also with the celebration of International Women's Year. This coincidence may explain the decision to base the movie on the Decembrists' wives. Yet upon inspection, this choice highlights the Decembrists' ambiguous position in Russian culture at the time, and deflects their subversive potentiality by valorizing the wives' traditional feminine images. The film depicts the wives' lofty sacrifice in a romanticized and sentimental manner—perhaps in response to the popularity of David Lean's *Dr. Zhivago* (1965)—idealizing their complete devotion. It features an all-star cast, with Aleksei Batalov in the role of Sergei Trubetskoi, Oleg Strizhenov as Volkonsky, Oleg Yankovsky as Ryleev, and Innokenti Smoktunovsky as Tseidler; the unknown actor, Igor Kostolevskii, playing Ivan Annenkov became famous immediately after the film's release. Though the critics panned the film's lack of historical accuracy, it was a popular success. Its impression survives to today in the minds of many former Soviet citizens, who, when queried about the Decembrists, immediately refer to the "wonderful" (*zamechatelnyi*) film. It has become a cult film and is frequently shown on Russian television.

The film's title borrows a memorable line from Pushkin's epistle, "To Chaadaev," and echoes the repeated refrain of Shaporin's *Decembrists* as a symbol of Russia's future release from autocratic tyranny. Given the rote memorization of Pushkin's poetry in Soviet schools, both the mass and intelligentsia audience would have recalled the original context, and perhaps also remembered the popular opera. The title takes on a sentimentalized nuance in its new context. The film opens with the dedication "to the women of Russia," associating the Decembrists' wives with all Russian women and underscoring the International Women's Year's celebration. The dedication also invokes Nekrasov's famous poem, *Russian Women*. Like Nekrasov, Motyl politicizes the women's action, insisting: "The main heroes of our film are the women—the Decembrists' wives and not the Decembrists themselves. In my opinion, the actions of the women were undoubtedly a continuation of the revolt of the men, a continuation of December 14."[48] With such disclaimers, it is not surprising that the first part of the film re-tells the story of the Decembrist uprising in a perfunctory fashion.[49] The film uses flashbacks to acquaint the viewers with the Decembrists' political views, intercutting between political discussions, intimate scenes of Volkonskii's and Trubetskoi's family lives and the romance between Annenkov and Gueble. After re-acquainting the viewer with the basic sequence of events leading to the uprising and its suppression, the second half concentrates on the well-known stories of Princess Ekaterina Trubetskaia (played by Irina Kupchenko), Pauline Gueble-Annenkova (the Polish actress Ewa Szykulska) and Princess Maria Volkonskaia (Natalia Bondarchuk, daughter of famed director Sergei Bondarchuk). The screenwriters borrow from Nekrasov's poem (especially in their conflation of the iconic scene of Volkonskaia's reunion with her husband and her descent into the mines) and from Annenkova's memoirs. It is notable she was included in the film dedicated to Russian women. One critic in all seriousness insists: "Her impulse makes even her—a French woman from a fashion atelier who did not know a word in Russian—a woman of Russia."[50]

Though the artistic director and designers used appropriate historical costumes and locations, they sacrificed historical accuracy for aesthetic impact, as one anecdote relates: "When the historical consultant arrived on Senate Square where they were shooting the scene of the uprising, he was outraged: 'The troops were not arrayed like that!' 'Well, never mind, it looks better that way,' he was told."[51] The actresses' demeanor, makeup and hairstyles reflect 1970s Soviet fashion, as does the music. The action takes place to the accompaniment of a romance written by Okudzhava, "The Cavalier Guard's Song" ("Pesnia Kavaler'garda" or "Kavaler'garda vek nedolog") rather than to historically appropriate strains of classical romances set to Pushkin's lyrics.[52] Film critics lamented the historical anachronisms: "It is very necessary to tell the contemporary viewer about what our people should genuinely be proud. But even so, historical truth must be placed first...and not the director's fantasy, even if it is very striking."[53] Yet despite these criticisms, several called it a success: "You leave the hall with a feeling of closeness to one of the most romantic, beautiful and tragic pages of our history. The spirit of the times, without a doubt, was successfully portrayed in the film...150 years is already far away—and, nevertheless—it is close."[54]

Why did Motyl and his colleagues focus on the Decembrists' wives rather than the rebels themselves? The primary reason had little to do with the fact that the anniversary coincided with the International Year of the Woman. Motyl's choice says far more about the destabilizing potential of the Decembrists, which was indeed borne out during 1975, and may explain why Gosfilm censors took several years before approving the script.[55] During the Thaw, the idea of the Decembrists as noble forefathers took a deeper hold upon the imagination of the disillusioned Russian intelligentsia and eventually led to dissent in the 1970s. Therefore, the filmmaker's focus on the wives—who through their personal sacrifice for their husbands fulfilled traditional roles in a patriarchal and conservative society—must be viewed as uncontroversial and appealing to a mass audience. This popularized version of the Decembrists' story suppressed their unsettling and ambivalent potential and reduced their role to figures in a love story with the uprising as a minor element. The portrayal could not be seen as advocating open rebellion against the establishment, as a film based on the Decembrist revolt could be interpreted in an atmosphere of increasing public dissent.

That these polarities of official and unofficial versions of the Decembrist myth coexisted—not always happily—in Soviet culture throughout the post–Stalin era testifies to the myth's staying power in the Russian imagination. Though challenges to the official myth re-emerged during this time they could not dominate because of censorship restrictions upon literature and the dissemination of information. Motyl's film kept the Decembrists' simplified and sentimentalized image alive in the masses' hearts and minds. That the myth remained malleable and vibrant attests to its depth and richness and to the fact that it continued to speak to Russian national identity during the post-Stalin era.

CHAPTER EIGHT

The Decembrists' Desacralization during the Glasnost and Post-Soviet Eras

> Myth is also a truth. In it one hears not the high priest's objective leaden intonation, but the stupid, naïve breathing of a human.
>
> —Kama Ginkas[1]

After Leonid Brezhnev's death in 1982, the Soviet Union plunged into a period of political uncertainty which was masked over by the Supreme Soviet and state media's assertions of "business as usual." Rapid changes in the country's leadership occurred after the untimely deaths of Brezhnev's successors, Iurii Andropov, former head of the KGB, who became General Secretary of the CPSU from November 1982 to February 1984, and Konstantin Chernenko, from April 1984 to March 1985. After Chernenko's death, with the appointment of a relatively unknown Party functionary, Mikhail Gorbachev, to the position of General Secretary a decidedly new phase began. Though fully-formed by the Soviet educational and political system, Gorbachev undertook political, economic and social reform to address the problems plaguing the system: a heavily bureaucratized, centralized economy, a lack of initiative and innovation, cultural and intellectual stagnation, alcoholism, and other social issues. The new policies—*perestroika* (restructuring) and *glasnost* (openness)—meant to effect gradual change from within the system from the top down. In comparison to the changes of the post–Soviet era, the Gorbachev-era changes now appear moderate, but at the time they seemed drastic.

In the cultural arena, *glasnost* had a wide-ranging impact. Suddenly, writers banned for decades were being published and unprecedented amounts of archival information became accessible. It was an exciting time—when each new literary journal was awaited with great antici-pation, when formerly taboo topics such as drug abuse, alcoholism, and society's deterioration became subject to open discussion in the press, literature and film, on television and the stage.

Because of the relaxation of censorship, the Decembrists' image was no longer necessary as a mirroring device for writers to discuss the present through allusions to the past. Yet it did not entirely recede to the background of cultural consciousness during this time. During *glasnost*, a "history boom" took place, which drew attention to previously suppressed elements of history and culture during the Soviet era.[2] Scholars still continued to publish monographs and articles on the Decembrists with new information gleaned from previously unavail-able archival materials. Eidelman played a large role in the renaissance of interest in nineteenth-century history, and several of his most well-known works emerged during this period.[3] Clark speculates that the intelligentsia was primed for the boom because of their obsession with the past, but history's popularity crossed over from the intelligentsia to the mass audience. As a part of this resurgence, Tynianov's novels were republished, and became best-sellers in the late 1980s, especially among the intelligentsia, but also among mainstream readers. A new writer, Mikhail Kuraev (b. 1939), also emerged, and recalling Gogol, Dostoevsky and Tynianov, created fantastic fictions about the little men of history. Kuraev's historical novellas met with immediate acclaim and distinguished him as one of the era's promising new voices.

As a part of the interest in filling in history's blank spots and increasing communication with the West, ties were strengthened between Soviet and émigré Russian communities. This improved relationship enabled Russian émigré nobility who were primarily Decembrists' descendents to visit the Soviet Union in the late 1980s. The public responded by greeting them with the claim that "you are ours" (*vy nashi*), as if it was a return of patrimony.[4]

Mikhail Kuraev's Excurses into Historical Truth

Mikhail Kuraev worked for 20 years as a screenwriter for Lenfilm and had six scripts produced before his first novella, *Captain Dikshtein: A Fantastic Narrative* (*Kapitan Dikshtein: Fantasticheskoke povestvovanie*) was published in 1987. His works ground their protagonists in their surroundings, be it Gatchina (in *Captain Dikshtein*) or Petersburg (in *Night Patrol* [*Nochnoi dozor*, 1988]) and ponder the meaning of historical events. Providing a key to Kuraev's oeuvre, the narrator says in *Captain Dikshtein*, "What sense is there picking the bones of history if you can't find the answer to the simplest question there. Why is it that a fantastic fate is given to certain people, or, for example to certain towns, and not others?"[5] In opposition to the teleologically-oriented approach of Marxist-Leninist historiography, Kuraev explores the way that individuals become swept up by history rather than influencing it. He demonstrates how chance can suddenly affect drastic change upon an individual's life and historical events.

In *Night Patrol: A Nocturne for Two Voices with the Participation of Comrade Polubolotov, Rifleman of VOKHR*, Kuraev interweaves the voice of the former NKVD rifleman Polubolotov with the implied author's voice. This authorial persona knows Soviet history well and provides an ironic counterpoint to Polubolotov's obtuse musings on his role as someone who "became one with the times and created history" (144). Polubolotov's descriptions of nighttime arrests and interrogations during the Stalin terror lead to a digression on Petersburg's landscape, specifically Peter-Paul Fortress, as a place for earlier executions:

> The nightingales are trilling above the quiet Kronwerk Canal, above the steep shores of the embankment. A hundred steps from the parade ground lies the so-far unidentified location, not yet adorned by an obelisk with five profiles, of the wicked and unskilled execution when rotten ropes choked the throats of five madmen who wished a different destiny for their fatherland than the one meted out by the single ruler, even though he may have been anointed to tsardom by Lord God himself.
>
> Beat nightingale's song; beat on the silent stone walls, beat on the thick prison gate, beat on the prison bolts that have locked up thousands of souls, some from the light of the world and others from the light of truth and goodness. May God let your whistling wake up someone who will start moving under the ooze of life's cares, let someone's soul be roused from its gray sleep and try to make its own life meaningful, strong and bold, and begin to abhor its own muteness, timidity, and endless chase after petty advantages. (162–63)

The nightingale stands guard over the location where the Decembrists were executed more than a century before the purges began. Kuraev recalls the Decembrists' execution as a blank spot of history, collapsing the eras in their similar urges for truth. Kuraev also contrasts the nightingale's song's potential to evoke man's best qualities with Polubolotov's earlier description of the nightingale's effect during his nocturnal burials of purge victims, again conflating the times. Kuraev interrogates those who justified their actions as "a part of history," rather than taking a moral stand and becoming apart from history. Though the narrator senses the song's redeeming quality and sees the Decembrists' deeds as an earlier response, Polubolotov says the song tears at his soul : "In this silence you begin to feel like the last human being in the world; when we return to the city there won't be anyone there and there's nobody in the rest of the whole wide world either, daylight will never come, there will only be white nights like this and an endless silence" (157–58). Polubolotov's perception of the nightingale's song as an apocalyptic omen reveals that despite his posturing, nostalgia and justification of his former job, deep down he knows he committed crimes against his people though he does not openly acknowledge his guilt. He is unredeemed and unredeemable.

Following in the footsteps of Gogol, Dostoevsky, Belyi, and Tynianov, Kuraev uses Petersburg's architecture as an independent character in his novella. In another Decembrist reference, Kuraev speaks of Revolution (formerly Troitsky) Square as an "ambiguous stage":

Another corner of the square touches the park where beyond the transparent stage scenery of tall trees you can just discern the area known by everyone, where during the white night of July 13 one of the most famous of all tragedies was played out without any spectators, but agitating the souls of contemporaries and plunging the fatherland into a silent torpor for many years.

A brick horseshoe as mighty as a fortress then occupied Kronwerk Square, where in accordance with the inspired com-position by the emperor himself, who also planned the procedure of its implementation, ninety-seven officers were subjected to civil execution and public dishonor for daring to doubt that tsars are appointed by God and for wanting to communicate to others the original meaning of the words "legality" and "justice." They had weakened and changed terribly from half a year of impris-onment, but without trembling and even triumphantly they went to meet their fate on the earthen banks that had settled and were crumbling, on which a scaffold had been constructed with two posts and one cross-bar for the five whom the tsar had graciously granted hanging and delivered from quartering. They saw how some youth grabbed a noose on the almost completed scaffold and hung on it to test the strength of the rope from which five hours after the execution they would remove the dead bodies that had before death been wrapped in white shrouds; but there strangled Russia would keep dangling who knows how long...

On that early morning there were no spectators at this perhaps most luxurious of all the executions that Troitsky Square and its surroundings had ever known and remembered. It was only the anointed organizer of the brutal spectacle who was awake at Tsarskoe Selo and received messengers every half hour, steaming from the long gallop, who reported on the premier performance. (178–179)

The ambiguous stage of Revolution Square echoes the ambiguity of the revolution's victory. The continuum of persecution and executions occurring in that space illustrates that history repeats itself, and that without acknowledgement of past sins and errors humankind cannot evolve. Kuraev insists that the area remains marked by the Decembrists' execution, a stain that cannot be cleansed generations later, but that it must be remembered and properly memorialized. Though in 1906 an army hospital was erected there, it could not erase the memory of the Decembrists' execution but instead reenacted it, literally, in its spatial organization: "It was a temple of mercy, an army hospital, whose geometrical design repeated the disposition in two squares of the officers of the guards and of the army who were condemned to exile and hard labor. The ever alert eye of the spiritual pastors must have been clouded, because the Vladimir Mother of God icon is looking down at us from the high hospital wall with the black eyes of Princess Volkonskaya, thanks to a whim of the young iconographer Kuzma from Khvalynsk, who rejected the thousand-year-old Byzantine canon that prescribes that the intercessor for the human race should be pictured with pale blue eyes" (178–179). Memory of the Decembrists is inscribed into Petersburg's architecture and the city's actual fabric, as in *Kiukhlia*.

Kuraev's equation of the Decembrists with the victims of Soviet repression is not new, but his manner for assuring their remembrance is, as Helena Goscilo suggests, "Kuraev's originality consists not only in perceiving contingency where others have claimed inevitability, but in revealing how the contingent and fantastic constitute so-called history."[6] Kuraev recreates the fantastic moments in past history to demonstrate that historical memory must be corrected for society to achieve progress.

Post-Soviet Deconstruction, Post-Modernism, and Commercialization

The Soviet Union experienced another cataclysm in the early 1990s, concluding Gorbachev's era. The August 1991 putsch by communist hard-liners to unseat Gorbachev and eradicate democratic reforms evoked memory of the Decembrists in some witnesses, according to Rosa Ianaeva, the wife of the coup's figurehead leader.[7] Though unsuccessful, the coup (along with challenges from non-Russian republics), precipitated the USSR's demise. Gorbachev resigned in December 1991, turning power over to Boris Yeltsin, the renegade Communist who led the mass resistance. The Decembrists came to mind again in October 1993, when President Yeltsin quashed opposition to his policies by shelling Moscow's White House, where Russian Parliament members, "defending the 1993 Constitution" had cloistered themselves. One commentator noted the parallels: "In both, vague and contradictory ideals prevailed; and 'the uprising' on the whole was limited to a sacrificial stand by important state buildings."[8] Despite the passage of time, the Decembrists' memory remained alive in Russian political culture.

With the change in leadership, from communism to Yeltsin's hybrid mix of democracy and authoritarian will, also came a radical economic shift, from a planned and centralized state-controlled economy to a chaotic, free-wheeling stab at capitalism. Artists and cultural institutions felt the harsh economic and social changes. Less state money was available to subsidize writers and artists; they began to learn about the vagaries of readership and the market, from which they had been shielded during the Soviet era. Writing and publishing according to state-approved plan was no longer necessary. In addition, people had unprecedented access to Western forbidden fruits—popular fiction, pornography, self-help books, action movies, soap operas, and fashion magazines—all became available to a starved reading public. One writer called the climate a "new Silver Age," in the multiplicity of available genres, writing styles, and topics, while others bemoaned the proliferation of sex and violence, and an editor of a prominent literary journal complained of impending bankruptcy because of new market demands.[9]

On a deeper level, people discovered how much information was still hidden from them, despite the many *glasnost*-era revelations about the USSR's secret past. Though more citizens questioned the past during *glasnost* than during the Thaw, with the Soviet Union's fall, many thought that the entire system was spiritually bereft and morally bankrupt, and they began to feel they had been living a lie. Movements and belief systems—spiritualism, religious sects, parapsychology, all of which had formerly been outlawed by the Soviet regime—that would help the average person come to terms with such critical questions of life and death, truth and falsehood, and legitimate and illegitimate power became more popular. People whose entire world view was shaped by the defunct and now dishonored system experienced a sense of extreme crisis.

Kama Ginkas's *The Decembrists' Execution*

Kama Ginkas's play *The Decembrists' Execution* (*Kazn' dekabristov*, written in 1980, first staged in 1995) straddles the boundaries between the *glasnost* and post–Soviet eras. Ginkas became interested in the Decembrists while writing his play *Pushkin and Natalie* in 1979: "I became fascinated by the whole era, and by chance, hit upon the material about the Decembrists. Here again, I wrote this play based not on live texts, but on dry reports, inquests, and the like. These were historical documents. People do not talk the way their speech is recorded in interrogations. I liked the fact that my characters would not be able to speak as a living person would. They must express themselves according to protocol."[10] These distancing techniques enabled Ginkas to gain a new perspective on the Decembrists. He began rehearsing at MKhAT in the early 1980s, but the play was not performed then because the MKhAT administration felt that it was "ideologically dubious."[11]

The topic appeared especially well-suited to Ginkas's theater as it contained "all the requisite ingredients...fact and myth, humor and the absurd, and playing with death."[12] After its premiere in 1995, the production was hailed as "a powerful and typically unorthodox presentation." Rather than realistically reenact the events, Ginkas has his actors "speak the language of interrogations, reports or letters from which the text has been cut and pasted," while an "Author" figure interrupts the action on stage and directs the actors' and audience's responses.[13] The actors wore the names of the characters they played on their chests. Ginkas spoke of the signs' dual function: "The nametags are labels.... There is the struggle of a living person with a title, of a real person with a historical personage. Some of my play's heroes directly name themselves, but others hide behind their title. I have always been interested in the clash between the sign and the living person."[14] The scenery included nooses, fetters, caps worn during a hanging and other objects associated with the execution. Ginkas calls his method "theater of the fact" (*teatr fakta*), emphasizing the importance of the objects as well as the actors. When queried about the play, Ginkas responded: "People are occupied with a simple task—getting to the bottom of the technology of an execution. Like anything else, an execution has its own technology. You need a wooden beam, a wrench, a rope. What kinds of rope? What kinds of knots? How do you grease them? It is all very simple. But we are talking about an execution—life and death."[15] He highlighted the execution's spectacular nature by including signs labeled "To the execution" in the theater's vestibule, directing the audience into the performance hall to their seats. Thus he conflates the theater and execution as two related performative acts and the stage and gallows as similar performance spaces: "A public execution is always theater: there are spectators, assistants, and, finally the main players. For that reason execution always had an edifying character."[16]

Ginkas engages the audience, making it feel the execution's horror and absurdity. He confronts his spectators with unambiguous physical objects while demonstrating the ambiguity of the "labels" applied to the execution's participants. His ultimate goal, however, is not to recreate historical truth but to defamiliarize clichéd conventions to lead to deeper understanding. Ginkas perceives the shading between myth and history that has taken place regarding the Decembrists: "Historical truth, slipping away from us, doesn't interest me. I'm interested in people. People's naïve, ambitious, touching, and funny attempts to dismember the truth; their lively intonations and affecting grimaces in the search of truth, their thirst or necessity of mythmaking."[17] Ginkas demonstrates the executed Decembrists' symbolic value by their unusual mode of representation. White nightshirts on hangers with nametags across their chests hang suspended against the brick wall backdrop of the theater. The figures become important specifically as emblems of the tsarist government's repressive act, rather than as embodied characters speaking and acting upon the stage. Despite the fact that these characters are represented and not living, the audience experiences a physiological reaction upon seeing the play. Ginkas explained:

> They bring in five sacks and we perceive them as corpses. But the actors open them up and it turns out to be sacks full of overcoats. They start slamming the coats against the wall as if they were

useless rags. And in that second we identify ourselves with those coats. We think, 'That's me they're slamming up against the wall!' When one of the characters takes a wooden hanger with an overcoat hanging on it and breaks it, we feel as though someone is snapping our spine. These are the elements that allow us to identify with what happens on stage.[18]

Ginkas provokes these reactions by appealing to primal instincts. Though not a faithful production in its historical depiction, it remains authentic in focusing on the actors' words from the historical documents. The play is not meant to be strictly representational or descriptive, but everything has been calculated for an artistic, psychological and emotional effect—to get at a higher or different Truth, rather than to get to the truth about what happened. Because of this search for Truth, or, to show that "myth is also a truth," the play resides in high art's realm, despite its reliance on historical sources. Though a postmodern, deconstructionist approach has been taken toward the topic, this work movingly treats the execution, peeling away at the layers of myth, reminding us of the humans behind the Decembrists' legendary image.

Pierre and Natasha and the Decembrists' Commodification

During the *glasnost* and post–Soviet era, the Decembrist myth's deep roots reached beyond high culture to Russian popular culture, where the Decembrists appear as comic book and pulp fiction heroes.[19] The post–Soviet popular challenges to the myth diverge from earlier satirical modes. In 1996, a literary scandal ensued with the publication of *Pierre and Natasha*, a sequel to Leo Tolstoy's, *War and Peace*, penned by a pseudonymous author, Vasilii Staroi. Panned by the critics and reviled by the intelligentsia, the two-volume sequel interrogates the Decembrists' lofty status in Russian history, collapsing under the weight of the Russian literary tradition. Yet unlike his predecessors, Staroi takes on not only the official Soviet view, but also the unofficial myth of the Decembrists as dissidents or challengers to established authority.

The publishers justified their sequel by citing the commonplace that Tolstoy originally intended *War and Peace* to be an introduction to a novel about the Decembrists. Obviously conversant with Tolstoy scholarship and historical sources on the Decembrist movement, Staroi writes his sequel using discarded plot developments from *War and Peace's* numerous draft versions.. Staroi portrays Pierre Bezukhov as a primary theoretician of the Decembrist movement, and presents his own interpretation of the revolt in a post–Soviet, postmodern text often bordering on the absurd in its mélange of popular fiction, historical documents and literary parody.

The author superimposes Tolstoy's fictional characters onto a depiction of the historical events, clumsily integrating them into the action, until the standoff between tsarist officials and the conspirators on Senate Square. Staroi launches into a surreal description of the revolt from Pierre's point of view. Though Pierre had sworn allegiance to the new tsar earlier in the day, he gets swept up in the rebellion. Staroi uses Pierre's involvement to explore the uprising's theatrical possibilities and to delineate its importance in Russian history.

Staroi blatantly imitates *War and Peace*'s Borodino scene and the scene of the uprising in Tynianov's *Kiukhlia* to illustrate that man cannot influence history. During the uprising, Pierre stumbles onto the square and unwittingly takes part in the revolt because a government spy, Mr. S, has gotten him drunk. Trivializing Pierre's revolutionary fervor by attributing it to inebriation, Staroi parodies the Decembrists' belief in revolution's positive value by naming this "liquor of the revolution," *The Twelve*, after Blok's famous poem on revolution's elemental force. Staroi expands his parody, satirizing Blok's philosophy of the connection between music and revolution: "In order to hear and understand the uprising's music, it is necessary to plug up one's ears and go mad—Mr. S said in a tenor voice...—The movement of people is the most demonic, that is the most speechless element, the murmuring of the deaf-mute, thirsting to lie" (1: 432–433). After this unusual exchange, Pierre sees things differently. Though he initially expects to go mad as a result of the revolution, he gains some clarity:

> And all the same, all the same,—Pierre thought—I feel that now something is happening, about which our descendants will speak. Pity that I, Count Bezukhov, am unprepared for the events and did not finish my main philosophical work about Russian democracy's particulars and capabilities using the Russian people's character as an example. As a result, the liberals are not armed with important knowledge and understanding as to which way to go and what to strive for.... But all the same, what is happening now? Is this how a revolution looks? And how should it look? A standing rebellion? There has been nothing like it before in Russia. There were palace coups. May we hope now for victory if on the liberals' side no organization is visible? (1:433)

Staroi grants Pierre the unusual perceptive capacity of distance, allowing him to place the rebellion in historical context and to question what future generations will think. Pierre plays a prophetic role in understanding the momentousness of the events he witnesses and in which he participates. Staroi ironically endows him with capacities similar to Pushkin, who, according to Soviet critics and historians, also foresaw the revolt's import for Russia's future.

Further complicating the depiction, Staroi piles on historical and literary references. The apocalyptic uprising recalls Merezhkovskii's portrayal of the revolt as *bezbozhnaia revoliutsiia* (godless revolution) in *December 14.* He also draws a parallel between the revolt and the fall of Jericho. Responding to Pierre's question about the sky's redness and an image of a horseman riding the waves of purple clouds, the mysterious Mr. S points out:

> Let us recall what happened there—Mr. S continued in the tone of a preacher, performing an exegesis of the episode from the Holy Scriptures.—The people howled, and the trumpets sounded, and the walls of the city fell. The entire native population was slaughtered, except the sinner Rahab, who betrayed her city and people. There she is on the right, at the walls. She is the first citizen of the world!
>
> Rahab really was standing...surrounded by smoke, in a white chiton. It was easy to take her for a priest. Pierre fell deep into thought, trying to somehow reconcile what was happening in the heavens and on earth. (1: 436)

In this context the revolt escalates from a disorganized rebellion to a cosmic event. References recur to the elemental nature of revolution. Adding a surreal note, Staroi animates the wind, which bears aloft monsters and naked women. All around the square, strange visions appear: "Girls with uniformly smooth small heads in uniformly white dresses swam in a tender dance onto the bared bayonets, and their dresses turned red as if from the sun's rays" (1: 439–440). Pierre again questions his guide, Mr. S, who "leads him along through the circles of Hell like Virgil": "Is it the end of the world? Our future? Hell?" (1: 440). This reference to Dante's *Inferno* completes the terrifying picture.

Just when the reader believes that another reference could not be added, s/he finds otherwise. Staroi apes the Tolstoyan technique of estrangement (*ostranenie*) in representing the revolt as an operatic performance. Narrated from the point of view of two actors, a tragedian and comic, who meet up with Pierre on the sidelines, they describe the uprising as a spectacle. The tragedian comments: "The noble count [Miloradovich] persuades the rebels. The opera's action depends on his role. So then, the count's aria. Basso. Two choruses—the rebels and the crowd. Listen to the music of the uprising!" (1: 441). Influenced by the actors, Pierre sees the encounter's theatrical quality. He witnesses the "heroic duet" between Miloradovich and young Prince Obolenskii (the tenor), which turns from a "dramatically begun scene to a comedy" when Miloradovich moves his horse so that Obolenskii needs to step back from its muzzle. The scene becomes a tragedy when Kakhovskii shoots Miloradovich. Theatrical allusions interweave with Pierre's musings on his inability to understand what he sees: "This is natural—any observation of an eyewitness suffers from one-sidedness and blindness. A man cannot faithfully and exactly encompass with a glance simultaneous actions. The impartial historian, who has documents, will also slip up, since he is immersed in another time's element, and the so-called documents are a drop in the sea of the true event. A drop, painted in a different color, since each time has its own hue" (1: 445). Pierre paraphrases postmodern theory in his commentary on the role of the embodied historian and the generic problems of history.

Pierre comes to a greater discovery regarding the uprising's essence: "It is not a play, badly staged by the Higher Dramaturge, but the merciless movement of history" (1: 445–46). He becomes so terrified by this insight that he goes mad, like Evgenii in Pushkin's *Bronze Horseman*, and shakes his fist at the distant statue of Peter the Great. Staroi parodies Evgenii's action in Pierre's repetition of the ultimate gesture of rebellion against tsar, God and city. Yet this imitation renders the gesture meaningless; Pierre threatens the statue in his delirium because he can no longer differentiate between earthly life and Hell. It is unclear whether Pierre holds the bronze horseman or its physical incarnation, the tsar, responsible for his condition.

Staroi continues his literary imitation with a stab at Tynianov's representation of Kiukhlia's role in the revolt. With Kiukhelbeker's entrance onto the square, Pierre gains new insight. Once the trickster or fool's role has been filled, Pierre can retain his grasp on reality. When Kiukhelbeker shoots at the Metropolitan, Pierre understands "the main thing:"

An unstable equilibrium reigned on the square, which could and must be broken. No one knows what to do and all the events so far are meaningless. He [Pierre] realized with clarity that the uprising lacks the smallest trifle—an insignificant push, direction, that is, he, Pierre, the main madman. However, it seems it's too late. Ah, no. Revolutions do not go according to plan but according to inspiration. Yes, yes, everything's going well, it needs a push! (1: 448)

Pierre conceives the revolution as an "unstable equilibrium," recalling Tynianov's representation of the battle of precariously balanced squares. Only after Pierre allows the revolution to overwhelm him, does he plunge into the middle of the revolt.

Echoing Sergei Muraviev-Apostol's musings on the interconnection between revolution and evil in Merezhkovskii's *December 14*, Pierre's philosophizes on the nature of revolutions after the revolt:

Each revolution and after it, unavoidable civil war, is an apocalypse: destructions, death, decay, bitter rivers, terrifying visions of turtles, squelching all the living, but in the last chapter, where one should see a "new heaven and earth" and "God will wipe each tear," and "there will be no more death,"—it turns out on the throne is not the Lamb, not Christ, but a man or group of people wasting their strength on the mutual battle for material things. This goes on for centuries." . . . "If it is not Christ on the throne,—he [Pierre] hit in the last nail into his intellectual structure,—then it is the anti-Christ, Satan. Any such man—Konstantin, Nikolai, Pestel, Napoleon, Drubetskoi, finally, I—can be the anti-Christ." (1: 460–1)

In his delirium, Pierre views all usurpers and pretenders who challenge legitimate succession as the Anti-Christ. For Pierre, the uprising takes on a meaning more profound than anything else: "Its unraveling may be the same as finding the solution to life itself" (1: 462). In his bizarre portrayal of the revolt, Staroi mocks Soviet historians' evaluation and distorts their general conclusions.

Again Staroi melds fact and fiction in a long footnote, grappling with the Decembrists' legacy. He recalls Tolstoy's literary excursus into the Decembrist movement which originally brought about the creation of Pierre's character:

Even his [Pierre's] nephew, the future great writer (who was not yet born in 1825), wanting to understand the events of 14 Dec. 1825, stops at 1820 in his great narrative, however, having the knowledge that Pierre never will discover. Another descendant of Pierre will try to look into that day from the twentieth century, when the power of the people, about whom Pierre thought so much, would not let one speak or write a word against the Decembrists—as they in time will call Pierre and his confederates—because they ostensibly awoke the people and someone else. This distant descendant of Pierre will suffer for his noble origins, not being able or not wanting to protest that the Decembrist in his forefather was stronger than the count in himself.... He will sit with head in hands in his room lit by an electric lamp in his communal apartment, having just returned from his place of confinement and, drunk on Moskovskaia vodka, will understand nothing. Why, serving the people, was he called the enemy of the people? And all this together is one endless strange dream about Russia. (1: 464)

The author telescopes past and future by alluding to Tolstoy's family history, since the Decembrist Volkonskii was his great uncle. Staroi compresses time to foretell the Decembrists' and Pierre's descendants' fates, conflating the fictional descendant with Leo Tolstoy. Staroi also collapses the fictional and historical in this combination of Pierre the literary personage with Volkonskii (and the fictional nephew Lev Rostov with Leo Tolstoy the writer). Staroi then posits a symbolic descendant who suffers in Soviet times: a camp returnee who takes the route of Erofeev's Decembrist and gets drunk because there is no greater meaning to his suffering. While citing Tolstoy as his authority, Staroi subverts that legitimation in his degraded portrayal of Tolstoy's successors, figurative and literal.

Synchronously with Pierre, the author considers the revolt's meaning. He filters all assessments through the lens of post–Soviet reality. Fractured because of the Soviet state's dissolution and the subsequent devaluation of society's central organizing myths, this lens reflects the crisis of legitimacy occurring in both times. Even if the myths had been questioned during the Soviet period, they were not openly debunked. Once Soviet central authority dissolved, the whole question of meaning resurfaced as irresolvable: who has the authority to decide what the events mean?

The first volume's final chapter posits a post-Soviet assessment, from the question of the revolt's origins to the issue of who is to blame:

What really happened on December 14, 1825 from 11 am until 3 pm? Why did this standing revolution occur? What meaning was there in the 2,000 frozen soldiers by the Governing Senate getting warm with cries of "Hurrah, Konstantin!" and the other side in many voices repeating that Konstantin himself abdicated and one should yell "Hurrah, Nikolai!"?

Who was to blame for this revolution? The imperial brothers, playing with the throne? The liberal gentlemen? Drubetskoi, who did not appear to command the troops that weren't there? Bulatov and Iakubovich, who got lost between the thirst for power and fear? Intrigues of "dark forces" (*temnye sily*)? What are the dark forces?

Could the uprising not have occurred? Or could it not have not happened? (1: 468).

Besides alluding to "Varshavianka," coincidentally Lenin's favorite song,[20] reference to "dark forces" demonstrates the millenarianism and "new age" sensibility in post-Soviet Russia. Zara Abdullaeva connects the destruction of primary Soviet myths to the occult's popularity: "We are living through extraordinary times today, when all the myths are dying. Witness all the sorcerers, astrologists, and witch doctors invading our TV screens.... At first we rejoiced when the myths began to fall by the wayside. Now that the floodgates of truth are open, we are desperately trying to stave off its tide, which threatens to engulf us. Even when we see through its deception, we do not want to see the myth explode and recoil from the sight of the mythological ruins."[21] In *Pierre and Natasha* the destabilizing effects of mythological destruction are displaced back to the nineteenth century. As in most historical fiction that exploits the past to discuss the present, the earlier age allows for reflection on the current day's crises of understanding.

Staroi desacralizes the Decembrist revolt, highlighting the chaos, indecision, and lack of planning. He asks: "Was everything that happened on December 14 a chain of senselessness? Or the law of the historical process of Russia's development?" (1: 470–71). The law of historical process allowed the Bolsheviks to use the Decembrists in their legitimizing genealogy. Yet Staroi goes beyond their pat formulation to reconsider the modes in which the past are evaluated. Like Pierre's discussion of the historian's task earlier, Staroi questions past appraisals, castigating historians for their biases: "With time historians will find reasons in this and that, will draw conclusions, will arrange these reasons and investigations in ranks, but will never exhaust the theme and will give more new interpretations of the events, in accordance with their own literary and philosophical gifts, their personal interests and times from which December 14, 1825 is visible to them" (1: 471). Ultimately, Staroi concludes that "December 14, 1825 is a bottomless and endless day," a day so important and great that it had a profound influence on Russian history and on the Russian people: "Each person living in Russia wove his own thread in the general cloth of the event. Before, during and after" (1: 471). Given his bizarre portrayal of the uprising, it appears that Staroi desacralizes the Decembrists more than he upholds their value.

Reflecting the Russian preoccupation with "shadow history," or, what "might have happened if the Bolsheviks had not seized control,"[22] Staroi asks: could the Decembrists have succeeded? His answer acknowledges their good intentions while insisting that they would have found it necessary to rule Russia with an iron fist according to the "laws of existence" (1: 476):

> No matter how you affirm that the Decembrists were terribly distant from the people, as if those who a century later took the Winter Palace were terribly close to them,—all the facts of Russian history persistently speak one repeated and simple truth, which no one wishes to notice: THE PEOPLE NEVER PLAYED AND DO NOT PLAY ANY ROLE IN THE SEIZURE OF POWER. Those play the main role whose forces, though they be few, approached the palace, the throne room, the bedroom, the living room, the wagon, where the carrier or carriers of power that is being annulled are located, in order either to kill, to arrest or to compel them to abdicate with one blow. (1: 477, author's emphasis)

Familiar with Soviet historical clichés, Staroi undermines the basic validating myth of Soviet legitimacy that the Bolsheviks were close to the people. Staroi insists the Bolsheviks won because of their political opportunism rather than because of their alliance with the people, demonstrating the significance of power's geographical loci, as seen earlier in Tynianov's *Kiukhlia*, but forgotten since. In desacralizing the Decembrists, Staroi chips away at Soviet power's edifice, founded on the maxim that the Decembrists were the forefathers of the Bolsheviks, who, unlike their predecessors, were able to unite with the masses. Echoing pre and post-Soviet assessments of the revolt as a "watershed in Russian history,"[23] Staroi asserts: "December 14 became the day from which the Russian revolution began. It continues, exhausting

generations with its ideas, intentions, fictions, conjectures and unpre-
dictability of events. Russia lives in it, first loving then hating it,
throwing her own children in its insatiable abyss. And it seems that
there is no end to the revolution, and it seems that there is no power
capable of stopping its step, run, victorious approach, its pursuit after
each individual soul, designated for torment and suffering" (1: 478).
For Staroi, the Decembrist uprising was only the first phase of the
Russian revolution; without it, the rest never would have taken place.
Staroi condemns all revolutions at the end of the first volume. He calls
into question the moments in Russian history which legitimated and/
or prefigured the success of the autocracy's overthrow. In other words,
now suspect are those very myths and figures chosen by Party historians who reevaluated Russian history for its usable past to illustrate
historical determinism. Staroi's anti-mythological urge seems directed
more at the excesses and falsehoods of the 1917 revolution than its
"first" revolutionary phase, though the Decembrists are tainted by
association. Staroi evaluates the Decembrists from his own historical
perspective, the failure of communism. His portrayal suggests that the
Decembrists have become morally and philosophically bankrupt; they
cannot provide a model of martyrdom because their suffering leads to
later Soviet excesses.

In the final volume Staroi details the disenchantments that each
protagonist suffers in a litany of deflation, running the gamut from
recanting to betrayal. Staroi depicts the Decembrists' less heroic acts
during their arrest, questioning and trial and contrasts those who
disavow their earlier ideals to Pierre who refuses to implicate others or
to change his thinking. Like Nekrasov and Tolstoy, Staroi focuses on the
aftereffects of the uprising on its participants' characters. Staroi depicts
Pierre in Siberia as a mature, distant, even hardened revolutionary,
anticipating the ascetics of the later Russian revolutionary movements
and their portrayal in Soviet socialist realism more than attesting to the
Decembrists' true character or the portraits handed down by Staroi's
literary predecessors. Pierre's sternness, aloofness and lack of awareness of his harsh surroundings recalls Chernyshevsky's Rakhmetov (of
What is to Be Done?, 1863) instead of the prevailing images of exiled
Decembrists. Akin to Rakhmetov, Pierre appears to be fortifying
himself for the long struggle ahead, impervious to human warmth and
compassion. Despite the final vignettes of Pierre's and Natasha's new
grim lives, the novel closes on an upbeat note. The last line tells of
the birth of Marie and Nikolai Rostov's son, Lev (read: Leo Tolstoy)

in 1828, followed by an ellipsis. In a strange twist, Staroi suggests that his sequel to *War and Peace* is really a prequel to Tolstoy's life story and oeuvre.

The novel takes a postmodern form in addition to its postmodern treatment of the Decembrist myth. *Pierre and Natasha* combines competing genres and voices, or *bricolage*, common to postmodern works.[24] In terms of plot, subplot and length, it imitates its predecessor's epic qualities and, like *War and Peace,* also defies generic definition. Sometimes it borders on the purely historical with direct transcription of letters, memoirs, diary entries and documents. Frequently, the author replaces historical figures with his own characters and casts them into actual events, substituting Tolstoy's Boris Drubetskoi for the Decembrist Trubetskoi, using Maria Volkonskaia's life story as the basis for Natasha's actions and Ekaterina Trubetskaia's for Julie Drubetskaia's. On one level then, the novel retells and expands on *War and Peace*'s plot line and the Decembrists' history.

At other times the novel mixes philosophical digression, detailed descriptions of nineteenth-century everyday life (*byt*), historical legend, gossip, and fantasy. Études on the masterpieces of Russian invention—the samovar and the Russian bath—interweave with the narrative of the conspiracy's aftermath. In these digressions, the author parodies Russian culture's sacred symbols and Russian literature's sacred texts. He demolishes the popular notions of Russian greatness and innovation and mocks the standard treatment of cultural icons, employing those canonical texts' imagery and vocabulary. One reviewer calls attention to this unsettling technique, calling it a theft of words: "What is the author to do if his own words are lacking? Here he steals first from Lenin and Stalin, then from Pushkin, Gogol, Tiutchev, Fet, Gorky, Blok, Mandelshtam, Pasternak, Vladimir Vysotskii, Evgenii Evtushenko, Mikhail Isakovskii, and Larisa Vasilieva."[25] The reviewer assumes that the author does this unknowingly. Yet Staroi could not have written this compendium of clichés without realizing what he was doing. The multitude of references begs the question: can this be anything other than parody, blatant though it may be? Should the author expect the mass audience to appreciate the references? Have some of these phrases become so ingrained in Soviet experience that they need to be defamiliarized to be seen anew? The aforementioned reviewer insists that the author's technique reflects a lack of historical sensibility (for example, when Empress Elizaveta Alekseevna asserts that "the tsar will show the true path," she misquotes Stalin).[26] The reviewer does not sense the parody's greater purpose. Staroi parodies the foundation texts of the Decembrist myth to deconstruct it. With the dismantling of the Decembrist myth, other important cultural myths affirming Soviet legitimacy lose their power.

Much of the reader's cognitive disjuncture stems from the generic confusion inherent in Staroi's novel. As a sequel to a classic, it manifests a generic ambivalence; it cannot be authoritative because it is not the original author's product. Instead it raises questions: Is it merely a work of pulp fiction or more meaningful? Is it parody or imitation? These questions arise from the sequel's generic implications. Gary Saul Morson discusses the sequel's psychological lure: "Readers often seek such additional 'information' about their favorite fictional characters as well, especially those from voluminous and riveting novels. A reader has lived so long, has identified so strongly, with beloved heroes or heroines that worries about them have become a treasured part of real life."[27] Morson calls this literary device "sideshadowing," which allows for the extrapolation of other possibilities for characters' actions.[28] Hinting at the unwelcome nature of the sideshadow (bordering on parody), Morson calls this genre the "paraquel": "One writer continues, fills in, or gives the prehistory of a famous story by another writer.... the original author is dead and we know these apocryphal continuations are written by someone else. They cannot be authoritative. Yet they do satisfy the desire for more of a favorite work. They are, in fact, almost entirely dependent on familiarity with the original or at least with some version of it (with knowledge of the plot, or in the case of *Scarlett*, with the film version)."[29] Indeed, *Pierre and Natasha* stems more from the popular Soviet version of *War and Peace* (with its omissions, adaptations and simplistic reductions of philosophical questions) than from the original. When asked about the work, Tolstoy scholar Sergei Dmitriyenko stated, "It's like taking a healthy, live human being and sewing on an additional arm." He himself had not read the sequel but was appalled by the presumption that someone would write one.[30] For literary purists, such a sequel will not do.

The publishers must have hoped for two things: to attract readers by capitalizing on their love of the original and to pique interest by inciting a controversy which would appeal to readers interested in sensationalism, since the publication could be seen as blasphemy. Gleb Uspenskii, senior editor of Vagrius (*Pierre and Natasha*'s publisher) remarked: "It's like writing a sequel to the Bible. Nobody wanted to do it."[31] Uspenskii said they had to keep the authorship secret because "people would burn the author's house down."[32] Whether this statement was true or a public relations ploy to fan the flames of controversy is unclear.

The advertisements for the novel reflect market concerns. They play up the sensational aspects while banking on love for Tolstoy's classic:

A new meeting awaits you with old friends—the heroes of *War and Peace*. 1825—Pierre Bezukhov, a member of the government council, belongs to an antigovernment secret society. Alexander I foresees the breath of Fate, dreams of distancing himself from worldly cares.

The author's unexpected discoveries: Alexander Pushkin, in love with the Empress Elizaveta Alekseevna, dedicates to her—his muse—the verses "I remember the miraculous moment," Natasha Rostova inspired Karl Briullov's painting "The Horsewoman," Nikolai Rostov, married to Princess Maria and, in contrast to Pierre, occupied not with state problems but with household and amorous affairs…Intrigues, gossip, conspiracies…."[33]

Though the advertisement promises familiar characters, unfamiliar, unbelievable characters who merely share the same names as the Tolstoyan originals inhabit the novel. Staroi trivializes the historical figures of the Decembrist movement and the Tolstoyan characters. There is no longer any divide between reality and fiction, nor is there any appeal in the sequel's personages. In highlighting the sequel's unexpected surprises, the publishers reveal its sensationalism and triviality compared to the original. This paraquel does not exploit what "may have been" but documents what could not have been, which in part explains its failure. Its sideshadowing techniques are clumsy and ineffective.

If the publishers anticipated that controversy alone might sell the books, then they were disappointed. Other than one article in the *New York Times* and one review in *Literaturnaia gazeta*, it generated little comment.[34] Despite a prediction made by the popular writer Larisa Vasilieva, *Pierre and Natasha* did not make the bestseller lists after its publication in March 1996.[35] Though this may suggest that the Russian reader of popular literature may be more discerning than expected, more likely it reflects a problem with marketing. The novel was pitched as a pulp romance and popular sequel when it should have been promoted as literary parody. Evidently, post–Soviet intelligentsia scorns popular fiction, and has no interest in the sequel, preferring the original over an inferior imitation. The mass audience, having had its fill of Russian classics during its school years, chooses other types of escapist reading, for example, detective novels, which consistently figure on bestseller lists.[36] Unlike *Pierre and Natasha*, the authorized sequel to *Gone with the*

Wind, Scarlett, was wildly successful in Russia and generated a whole Russian cottage industry of sequels. Yet it came as a continuation to a popular novel, not to a classic per se. *Pierre and Natasha* may have deterred readers by its attempt to add to and reevaluate the canon. It did not bridge the gap between high and popular literature, despite appeals to both audiences. Regarding the question of audience, the novel's reception confirms that a fictional work with a dissertation about the Decembrists will not find a mass audience despite associations with Tolstoy's familiar characters. The sequel's reception suggests that post–Soviet society had enough of reading about revolutions and revolutionaries.

This work also reflects the post–Soviet mass-market trend to sensationalize history to sell books. Historians who formerly wrote scholarly texts now produce books ferreting out the steamy secrets of bygone eras. These books sell on the street alongside reprints of formerly banned, early twentieth-century Russian philosophy and literature, crime novels and soft porn. This context reflects the postmodern fragmentation of aesthetic and generic conventions and the crisis of the authority of prior categories of valuation and meaning. These attempts to popularize history echo to a degree the endeavors of the 1920s, when the party ideologues and Communist intelligentsia wanted to educate the masses about the Decembrist movement. Yet the current sensationalization of history takes a different turn from earlier efforts. The 1925 centennial's campaign to educate the general public about the Decembrists to demythologize them had a reverse effect. At that point, the public's knowledge increased, but the mythologization did not decrease. However, in the post–Soviet era there is a complete trivialization and desacralization of the Decembrists, which may well deconstruct the myth in the end.

Frederick Starr suggests, "In retrospect, it is clear that Western observers failed adequately to appreciate the extent to which the endless droning of those same myths in the public sphere continued to define the values of official life long after they ceased to be taken seriously by millions of ordinary people in their private realms."[37] *Pierre and Natasha* reflects the duality and ambivalence of Soviet myths that Starr discusses. Partly devalued, partly honored, they teeter precariously on the edge of cultural consciousness. These myths were exploited for three-quarters of a century to legitimate Soviet power. Now their status remains uncertain in an era of cultural and political transition. Will the Decembrist myth survive as part of the next era's "usable past?" Starr suggests: "History's winners will become its losers, and its losers will stand forth as winners."[38] The Decembrists' association with the Soviet regime's legitimating myths may well have tainted them beyond re-integration.

The Myth in the New Millennium

So far the new millennium has continued the trends of the early post–Soviet era. In political culture, another analogy was made between the Decembrists and a group of 40 young members of the National Bolshevik Party, called "young Decembrists" (*mladodekabristy*), who on December 14, 2004 "stormed and occupied" the Presidential Administration building. Less than 15 minutes later they were captured by the police, beaten, and put into Moscow prisons.[39] The Decembrists continue to be commodified, as in the mass-market novel, *Onegin Code* (*Kod Onegina*, 2006), by a pseudonymous author, "Brein Daun" (pronounced "Brain Down") a blatant and clumsy literary parody of Dan Brown's *DaVinci Code*, and a crude reference to Down's syndrome.[40] The author uses the Decembrists' relationship with Pushkin and their well-known role in the tenth chapter of *Eugene Onegin* as a motivating device for his conspiracy plot. Like *Pierre and Natasha*, the novel suffers from poor writing and a pastiche of literary genres. *Onegin Code* did not become a bestseller nor did it receive any accolades for its literary parody. The system of prizes for literature, a new resource for fueling the book market since the institution of the Booker Prize in 1994, rightly ignored the work in its 2006 and 2007 competitions. Also reflecting the search for books that will sell, Vagrius press (publisher of *Pierre and Natasha*) has since 2004 begun reissuing Eidelman's popular histories from the 1960s–1980s, many of which treat the Decembrists.[41]

The desacralizing trend continues along with the commercialization of the last decade. Sensationalist popular histories of the Decembrists, such as the incendiary *Decembrists: Conspiracy against Russia* by the young journalist Aleksei Shcherbatov and *Myths and Truth about the Decembrist Uprising* by Vladimir Briukhanov, take the Decembrists off their lofty pedestal by emphasizing the movement's weakness, lack of organization and defined political goals and the participants' alleged cowardice. Shcherbatov cites the memoirs of the Decembrists' reactionary contemporaries and employs pseudo-scientific jargon to assert that the Decembrists were banal rebels, the "Manilovs" of high society who exploited their troops and were justifiably sent into exile and "cheerful penal servitude." Briukhanov resurrects a conspiracy theory popular in the early 1900s, that the Decembrist uprising was part of a larger Masonic plot against the tsar and implicates General Miloradovich, Dibich, and Arakcheev in its workings.[42]

On the scholarly front, an active cohort of Russian academics still publishes on the Decembrists. V. M. Bokova delineates two trends in current historical discourse, one she calls "negative," that seeks to blame the Decembrists for the excesses of later revolutionaries and their oppositional stance against authority, up to and including the overthrow of the autocracy and the establishment of Communism. (This trend is not new and emerged immediately after the October Revolution only to resurface during *glasnost*.) The second she calls "objective" in the sense that the Decembrists have become "objectified" as a part of a larger theoretical framework and frequently are examined outside an appropriate historical context. Though some scholars still concentrate on publishing valuable archival materials, several offer new approaches to the Decembrists. One of the most important topics for these scholars is to correct earlier broad categorizations about the Decembrists by calling into question the very usage of the appellation "Decembrist" as Bokova[43] and O. I. Kiianskaia insist.[44] In tsarist and Soviet historiography, there was little discrimination between the political views of the participants in the uprising and their proto-organizational groups. This corrective step would permit meaningful distinction among individuals since the Northern and Southern Societies members' held a wide spectrum of political views. This differentiation after a century of viewing the Decembrists as a monolithic group should be fruitful and allow for new perspectives to emerge. *The Decembrists: Actual Problems and New Approaches,* the newest compendium of research from a group of scholars out of the Russian State Humanities University (RGGU) in 2008, addresses the concerns above and marks the hundredth anniversary of Decembrist studies as well, pinpointing 1905 as the discipline's starting point. The editor Kiianskaia recognizes the mythic basis of both prerevolutionary and Soviet scholarship, but admits that most scholars even at the beginning of the twenty first century are not disposed to destroy the myth in its entirety, since many are "children of that myth" themselves.[45]

What then will become of the Decembrist myth in the new millennium? Clark's discussion of Soviet culture's changing historical paradigms pertains to the "temporal confusion and re-orientation" occurring in the post–Soviet period. Though the same "master model" dominated the political and intellectual discourse of a given period, the historical moments were contextualized differently with each shift.[46] It was easy to see the shifts when history had a single authorized version for most of the Soviet period which could be polemicized with depending on one's orientation. Since 2000, the time of Vladimir Putin's presidency, the course is not so clear. It appears that the scene is changing in reaction to the lack of a master narrative. A 2002 article bemoaned the current state of history textbooks in Russia, which are published "without limitations and practically without any control on the part of the government."[47] Thomas Sherlock argues that history textbooks are "powerful weapons in this struggle to shape the identity of the new state and nation," as evident in Putin's 2003 remarks on the goal of history textbooks to "help raise young people in the spirit of pride for their fatherland and in its history."[48] If the government takes a more active role in codifying school textbooks, then in this renewed age of authoritarian rule and governmental control of the press, it is likely that the Decembrists' mythic image will fall from favor given their oppositional stance to authority. Putin favored the revival of tsarist traditions and during his presidency "fostered the idea that Russia's traditions of authoritarian rule are morally equal to democratic Western traditions."[49] Given his influence as the current Prime Minister, "Tsar" Vladimir will likely brook no opposition to his call for "common standards" in Russian schools and will develop a "patriotic narrative" that "has serious implications for the ability of Russian society to identify democracy and authoritarianism as very different systems of rule, and to properly choose between them."[50] At best then, the Decembrists may be relegated to minor mention in history textbooks as opponents of autocracy and serfdom and as friends of the great national poet Pushkin. Or, at worst, they may become suppressed and/or vilified as the progenitors of revolutionary unrest. This treatment may well lead to another resurgence of the Decembrists' image in high literature and a reinvigoration of the myth of the Decembrists as tricksters. Until writers of higher caliber than those producing the mass-market literary parodies of the 1990s–mid-2000s take up the task, we will have to wait and see.

EPILOGUE

"The Decembrists Are Our All"

> The Decembrists are our all.
> —Russian blogger, "haspar_arnery"[1]

Reconfiguring Apollon Grigoriev's celebrated maxim of 1859 that "Pushkin is our all," one Russian thus commemorated the Decembrist anniversary in 2008, speaking of the myth's universality. Invocations of the Decembrists cross political spectrums during the late twentieth and early twenty-first centuries, as evident in comparisons made between the Decembrist coup and the Communist putsch of 1991, the stand at Moscow's White House in 1993 by renegade members of the Russian Parliament, the 2004 protests of the National Bolshevik Party, and most recently, the 2008 march of "Other Russia" party members in opposition to recent government elections.[2] It has become part of the national dialogue to cite the Decembrists at significant moments of political unrest, and for opponents of those in authority to lay their claim as heirs to the Decembrists. Yet the Decembrist myth still figures largely in Russian culture for reasons beyond their political resonance.

Though O. I. Kiianskaia insists "In Russia there is not a person who, considering himself an *intellectual*, has not heard of the Decembrists,"[3] frequent references to the Decembrists transcend the scholarly disciplines of literature and history and have filtered down into Russian popular culture, as more than 3,000 web pages devoted to Decembrists on one Russian search engine, Yandex, attest. These references range from a virtual "Decembrist museum" to humorous anecdotes to scholarly citations to recent news on Decembrists' descendants' 2006, 2007, and 2008 trips to Siberia,[4] and in some ways repeat the oral tradition on the Decembrists of nearly two centuries earlier. The internet serves as a convenient repository for this ephemeral material, as S. E. Erlikh reflects in a recent article on the surprising amount of material on the Decembrists in cyberspace.[5]

Most important, the majority of internet blogs and chat rooms that discuss the Decembrists are not comprised of scholars alone. The organizer of the virtual Decembrist museum on the web is a non-specialist, who constructed the site because of her interests and provides links to scholarly articles and Decembrist iconography. The Decembrists resurface in anecdotes taken from Russian students' schoolwork, which paraphrase Lenin's axiom on the Decembrists' awakening Herzen: "The Decembrists roused Herzen. Herzen, in his bathrobe, went in to them and said: 'Have you lost your mind? It's three a.m.!—And went back to sleep."[6] Count Rostopchin's quip that "hitherto revolutions had been made by peasants who wanted to become gentlemen; now gentlemen tried to make a revolution so as to become cobblers,"[7] found a variant which satirized the Bolsheviks instead. During the October Revolution, a countess who was a granddaughter of a Decembrist heard a demonstration outside her window. She asked her maid to find out what was happening. The maid returned and said: "the people don't want the tsar anymore." The countess responds: "My grandfather the Decembrist wanted that too. What else?" The maid says: "they want freedom!" The countess: "Oh, that's interesting—my grandfather said they fought for freedom too! What else?" "They also don't want to have any more rich people, countess!" The countess: "Strange. My grandfather wanted no one to be poor in Russia."[8] This remark speaks to the cultural resonance of the Decembrists' "mission"—they proclaimed themselves as opponents of tyranny and proponents of freedom. Their image as freedom fighters who dared to take a moral stand against the autocracy despite the knowledge that they would fail spoke to later generations and provided a productive model of self-sacrifice to radical revolutionaries, members of the nineteenth-and twentieth-century intelligentsia, and to regular people across the centuries. Though some saw them as harbingers of the bloodshed of twentieth-century revolutionary cataclysms, as for example asserted at the 2000 conference: "The Decembrists: Heroes or Criminals?",[9] more often they were appreciated for their sense of personal honor and moral obligation, especially during Soviet times, when many felt that those qualities had literally been purged by the exile and extermination of former nobles and elites of the prerevolutionary era. It appears that the Decembrist myth is alive and well in Russia. It remains to be seen if and how the post-Putin regime will re-cast the myth for its own purposes.

NOTES

Preface

1. Henry Tudor, *Political Myth* (New York: Praeger Publishers, 1972), 36–37.
2. Paul Debreczeny makes a similar argument regarding the Pushkin myth's richness: " 'Zhitie Aleksandra Boldinskogo': Pushkin's Elevation to Sainthood in Soviet Culture," *South Atlantic Quarterly* 90, no. 2 (Spring 1991): 269–292.
3. Venturi, *The Roots of Revolution: A History of Populist and Socialist Movements in Nineteenth-Century Russia* (Chicago, IL: University of Chicago Press, 1960), Walicki, *A History of Russian Thought from the Enlightenment to Marxism* (Stanford, CA: Stanford University Press, 1979), Pomper, *The Russian Revolutionary Intelligentsia* (Arlington Hts., IL: Harlan Davidson, Inc., 1970) Raeff, *The Decembrist Movement* (Englewood Cliffs, NJ: Prentice Hall, 1966) and Zamoyski, *Holy Madness: Romantics, Patriots, and Revolutionaries, 1776–1871* (New York: Penguin, 1999), especially 245–254.
4. Victor Turner, *Dramas, Fields, Metaphors: Symbolic Action in Human Society* (Ithaca, NY: Cornell University Press, 1974), 35.
5. Iurii Lotman, "The Decembrist in Everyday Life," 71–123 and "Theater and Theatricality as Components of Early Nineteenth-Century Culture," 141–164, in Iu. M. Lotman and B. A. Uspenskii, *The Semiotics of Russian Culture* (Ann Arbor: Michigan Slavic Contributions, 1984) and Lydia Ginzburg, *On Psychological Prose*, translated by Judson Rosengrant (Princeton: Princeton University Press, 1991). Chapter 7 discusses Lotman's seminal works in detail.
6. T. V. Orlova, "Dvizhenie dekabristov s tochki zreniia istorii mental'nostei," in O. I. Kiianskaia (ed.), *Dekabristy: aktual'nye problemy i novye podkhody* (Moscow: RGGU, 2008), 529.
7. Eric Hobsbawm (ed.), *The Invention of Tradition* (Cambridge: Cambridge University Press, 1983), 1.
8. Ibid., 2.

Introduction

1. N. K. Piksanov, *Griboedov i staroe barstvo* (Moscow: Nikitinskie subbotniki, 1926), 73.
2. *The Times* (London), Jan. 7, 1826, p. 2, col. 3, cited in Anatole G. Mazour, *The First Russian Revolution, 1825, the Decembrist Movement: Its Origins, Development, and Significance* (Stanford, California: Stanford University, 1937), 156.

3. The Manifesto of 1823 was revealed to the public after Constantine's younger brother, Nicholas, ascended the throne.

4. Pestel' and Nikita Muraviev authored documents on the possible form of government after their coup. These works have been analyzed thoroughly in a variety of Russian and English sources. See especially Patrick O'Meara, *The Decembrist Pavel Pestel: Russia's First Republican* (Houndmills and New York: Palgrave Macmillan, 2003) and S. S. Volk, *Istoricheskie vzgliady dekabristov* (Moscow: Izdatel'stvo Akademii Nauk SSSR, 1958).

5. In my account of the uprising, I rely primarily on Mazour's *The First Russian Revolution* and W. Bruce Lincoln's *Nicholas I: Emperor and Autocrat of All the Russias* (DeKalb, IL: Northern Illinois University Press, 1989) 17–47. See Mazour for a detailed discussion of the secret society's branches and their various aims, 66–116. Mazour emphasizes that the Decembrists' testimony during their incarceration gives contradictory portrayals of the secret societies' goals.

6. For an account of the execution's impact on Russian culture see my article, "The Spectacle of the Scaffold: Performance and Subversion in the Decembrists' Execution" in Marcus Levitt and Tatyana Novikov, *Times of Trouble: Violence in Russian Literature and Culture* (Madison, WI: University of Wisconsin Press, 2007). See also *Pisateli-dekabristy v vospominaniakh sovremmenikov* (Moscow: Khudozhestvennaia Literatura, 1980), 1: 430 n. 2, hereafter *PD*.

7. They were: Ekaterina Trubetskaia, Maria Volkonskaia, Alexandra Muravieva, Elizaveta Naryshkina, Alexandra Ental'steva, Alexandra Davydova, Natalia Fonvizina, Anna Rozen, and Anastasia Iushnevskaia. Pauline Gueble and Camille LeDantu both journeyed to Siberia to marry their respective beaux. After 1838, the mother and sister of K. P. Torson joined him once his term ended as did Elena, Maria, and Olga Bestuzheva, the Bestuzhev brothers' unmarried sisters. A. N. Muraviev's wife, Praskovia Shakovskaia came to Siberia without loss of title, unlike the others who arrived earlier (E. A. Pavliuchenko, *Zhenshchiny v russkom osvoboditel'nom dvizhenii: ot Marii Volkonskoi do Very Figner* (Moscow: Mysl', 1988), 21–26 and *Zhenshchiny v dobrovol'nom izgnanii: o zhenakh i sestrakh dekabristov* (Moscow: Nauka, 1976).

8. Turner, *Dramas*, 38.

9. Lewis Bagby, *Alexander Bestuzhev-Marlinsky and Russian Byronism* (University Park, PA: Penn State University Press, 1995), 154. December 14 coincided with the celebration of the winter solstice, but it figures most importantly as the announcement of the succession (and not the coronation day, as Bagby suggests) and was distinct from the crowning of the new tsar. Though the theme of regicide is deeply embedded in the carnival tradition, the uprising's immediate context must be privileged. Alexander I's death, which some people believed suspicious, and the uncertainty of succession provided enough justification for thoughts of regicide to arise in the contemporary Russian consciousness.

10. René Girard, *Violence and the Sacred* (Baltimore, MD: Johns Hopkins University Press, 1977), 105–107.

11. N. Shil'der, *Imperator Nikolai Pervyi: ego zhizn' i tsarstvovanie* (St. Petersburg, 1903), 1: 454, quoted in Richard Wortman, *Scenarios of Power: Myth and Ritual in the Russian Monarchy* (Princeton, NJ: Princeton University Press, 1994), 1: 276.

12. G. Nevelev, *Dekabristy i dekabristovedy* (St. Petersburg: Technologos, 2003), 6.

13. Bludov's article appears to have been reprinted by newspapers such as *The Russian Invalid* days later. See *Russkii invalid ili Voennye vedomosti*, No. 300, 19 dekabria 1825 g. in V. A. Algasov, *Dekabrizm i dekabristy: 1825–1925. Khrestomatiia* (Kiev: Gosudarstvennoe izdatel'stvo Ukrainy, 1925), 140.

14. Algasov, 141.

15. Ibid., 142.

16. *Posledovanie blagodarstvennago i molebnago penie: ko Gospodu Bogu...* (Moscow: Sinodal'naia tipografiia, 1826), unnumbered.

17. Shil'der, 1: 704.

18. Wortman, 1: 265–266.

19. Though Nicholas felt compelled by the impending revolt to take control, he violated the succession law by taking his decisive action. Wortman asserts: "The insurgent regiments on the square, paradoxically, were now the only defenders of the letter of the law on the succession" (1: 266–267).

20. "[Nicholas] used the court and the drill field to give constant revalidation to the mythical grounding of his power. His ceremonies presented his dynastic scenario as a heroic triumph of good and morality, embodied in the imperial family, over the subversive forces of evil" (Wortman, 1: 269). See Leonid Frizman, *Dekabristy i russkaia literatura* (Moscow: Khudozestvennaia. literatura, 1988) and N. L. Brodskii, "Dekabristy v russkoi khudozhestvennoi literature," *Katorga i ssylka* 21 (1925): 187–226 for the poetry and prose celebrating Nicholas's victory.

21. Shil'der, 1: 456–458, cited in Wortman, 1: 277.

22. "At moments of crisis, Nicholas appeared in public and reenacted the heroic scene of December 14. His acts, as lone hero appearing among his people to crush the forces of subversion and ignorance, were quickly made part of his mythology of rule" (Wortman, 1: 301).

23. Ibid., 1: 408.

24. Turner, *Ritual Process: Structure and Anti-Structure* (Ithaca, NY: Cornell University Press, 1969), 110.

25. Korf completed the narrative shortly before the autumn of 1848; it existed in a single manuscript copy in the Tsarevich's possession. Soon thereafter, at Grand Princess Olga Nikolaevna's suggestion, the first edition (25 copies) was published so that imperial family members could have a readable, well-preserved text and incorrect manuscript copies would not be made. For publication history and Korf's sources, see Modest Korf, *Vosshestvie na prestol Imperatora Nikolaia I-go*, 5th edition, third for the public (St. Petersburg: Tipografiia III-ogo otdeleniia sobstvennoi ego Imp. Vel. Kantselarii, 1857), xi–xv. Henceforth references will be included in the text. See also I. V. Ruzhitskaia, *Baron M.A. Korf—istorik: Po materialom ego arkhiva* (Moscow: Arkhiograficheskii tsentr, 1996), 32–38.

26. "Iz zapiski barona M. A. Korfa," *Russkaia starina* 101 (Mar. 1900): 549.

27. Ibid.

28. Louis Marin, *The Portrait of the King*, trans. Martha Houle (Minneapolis, MN: University of Minnesota Press, 1988), 71.

29. See Nikolai Piksanov, "Dvorianskaia reaktsiia na dekabrizm," *Zven'ia* 2 (1933): especially 155–159.

30. The preface to the first edition mentions foreigners' accounts of the uprising as a concern (including, specifically, Jean-Henri Schnitzler's *Histoire intime de la Russie sous les Empereurs Alexandre et Nikolas* [Paris: J.P. Meline, 1847]). Korf also read Herzen's journalistic attacks on Nicholas' regime, begun abroad in 1853 with his establishment of the Free Russian Press. Herzen's journal dedicated specifically to the Decembrists, *The Polar Star (Poliarnaia zvezda)*, began its print run in 1855. His refutation of Korf's book, *14 dekabria 1825 i imperator Nikolai. Izdano redaktsiei 'Poliarnoi zvezdy.' Po povodu knigi barona Korfa* appeared in 1858. See *14 dekabria 1825 goda i ego istolkovateli (Gertsen i Ogarev protiv barona Korfa)* (Moscow: Nauka, 1994).

31. Korf claims the rebels hoped to gain the soldiers' support by suggesting the word *konstitutsiia* was the name of Constantine's wife (195).

32. RNB (Manuscript Division of the Russian National Library) f. 380, d. 50, l. 50, quoted in Nevelev, *Dekabristy i dekabristovedy*, 114.

One   The Decembrist Myth in the Nineteenth Century

1. N. Eidel'man, *Pushkin i dekabristy* (Moscow: Vagrius, 2005), 474.

2. Cited in S. Shtraikh, *K iubileiu dekabristov* (Moscow: Transpechat', 1925), 15.

3. See Eidel'man, 356–368.
4. I. D. Iakushkin, *Zapiski* (St. Petersburg: Obshchestvennaia pol'za, 1905), 51–52.
5. Pushchin, *Zapiski*, 62–63.
6. Ibid., 76.
7. Iakushkin, 52.
8. V. A. Zhukovskii to Pushkin, Apr. 12, 1826, in Aleksandr Pushkin, *Polnoe sobraniie sochinenii* (Moscow: Izd. Akademii Nauk, 1937–1959), 13: 271. Henceforth references will be to this edition and will be included in the text.
9. A. Slezkinskii, "Prestupnyi otryvok elegii 'Andrei Shen'ie,'" *Russkaia starina* 8 (1899): 313–326, includes government documents regarding the case.
10. A. G. Khomutova, *Russkii arkhiv* (1867): 1066 cited in V. Veresaev, *Pushkin v zhizni: sistematicheskii svod podlinnykh svidetel'stv sovremennikov* (Moscow–Leningrad: Akademiia, 1932), 1: 204. See 204–205 for the different accounts.
11. Veresaev, 192. In some versions, Pushkin also met a monk, an omen of death in Russian folk belief.
12. In addition to his portrayal of the meeting in "Vstrecha s Kiukhel'bekerom," Pushkin referred to their encounter in the last two lines of the poem "Farewell" (*Proshchanie*, 1830): "as one friend silently embraces another / Before his imprisonment."
13. *Materialy dlia biografii A. S. Pushkina i pis'ma ego k Ryleevu i drugim* (Leipzig: E. L Kaspirovich, 1876). The courier's report was also published in *Russkaia starina* 3 (1901): 578.
14. G. A. Nevelev, "*Eksizy raznykh lits..*": *Dekabristy v risunkakh A. S. Pushkina* (St. Petersburg: Izdatel'stvo IKS, 1993), 33–34.
15. Beginning with Anna Akhmatova, commentators note that Pushkin actively attempted to find out more about the Decembrists' execution and burial site. G. A. Nevelev speculates that both Pushkin and Griboedov visited the purported grave site at separate times (cf. "Pushkin o meste pogrebeniia kazennykh dekabristov," *Voprosy istorii* 5 [1984]: 179–184).
16. Lidiia Ginzburg, *O lirike* (Leningrad: Sovetskii pisatel, 1964), 17–22. Ginzburg discusses the Decembrists' vocabulary in the first decades of the nineteenth century to indicate the "freedom-loving subtext" of their poems. Words like liberty (*vol'nost'*), law (*zakon*), citizen (*grazhdanin*), chains (*tsepi*), dagger (*kinzhal*), tyrant (*tiran*) and autocracy (*samovlast'e*) "unmistakably bring to the reader's consciousness a series of freedom-loving, tyranny-battling representations" (20).
17. V. E. Iakushkin, *O Pushkine*, 52.
18. Ibid., 53.
19. Paul Debreczeny, "Pushkin's Reputation in Nineteenth-Century Russia," in *Pushkin Today*, ed. David M. Bethea, (Bloomington: Indiana University Press, 1993), 211. For more on the 1899 centennial, see Marcus Levitt, *Russian Literary Politics and the Pushkin Celebration* (Ithaca: Cornell University Press, 1989).
20. Levitt, 159.
21. A. L. Slonimskii, "Pushkin i dekabr'skoe dvizhenie," 528 in A. S. Pushkin, *Polnoe sobranie sochinenii,* ed. S. A. Vengerov (St. Petersburg: Brokgauz-Efron, 1908), 503–528. Slonimskii already discussed Pushkin and Decembrists in his earlier article, "Politicheskie vzgliady Pushkina," *Istoricheskii vestnik* 96 (1904): 970–986.
22. Leslie O'Bell, "Through the Magic Crystal to *Eugene Onegin*," in *Pushkin Today*, 165 and N. O. Lerner, "Pushkinskie etiudy," *Zven'ia* 5 (1935): 140.
23. B.V. Tomashevskii, "Desiataia glava *Evgeniia Onegina* (Istoriia razgadki)" in B.V. Tomashevskii, *Pushkin* (Moscow-Leningrad: Izd. Akademii Nauk SSSR, 1961), 2: 208. See also V. V. Pugachev, "Onegin-dekabrist ili Onegin 'chaadaevets'?," *Studia Slavic Hung.* 37 (1991–1992): 273–285.
24. Waclaw Lednicki, *Pushkin's Bronze Horseman: The Story of a Masterpiece* (Berkeley, CA: University of California Press, 1955), 14.
25. *Dekabristy: biograficheskii spravochnik* (Moscow: Nauka, 1988), 59.

26. See Nechkina, *Griboedov i dekabristy* (Moscow: Khudozhestvennaia literature, 1977), 482–491.
27. Pushchin, *Zapiski*, 82–83.
28. See S. A. Fomichev, "K istorii teksta 'Gore ot uma,'" in Bazanov, *Literaturnoe nasledie*, 301–313 for the publication history of the play. Nechkina discusses Griboedov's relationship with the Decembrists and the play's reception in the nineteenth century (5–52). Makogonenko briefly treats the subject of Griboedov and the Decembrists in *A. S. Pushkin: ego tvorchestvo v 1830-kh godakh*, 313–315.
29. A. A. Bestuzhev, "Moe znakomstvo s Griboedovym," *Vospominaniia Bestuzhevykh*,ed. M. K. Azadovskii (Moscow: Izdatel'stvo Akademii nauk, 1951), 526–527.
30. Nechkina, *Griboedov*, 501.
31. Ibid, 490.
32. A. P. Beliaev lists Griboedov's play, the almanac *Poliarnaia zvezda*, Ryleev's poems "Voinarovskii" and "Nalivaiko," and Pushkin's "Liberty." (A. P. Beliaev, *Vospominaniia dekabrista o perezhitom i perechuvstvovannom* [St. Petersburg: Izd. A.S. Suvorina, 1882], 154–155, cited in Nechkina, 488.) Shteingel' lists Griboedov and Pushkin but claims that they were amusing but not influential (Nechkina, 495.)
33. Alexander Herzen, *Polnoe sobranie sochinenie v 30-ti tomakh* (Moscow: Izd. Akademii Nauk, 1959), 18: 180. Henceforth references will be made to this edition and included in the text.
34. N. Brodskii, "Dekabristy v khudozhestvennoi literature," *Katorga i ssylka* (hereafter *KS*) 21 (1925): 187.
35. F. M. Dostoevskii, "Zimnye zametki o letnykh vpechatleniakh," *Polnoe sobranie sochinenii v 30-ti tomakh* (Leningrad: Nauka, 1973), 5: 61. All further references will be made to this edition and included in the text.
36. A. V. Arkhipova, "Dvorianskaia revoliutsionnost' v vospriatii F. M. Dostoevskogo," in Bazanov, 220.
37. F. M. Dostoevskii, *Zapisnye tetradi* (Moscow: Akademia, 1935), 131–132. For discussion of Dostoevskii's views on revolutionary activity, see F. Ia. Priima, "Dvizhenie dekabristov i ego rol' v razvitii russkoi kul'tury," *Slavianskie kul'tury v epokhu formirovaniia i razvitiia slavanskikh natsii XVIII–XX vv.* (Moscow: Nauka, 1978) 86–100 and Arkhipova, 219–245.
38. See *Neizdannyi Dostoevskii. Literaturnoe nasledstvo* 83 (Moscow: Nauka, 1971), 316 as cited in Frizman, 254. "We saw these great sufferers, who willingly followed their husbands to Siberia" (*PSS*, "Dnevnik pisatelia," 21: 12). The wives greeted and blessed the Petrashevtsy, Dostoevskii included, and gave them each a copy of the Gospels with money hidden inside.
39. Margaret Ziolkowski, *Hagiography and Modern Russian Literature* (Princeton, NJ: Princeton University Press, 1988), 70.
40. To limit the scope of this study, I do not discuss Herzen's *14 dekabria 1825 i Imperator Nikolai* (London: Free Russian Press, 1858) his response to Korf's *The Accession of Nicholas I*. Suffice it to say that Herzen called Korf's representation a "servile brochure." To rebut him, he published the documentary materials related to the uprising (*Donesenie Sledstvennoi Kommissii*, 1827) and his own assessment. For discussion of Herzen's political and historical writings on the Decembrists see: Frizman, 155–161 and *14 dekabria 1825 goda i ego istolkovateli*. S. E. Erlikh's recent study, *Istoriia mifa ('Dekabristskaia legenda' Gertsena)* (St. Petersburg: Aleteia, 2006) details the pagan and Christian elements of Herzen's myth.
41. Martin Malia, *Alexander Herzen and the Birth of Russian Socialism: 1812–1855* (Cambridge, MA: Harvard University Press, 1961), 44.
42. N. P. Ogarev, *Izbrannye sotsial'no-politicheskie i filosofskie proizvedeniia* (Moscow: Gosudarstvennoe izdatel'stvo politicheskoi literatury, 1952), 2: 22.
43. Frizman, 161. Maxim Gorky repeats Herzen's formula in the twentieth century.
44. Malia, 40.

45. Ginzburg suggests Herzen is not "an elect personality in the old romantic sense," but a "*representative*... the best representative of the 'educated minority' that has been called upon to lead the Russian liberation movement" (*Psychological Prose*, 212). I disagree, in that Herzen points to several moments in his life at which point he seems to be "chosen" specifically: the fact that he survived the siege of Moscow during the Napoleonic wars and the special "sign" of imperial greeting from Alexander I when he was a small child.

46. Herzen continues with a mythic statement about the women, who were the only ones who dared to show sympathy toward the captured conspirators, comparing them to the women who stood by Christ during his crucifixion.

47. Alexander Herzen, *Poliarnaia zvezda*, 1855, facsimile edition (Moscow: Izdatel'stvo 'Nauka,' 1966), 1: 228.

48. Herzen bestowed a copy of the engraving to his son Sasha for his nameday and "initiation into revolutionary adulthood" (Judith E. Zimmerman, *Mid-passage: Alexander Herzen and European Revolution, 1847–1852* [Pittsburgh: University of Pittsburgh Press, 1989], 212).

49. Ginzburg, *Psychological Prose*, 217. This notion reflects the perception of a collective historical consciousness that came to the forefront during the Romantic period.

50. Harriet Murav, "Vo Glubine sibirskikh rud': Siberia and the Myth of Exile," in *Between Heaven and Hell: The Myth of Siberia in Russian Culture* (New York: St. Martin's Press, 1993), 109 n. 22.

51. N. Ogarev, *Stikhotvoreniia i poemy* (Leningrad: Sovetskii pisatel', 1956), 291. Henceforth references will be made to this volume and included in the text.

52. The wives' decision to go to Siberia played an enormous role in validating the Decembrists in contemporaries' eyes. Their mythologization occurred simultaneously with the Decembrists' and became an inseparable part of the myth. Because of space limitations I limit my comments here to Nekrasov's poem, though the wives are worthy of a separate chapter, let alone a separate volume. See Anatole Mazour, *Women in Exile: Wives of the Decembrists* (Tallahassee, FL: Diplomatic Press, 1975) and Pavliuchenko, *V dobrovol'nom izgnanii*.

53. Nechkina, *Dekabristy*, 169.

54. Murav, 103.

55. See Murav for Nekrasov's treatment of Siberia as "sacred topography," 103–106.

56. Lotman, "The Decembrist," 94.

57. N. A. Nekrasov, *Polnoe sobranie sochinenii i pisem* (Moscow: OGIZ, 1949), 23–85. Further references will be included in the text.

58. M. M. Khin, "Zheny dekabristov," *Istoricheskii vestnik* 18 (1884): 651–683, P. Shchegolev, "Podvig russkoi zhenshchiny," *Istoricheskii vestnik* 96 (1904): 530–550, and V. Pokrovskii, *Zheny dekabristov* (Moscow: G. Lissner i D. Sobko, 1906).

59. Volkonskaia's son died less than a year after her departure in 1828. Pushkin wrote the poignant epitaph for the child's grave and sent it to Volkonskaia in Siberia: "In radiance, in joyful peace / at the Eternal Creator's throne, / He looks with a smile to earthly exile, / Blesses his mother and prays for his father." The epitaph remained unpublished during Pushkin's lifetime.

60. Rozen, 228. Odoevskii memorialized the Decembrists' wives as angels in his 1829 poem dedicated to Volkonskaia. See *Dekabristy: Izbrannye sochineniia v dvukh tomakh* (Moscow: Pravda, 1987), 2: 347–348.

61. The reference recalls the Old Russian apocryphal text *Descent of the Virgin into Hell* (*Khozhdenie bogoroditsy po mukam*). M. S. Volkonskii read Nekrasov his mother's memoirs. See Frizman, 197–198.

62. Frizman, 194.

63. Yury Slezkine, "Lives as Tales," in *In the Shadow of Revolution: Life Stories of Russian Women* (Princeton: Princeton University Press, 2000), 19. Volkonskaia's memoirs, *The Way of Bitterness*, are excerpted in this volume, 139–165. See 158 on Dzerzhinsky, head of the

Soviet secret police from 1917–1923. For more on other women who modeled their actions on the Decembrists' wives, see 22 and n. 14.

64. Kathryn B. Feuer, *Tolstoy and the Genesis of War and Peace* (Ithaca, NY: Cornell University Press, 1996), 32. Feuer asserts that the unfinished story "The Distant Field" is the Decembrist tale of which Tolstoy spoke.

65. Tolstoy's letter to Herzen, Mar. 14/16, 1861 in L. N. Tolstoi, *Polnoe sobranie sochinenii* (iubileinoe) (Moscow: Gosudarstvennoe izdatel'stvo, 1936), 60: 374. Henceforth references will be included in the text.

66. Feuer, 197.

67. See Ibid., especially 40–53.

68. B. Eikhenbaum, *Lev Tolstoi: 60-ye gody* (Moscow-Leningrad: Gosudarstvennoe izdatel'stvo Khudozhestvennoi literatury, 1931), 2: 208–211.

69. All further references will be made to this version of 1863/1884 (without its variants) and will be included in the text.

70. M. A. Tsiavlovskii, "*Dekabristy*: Istoriia pisaniia i pechataniia romana," in Tolstoi, *PSS*, XVII, 469–513. Tsiavlovskii examines the draft chapters, outlines, and notebooks Tolstoy accumulated from 1877–1884. He believes Tolstoy planned to incorporate a "peasant theme" in his unfinished novel. According to fragmentary chapters, one of which Tolstoy published in 1884, peasants from the Chernyshev estate were sent to Siberia for appropriating their landlord's lands. The exiled Decembrist Chernyshev ends up in the same settlement and shares the peasants' fate.

71. A. B. Goldenveizer, *Vblizi Tolstogo* (Moscow: Kooperativnoe izdatel'stvo, 1922–1923), 1: 126.

72. Brodskii, 209.

73. N. Leonov, "Dekabristy (po khudozhestvennoi literature i dokumentam)," *Narodnyi uchitel'* 12 (1925): 101. This article appeared in a journal for provincial teachers, supporting my conclusion that in 1925 an effort to control the presentation of the Decembrists develops among party propagandists.

74. Leonov, 209.

Two Literariness and Self-Fashioning in the Decembrists' Memoirs

1. Rozen, 25.

2. M. K. Azadovskii, "Zateriannye i utrachennye proizvedeniia dekabristov," *Stranitsy istorii dekabrizma* (Irkutsk: Vostochno-Sibirskoe knizhnoe izdatel'stvo, 1992), 2: 178.

3. Rozen, 22. Nikolai Bestuzhev must have begun "Reminiscence of Ryleev" no later than 1832, but the exact date of composition cannot be ascertained (*Vospominaniia Bestuzhevykh*, 679). Trubetskoi's bound manuscript is dated 1844–1845; his essay, "Notes on Baron Korf's book," insists Korf's portrayal was a distortion of the facts (S. Trubetskoi, *Zapiski*, 1: 310–319).

4. M. I. Semevskii met Elena Alexandrovna Bestuzheva in 1859 and became interested in her brothers' legacy. Semevskii urged Mikhail Bestuzhev to write his memoirs in the 1860s. When Semevskii became the editor of the journal *Russkaia starina* in the 1870s he published reminiscences by several Decembrists, including the Bestuzhev brothers, Rozen, Beliaev, and Fonvizin. See *PD*, 1: 14 and N. Ia. Eidel'man, *Tainye korrespondenty 'Poliarnoi zvezdy'* (Moscow: Mysl, 1966).

5. Azadovskii, *Vospominaniia Bestuzhevykh*, 694 n. 1.

6. Ginzburg, *On Psychological Prose*, 7.

7. Ibid, 8–9.

8. Ibid., 9.
9. Ibid., 7.
10. Stephen Greenblatt employs this term in *Renaissance Self-Fashioning from More to Shakespeare* (Chicago, IL: University of Chicago Press, 2005 rev.ed.).
11. I. I. Pushchin, quoted in Sergei Gessen, *Dekabristy pered sudom istorii* (Leningrad: Izdatel'stvo "Petrograd", 1926), 129.
12. Rozen, 132.
13. Ibid, 23–28.
14. I. D. Iakushkin, *Memuary, Stat'i, Dokumenty* (Irkutsk: Vostochno-Sibirskoe knizhnoe izdatel'stvo, 1993), 178.
15. Ginzburg, emphasizing the memoir's retrospective dynamic and novelistic nature, asserts: "memoirs, autobiographies, and confessions are almost always literature presupposing readers in the future or the present" (*Psychological Prose*, 9).
16. Trubetskoi, 250. Most commentators agree that Trubetskoi blunted the radicalism of the conspirators' intentions. See N. Druzhinin, "S. P. Trubetskoi kak memuarist" in *Dekabristy i ikh vremia* (Moscow, 1932), 2: 23–43 and Trubetskoi, 352–382.
17. E. P. Obolenskii, "Vospominaniia o Ryleeve," *PD*, 2: 106. Obolenskii's memoirs were first translated into French by Prince Auguste Galitzin and printed abroad as *Souvenirs d'un Exile en Siberie*, (Leipzig: A. Franck'sche, 1862).
18. M. K. Azadovskii, "Memuary Bestuzhevykh, kak istoricheskii i literaturnyi pamiatnik" in *Vospominaniia Bestuzhevykh*, 631–632. Plutarch's *Lives* may have been the model for some Decembrist memoirists in "their purposeful heroicization, pathetic tone of narration and their elevated style" (*PD*, 1: 16).
19. M. Bestuzhev, "14 dekabria 1825," in *PD*, 1: 60–61.
20. V. I. Shteingel', *Sochineniia i pis'ma* (Irkutsk: Vostochno-Sibirskoe knizhnoe izdatel'stvo, 1985), 1: 150–151.
21. M. Bestuzhev, *PD*, 1: 60.
22. N. Bestuzhev, "Vospominanie o Ryleeve," *Vospominaniia Bestuzhevykh*, 34.
23. Rozen, 123. N. Bestuzhev confirms Ryleev's words (*PD*, 2: 154).
24. Rozen, 422, in Gessen, 131.
25. Turner, *Dramas*, 122.
26. Trubetskoi, 287–288.
27. Michael Cherniavsky, *Tsar and People: Studies in Russian Myths* (New Haven, CT: Yale University Press, 1961), 6–12.
28. Turner, *Dramas*, 258–259.
29. Trubetskoi, 241.
30. Raeff, *Decembrist Movement*, 15–16.
31. See N. Bestuzhev's "Vospominanie o Ryleeve" (10, 28), Lotman, "The Decembrist" and my article "Historical Models of Terror in Decembrist Literature," in *Just Assassins: The Culture of Russian Terrorism*, ed. Anthony Anemone (Evanston: Northwestern University Press, forthcoming).
32. Jacques Le Goff, *History and Memory* (New York: Columbia University Press, 1992), 151.
33. N. Bestuzhev, *Vospominaniia Bestuzhevykh*, 7.
34. Shteingel', 166–167, cf. 162, 172, 180. Shteingel' refers to the executed leaders and other Decembrists as victims. See also N. P. Tsebrikov, "Vospominaniia o kronverkskoi kurtine, *PD*, 1: 240.
35. Tsebrikov, *PD*, 1: 241.
36. For treatment of self-sacrificial models in the Decembrists' poetry, see Lotman, 94–96, Margaret Ziolkowski, "Hagiography and History: The Saintly Prince in the Poetry of the Decembrists, *Slavic and East European Journal* 30, no. 1 (1986): 29–43, and Murav, especially 96–100.
37. Ginzburg, *Psychological Prose*, 17.

38. See Abby M. Schrader, "Containing the Spectacle of Punishment: The Russian Autocracy and the Abolition of the Knout, 1817–1845," *Slavic Review* 56, no. 4 (Winter 1997): 613–644, Alan Wood, "Crime and Punishment in the House of the Dead," in Olga Crisp (ed.), *Civil Rights in Imperial Russia* (Oxford: Oxford University Press, 1989), 215–233, and Cyril Bryner, "The Issue of Capital Punishment in the reign of Elizaveta Petrovna," *Russian Review* 49, no. 4 (Oct. 1990): 389–416.

39. Viazemskii stated: "Everything remained in words and on paper, because in the conspiracy there was not a single regicide. I did not see them on Senate Square, just as I did not see a single hero in any war on the field of battle.... You don't give a St. George's cross for intention alone and in the hope of future heroic deeds, why should you execute prematurely?" (Cited in Iu. M. Lotman, "P. A. Viazemskii i dvizhenie dekabristov," *Trudy po russkoi i slavianskoi filosofii t. III, Uchennye zapiski Tartuskogog gosudarstvennogo universiteta* 98 [Tartu: Tartuskii gosudarstvennyi universitet, 1960]: 94).

40. Michel Foucault, *Discipline and Punish: The Birth of the Prison*, trans. Alan Sheridan (New York: Vintage Books, 2nd ed., 1995), 34.

41. Ibid., 9.

42. Ibid., 14.

43. Ibid, 57–59; 130.

44. Pieter Spierenburg, *The Spectacle of Suffering: Executions and the Evolution of Repression: from a Preindustrial Metropolis to the European Experience* (Cambridge: Cambridge University Press, 1984), vii; 109.

45. George L. Yaney, *The Systematization of Russian Government: Social Evolution in the Domestic Administration of Imperial Russia, 1711–1905* (Urbana, IL: University of Illinois Press, 1973).

46. "Donesenie tainogo agenta o nastroenii umov v Peterburge posle kazni dekabristov," *Dekabristy: neizdannye materialy i stati* (Moscow: Vsesoiuznoe obshchestvo politkatorzhan i ssylno-poselentsev, 1925), 38.

47. *PD*, 1: 419.

48. Rozen, 175.

49. *PD*, 1: 249.

50. Tsebrikov, *PD*, 1: 246.

51. See *PD*, 1: 249–268.

52. Spierenburg posits several explanations, from the survival of pagan popular beliefs to the subconscious rejection of a system of physical punishment, which is transformed to hatred for its active agent (21–23).

53. Shil'der, 1: 456–458, in Wortman, 270.

54. "Donesenie," 38–39. Herzen also recounts the active role played by the Decembrists' wives and female relatives in expressing their outrage at the punishment and supporting their husbands and friends (8:58).

55. Foucault, 66–68.

56. *PD*, 1: 259.

57. *PD*, 1: 246, 1: 425 n. 7. The poet N. M. Iazykov penned these lines.

58. Schnitsler, *PD*, 1: 268. Rozen confirms the second variant (*PD*, 1: 171).

59. *Mezhdutsarstvie 1825 goda*, 102.

60. "Kazn' Ryleeva," *PD*, 1: 253. Bestuzhev received information from prison attendants Podushkin and Trusov as well as Trubetskaia and Muravieva.

61. Foucault, 67. This sanctification is more likely to occur if the criminal became penitent at his execution. Myslovskii referred to Pestel and Ryleev as "perfect Christians" because of their penitence. See "Rasskaz samovidtsa o kazni, sovershennoi v Peterburge 1826 goda 13 iulia," *PD*, 1:271.

62. Rozen, 175. Multiple copies of Ryleev's last letter were disseminated. An incorrect version was published in N. I. Grech's memoirs in *Russkii vestnik* 6 (1868): 384–385. See Rozen, 430 n. 51.

63. Rozen, *PD*, 1: 168.
64. "Rasskaz samovidtsa," *PD*, 1: 271. The witness continues: "These words show him as an impenitent sinner." He also attributed these last words to Ryleev after his fall from the gallows: "God grants me another minute to pray for the tsar."
65. *PD*, 1: 246.
66. See Luke, 23:39–43.
67. Tsebrikov, *PD*, 1: 240; N. Bestuzhev, *PD*, 2: 75.
68. Turner, 123–124.
69. I. M. Gorbachevskii, letter to M. A. Bestuzhev (Jul. 12, 1861), *PD*, 1:250, 426–427. Gorbachevskii provides details to Bestuzhev, who asked in June 1861 for more information. Gorbachevskii purportedly saw the condemned men's processional from his prison window.
70. Rozen, 52.
71. M. Bestuzhev, "Iz zapisok M. A. Bestuzheva v vide otvetov na voprosy M. I. Semevskogo. 1860–1861," *PD*, 1: 119.
72. Iakushkin, *Memuary*, 145.
73. D. I. Oleinikov, "Don Kikhot i Gamlet kak tipy istoricheskogo samosoznaniia pokolenii dekabristov i idealistov 30kh godov,' *Ekonomicheskaia i obshchestvennaia zhizn' Rossii novogo vremeni* 2 (Moscow, 1992): 167–178.
74. Iakushkin, *Memuary*, 162.

Three   The Image in Flux in the Early Twentieth Century

1. Cited in Jane Burbank, *Intelligentsia and Revolution: Russian Views of Bolshevism, 1917–1922* (Oxford: Oxford University Press, 1986), 3–4. Shingarev, a member of the Kadets' central committee, was imprisoned by the Bolsheviks in Peter-Paul Fortress after the October revolution.
2. M. Bestuzhev, "Iz 'Dopolnitel'nykh otvetov 1869–1870,' " *PD*, 1: 140–142.
3. See Zamoyski, 276, 320, 385.
4. V. I. Vlasov, "I. S. Turgenev i dekabristy," *Orlovskaia pravda*, no. 291–292, 14 December, 1975, 8.
5. G. Plekhanov, *14-e dekabria 1825 goda. Rech' proiznesennaia na russkom sobranii v Zheneve 14/27 dekabria 1900 goda* (Petrograd: Gosudarstvennoe izdatel'stvo, 1921), 3.
6. The Social Democrats' regional committees in Odessa, Tver', Kiev, Kharkov, and Perm celebrated the anniversary from 1901–1905. One pamphlet exhorted the workers: "We will erect a monument to them [the Decembrists] with our great struggle for liberation" (Frizman, 282). See Frizman, 282–285.
7. See Leonard Schapiro, *The Communist Party of the Soviet Union*, 2nd ed. (New York: Random House, 1971), 37–71, on *Iskra*'s role in Social Democratic politics and party organization.
8. N.K. Krupskaia, *Vospominaniia o Lenine* (Moscow: Partizdat, 1932), 32.
9. See A. I. Iezuitov, "K istoriia epigrapha Leninskoi gazety 'Iskra'," in Bazanov, 382–389.
10. Nevelev, *Dekabristy i dekabristovedy*, 232.
11. See Ibid., 218–269.
12. Iakushkin, *Memuary*,312. Excerpts from Volkonskaia's memoirs (in French) were first published in *Russkaia Starina* 6 (1878): 336–342; the full text was published in 1906 in St. Petersburg after an incomplete first edition in 1904. The memoirs were retranslated and republished in 1914 and 1924.
13. Brodskii, 217. S. V. Balmashev (1881–1902) was the revolutionary terrorist who was hanged for assassinating the Minister of the Interior, D. S. Sipiagin, in 1902. N. I. Sazonov

(1815–1862), a member of the Herzen circle at Moscow University, emigrated and became a writer for European radical newspapers and political activist who participated in the 1848 revolutions in Europe. Lieutenant P. P. Shmidt (1867–1906) was executed by firing squad in 1906 for his leadership of the 1905 Sevastopol uprising.

14. Zenzinov issued *Pamiati dekabristov* (Moscow, 1907), a commemorative album of Decembrist portraits and drawings.

15. "Muzei dekabristov v Moskve (k godovshchine 14 dekabria 1825 g.)," *Utro Rossii*, no. 291, Dec. 18, 1911, 4.

16. V. Lenin, "Pamiati Gertsena," *PSS*, 21: 261.

17. D. S. Merezhkovskii, *Perventsy svobody: istoriia vosstaniia 14-o dekabria 1825 g.* (Petrograd: Narodnaia vlast', 1917), 2.

18. *Ustav obshchestva pamiati dekabristov* (Petrograd, 1917), 3–4, K.G. Liashenko, "1917 g. Obrashchenie obshchestva pamiati dekabristov k grazhdanam Rossii", *Sovetskie arkhivy* 6 (1991): 71–73.

19. Liashenko, 72.

20. Ibid., 73.

21. Ibid., 72.

22. Richard Stites, *Revolutionary Dreams: Utopian Vision and Experimental Life in the Russian Revolution* (Oxford: Oxford University Press, 1989), 88–89.

23. Frizman, 298, cf. also Brodskii, 222–226.

24. *Dekabristy: Khudozhestvennyi al'bom: 36 portretov ispolnennykh khudozhnikami G. M. Manizer i V.A. Taburin s originalov togo vremeni. Tekst I. N. Bozherianova.* (Petrograd: Rus,' 1917), 5–6.

25. Ibid.

26. "Pamiati dekabristov," *Muzei revoliutsii, Sbornik I* (Petrograd, 1923), 68. Gor'kii, Lunacharskii and Shchegolev also spoke.

27. *Petrogradskaia pravda*, no. 7, Jan 11, 1920, 1.

28. Ozouf, *Festivals and the French Revolution* (Cambridge: Harvard University Press, 1988), Stites, *Revolutionary Dreams*, Von Geldern, *Bolshevik Festivals, 1917–1920* (Berkeley: University of California Press, 1993), Clark, *Petersburg: Crucible of Cultural Revolution* (Cambridge: Harvard University Press, 1995). Ozouf, unlike the others, emphasizes that most celebrations (except state-sponsored funerals) did not elicit the desired support.

29. Von Geldern, 8–10.

30. Ibid., 13.

31. Cherniavsky, 41.

32. Von Geldern, 3.

33. Ibid., 12.

34. Ibid., 46.

35. Ibid., 12.

36. P. M. Kerzhentsev, *Tvorcheskii teatr* (Moscow-Leningrad: Gosudarstvennoe izdatel'stvo, 1923), 124–125.

37. Stites, 97.

38. Clark, 189.

39. D. S. Merezhkovskii, *Sobranie sochinenii v 4-x tomakh* (Moscow: Pravda, 1990), 4: 43. Henceforth references will be included in the text.

40. The winner in playing at give-away is the first player to lose all his pieces in the game of draughts (*Oxford Russian Dictionary*, 2nd ed., Oxford: Clarendon Press, 1984, 535).

41. Cossack heroes took center stage in Bolshevik propaganda during the 1920s, when the Bolsheviks had to unite the workers, peasants, and Cossacks in a collective force during the Civil War period. See Judith Kornblatt, *The Cossack Hero in Russian Literature: A Study in Cultural Mythology*, (Madison: University of Wisconsin Press, 1992), 104–105.

Four   The Battle over Representation
during the Centennial

1. "Pamiati piati," *Leningradskaia pravda,* no. 170, Jul. 27, 1926, 5.
2. *Zhizn' isskustva,* No. 316–317, Dec. 14, 1919, 3.
3. See M. Ol'minskii, "Rasrushennye legendy," *Vestnik zhizni,* no. 3 (Mar. 1907): 72–83 for his first attack on the Decembrist myth. That article anticipates many points brought up by M. Pokrovskii in later iconoclastic articles on the Decembrists.
4. "Dve godovshchiny: 1905 i 1825,"*Rabochaia Moscow,* No. 283, Dec. 16, 1923, 3.
5. "Sleduet li prazdnovat' 100-letnei iubilei vosstaniia dekabristov, *Izvestiia TsIK,* no. 290, Dec. 19, 1923, 3.
6. G. Zinoviev, *Istoriia Rossiiskoi kommunichesticheskoi partii bol'shevikov,* quoted in "Sleduet li prazdnovat'," 3.
7. "O stoletnem iubilee dekabristov," *Rabochaia Moscow,* no. 8, Jan. 10, 1924, 3.
8. M. Pokrovskii, "Nuzhno li prazdnovat' iubilei dekabristov?" first published in *Molodaia gvardiia,* no. 5, 1923, reprinted in S. Shtraikh (ed.), *Dekabristy: K stoletiiu zagovora 1825–1925.* (Moscow: Transpechat', 1925) 19–20.
9. The United Slavs, composed primarily of small landowners and low-ranking military officers, desired the eradication of the autocracy, the abolition of serfdom and the wholesale distribution of all land to peasants. See Mazour, *First Russian Revolution,* 139–153.
10. Ibid., 21. Pestel sought to insure the peasants' economic and social stability in the communal ownership of land, but also to allow for private land ownership for those with the desire and means to work it. He saw historical precedent in the Russian peasant commune's existence alongside of private ownership. See also Venturi, 3–7 and Walicki, 62–66.
11. Ibid., 32.
12. Pokrovskii sought to assert his claim against such "White Guard" views as espoused by A. Shingarev, who drew a parallel between the Decembrists and Kadets while imprisoned after the October revolution (see n. 1, chapter 3). Even a year after the jubilee, the Bolsheviks defended their inheritance, as evident in M. Nechkina's vituperative article, "Portreti 'predkov': iubilei dekabristov za rubezhom," *Pechat' i revoliutsiia* 8 (Dec. 1926): 28–38.
13. Katherine Verdery, *The Political Lives of the Dead: Reburial and Postsocialist Change* (New York: Columbia University Press, 1999), 33.
14. Verdery, 41.
15. Ibid., 31.
16. See Tumarkin, 165–206, for discussion of the decision to embalm Lenin's body and display it permanently.
17. Tumarkin, 135.
18. At this time there was great interest in the fact that another important nineteenth-century ancestor, Pushkin, did not have a proper burial. See Osip Mandel'shtam's reference to the "buried sun" in "We shall meet again in Petersburg" (1920).
19. The first meeting took place on October 19, 1923 ("Protokoly zasedanie komissii po podgotovke prazdnovaniia stoletiia dekabristov," GARF [State Archive of the Russian Federation], f. 533, ed.khr. 86, op. 1, l. 1). VOBPKS was slightly less important than the Communist Academy and the Institute of Red Professors in the hierarchy of Soviet research institutions. Unlike the first two Marxist institutions, VOBPKS included both Marxists and Populists. See Enteen, *The Soviet Scholar-Bureaucrat,* chapters 4 and 8.
20. *KS* 6, no. 13 (1924): 268–269.
21. "O stoletnem iubilee dekabristov," *Izvestiia TsIK,* no. 278, Dec. 5, 1923, 7. Later, an arts committee was established that included K.S. Stanislavksii and G. Meyerhold ("Protokol from 24 April 1925," GARF, f. 533, ed. khr. 86, op. I, l. 39).

22. Thomas Sherlock, *Historical Narratives in the Soviet Union and Post-Soviet Russia* (New York: Palgrave Macmillan, 2007), 149.

23. "Protokol. No. 18, 29 January 1925," GARF, f. 533, ed.khr. 86, op. I, l. 25.

24. Shtraikh, *K iubileiu dekabristov* was first published in *Molodaia gvardiia* 7 (1925). In the centennial's honor, M. Nechkina and E. Skazin also organized materials for pedagogical use in educational institutions: *Seminarii po dekabrizmu* (Moscow: Prometei, 1925).

25. Shtraikh, 3.

26. "Kratkii obzor deiatel'nosti 'Dekabristskoi komissii,'" *KS* 6, no. 13 (1924): 268–269. For more on Lenin corners, see Tumarkin, 3.

27. "K stoletnemu iubileiu dekabristov. Ot komissii Vsesoiuznogo obshchestva politkatorzhan i ss.-poselentsev po prazdnovaniu stoletnego iubileia vosstaniia dekabristov," *K S* 1, no. 14 (1925): 178–184.

28. Ibid., 179. All further references are included in the text.

29. GARF, f. 533, ed. khr. 86, op. 1, l. 44. The request was submitted in April 1925. The protocols do not include a response from the state indicating how much money was given to subsidize the celebration.

30. "Podgotovka k prazdnovaniiu 100-letnego iubileia vosstaniia dekabristov," *KS* 4, no. 17(1925): 296–299, 297.

31. Clark, 193 and 344 n. 46. Clark compares the coverage in the commemorative issue of *Zhizn' iskusstva*, no. 41, Dec. 14–17, 1925.

32. On the "cultural dialogue," between Moscow and Petersburg, see Clark, 192, 262–265, 297–307. For discussion of the nineteenth-century rivalry, see Richard Wortman, "Moscow and Petersburg: The Problem of Political Center in Tsarist Russia, 1881–1914," in Sean Wilentz (ed.), *Rites of Power: Symbolism, Ritual, and Politics Since the Middle Ages* (Pennsylvania: University of Pennsylvania Press), 1985. The 1926 guide *Po revoliutsionnoi Moskve* also asserts Moscow's centrality. It guides readers through neighborhoods important to the revolutionary movement. The tour notes the Decembrists' Moscow locales, listing by region their homes and graves (22–25; 62–63; 130–133; 172, 211, 269–270).

33. The Academy of Sciences organized events in Leningrad: a commemorative meeting (December 28) and an exhibition at Pushkinskii Dom (Pushkin House). See *Izvestiia TsIK SSR*, no. 296 (2629), Dec. 29, 1925, 3.

34. The centennial renaming followed changes in street names near the square in the Decembrists' honor immediately after the 1917 revolution. In 1918 Officer's Street (*Ofitserskaia ulitsa*) became Decembrists' Street (*Ulitsa dekabristov*). In 1923 both Pestel and Ryleev were similarly honored: Panteleimonov street (*Panteleimonovskaia ulitsa*), was renamed Pestel Street (*Ulitsa Pestelia*) and Spasskaia street (*Spasskaia ulitsa*) became Ryleev Street (*Ulitsa Ryleeva*). See K. S. Gorbachevich and E. P. Khaldo, *Pochemu tak nazvany? O proiskhozhdenii nazvanii ulits, ploshchadei, ostrovov, rek i mostov v Leningrade* (Leningrad: Leninizdat, 1967), 262; 300.

35. *Vsesoiuznoe ob-vo politicheskikh katorzhan i ssyl'no-poselentsev. 1825–1905–1925. Sto let politicheskoi katorgii. 2-i Vsesoiuznyi s"ezd politkatorzhan. 26–29 dek. 1925 g.* (Moscow: 1926), 18. Feliks Iakovlevich Kon (1864–1941) was an elder revolutionary (Old Bolshevik) who was exiled to Irkutsk in 1897 for his membership in the Polish Socialist Party. He worked as a journalist and historian as well.

36. An excerpt of Figner's speech was published in *Rabochaia Moscow* ("Ot dekabristov k Oktiabriu," No. 296, Dec. 29, 1925, 6). Though Trotskii's speech has been widely reproduced in newspaper accounts and in the above publication, I have not found Figner's full text. Figner admits that both the Decembrists and the People's Will failed because of their distance from the masses, and seems to assert the primacy of 1905 over 1825. Yet Figner's activism first occurred as a member of People's Will and her involvement in the centennial stemmed from her interest in the Decembrists, not in 1905. Hoogenboom has suggested that Figner may have alluded to the connection between the two groups to subvert the Bolsheviks.

37. *Vsesoiuznoe ob-vo politkatorzhan*, 18.
38. "1825–1905–1925. Na vsesoiuznom s'ezde ob. politkatorzhan i ssyl'noposylentsev. Rechi t.t. Trotskogo, Feliksa Kona i Very Figner," *Rabochaia gazeta*, no. 296, Dec. 29, 1925, 6.
39. "Vsesoiuznyi s"ezd politkatorzhan i ssylno-poselentsev," *Izvestiia TsIK SSR*, no. 294 (2627), Dec. 24, 1925, 4.
40. 32 titles were published on the Decembrists compared to 21 on the 1905 revolution ("K iubileiu dekabristov," *Knigonosha*, no. 39–40 (120–121), Dec. 31, 1925, 12–13).
41. "Potomki dekabristov," *Krasnaia gazeta*, vech. vyp., no. 310 (998), Dec. 23, 1925, 5.
42. "Vnuchka dekabrista Muravieva," *Isvestiia TsIK SSR*, no. 296 (2629), Dec. 29, 1925, 3.
43. K. Stanislavskii, "Vstupitel'noe slovo na utre pamiati dekabristov v MKhAT, 27 dekabria 1925 g," *Sobranie sochineniia* (Moscow: Iskusstvo, 1959), 6: 212.
44. A. Cherkasskii, "O poslednikh moskovskikh postanovkakh," *Komsomoliia*, 2 (Feb. 1926): 66–70. For reviews see: *Izvestiia*, no. 9 (2640), Jan. 12, 1926, 7; *Rabochaia gazeta*, no. 296, Dec. 29, 1925, 6; *Vecherniaia Moscow*, no. 296, Dec. 29, 1925, 3.
45. P. Kudelli, cited in Arkadii Selivanov, "Vecher pamiati dekabristov (V Akteatre opery i baleta)," *Krasnaia gazeta*, no. 315 (1003), Dec. 30, 1925, 5.
46. For detailed discussion of Shaporin's work, see chapter 6.
47. *Krasnaia gazeta*, no. 313 (1001), Dec. 28, 1925, 5.
48. N. Vselkov describes the exhibition in *Trud* (no. 2, Jan. 3, 1926). On entering one saw a large poster with a citation from Lenin's Zurich speech. Pokrovskii, Plekhanov and other historians were also quoted. Another part of the exhibition focused on Pushkin and the Decembrists. Vselkov criticized the curators' choices, lack of proper labeling and the poor quality of reproductions.
49. *Bibliotechnoe obozrenie* (Leningrad) 1–2 (1926): 136–137. The visitors included youth from higher educational institutions, middle schools and factory workers.
50. *Krasnoe Znamia* (Tomsk), no. 157, Jul. 14, 1925, 2.
51. If the organizers coordinated the centennial with the release of films about the Decembrists their commemoration might have been more successful. See chapter 5 on the popularity of the films which came out in 1926–1927. See T. Lozinskaia, *Dekabristy— Ekskursiia* (Leningrad: Iz-vo knizhnogo sektora LGONO, 1925, Seriia ekskursionnaia praktika, Leningradskogo otdela narodnogo obrazovaniia), for discussion of the Museum of Revolution's exhibition. Rather than exploring Leningrad sites related to the uprising, the guide gives cursory discussion of Senate Square before going to the museum. Only during the 1937 Pushkin centennial was the potential of Decembrist excursions exploited in N. R. Levinson, *Pushkinskaia Moskva. Putevoditel'* (Moscow: Moskovskii rabochii, 1937).
52. Clark, 196. See 143–200 for the conflict between mass and intellectual culture during the 1920s.
53. "100-letie vosstaniia dekabristov: prazdnovanie stoletiia vosstaniia dekabristov v Kieve," *KS* 22 (1926): 284; "K iubileiu vosstaniia dekabristov: Otkrytiia zasedanie nauchno-issledovatel'skoi kafedry," *Kievskii proletarii*, no. 165, Jan. 5, 1926, 5.
54. See "Dekabristy v Omske," *Rabochii put'* no. 296, Dec. 25, 1925, 3.
55. For a discussion of the polemical battles in Soviet historiography, see Enteen, *The Soviet Scholar-Bureaucrat*, especially 64–164.
56. See "14/26 dekabria 1825 goda," *Pravda*, no. 297 (3228), Dec. 30, 1925, 10 and "Dva iubileia," *Rabochaia gazeta*, no. 290, Dec. 19, 1925.
57. Pokrovskii, "14 dekabria 1825," *Leningradskaia pravda*, no. 1, Jan. 1, 1926, 4.
58. "Vekovoi iubilei 14(27) dekabria 1825 g-27 dekabria 1925 g," *Krasnoe znamia*, no. 296, Dec. 25, 1925, 1. This is the only other article I have seen that explicitly states that a legend had been created which did not correspond to historical reality.
59. E. Skazin, "Vosstanie dekabristov," *Krasnoe znamia* (Tomsk), Nov. 22, 1925, 1.

60. Skazin's article was first published on 11 November 1925 in the Press Bureau's bulletin "A Division of Publications" (Press-biuro Otdela Pechati, TsK RKP, Moscow). It was subsequently reproduced in 12 local newspapers across the union. Versions of Shtraikh's article "K iubileiu" appeared in various local newspapers and Moscow journals, including *Prozhektor, Smena, Ogonek,* and *Gorod i Derevnia.* See N. M. Chentsov, *Vosstanie dekabristov: bibliografiia* (Moscow-Leningrad: Gosudarstvennoe izdatel'stvo, 1929), 583–688.

61. Verdery, 58.

62. Stephanie Sandler, "Remembrance in Mikhailovskoe," in Gasparov, 245–246.

63. "Mogily kaznennykh dekabristov," *Vecherniaia Moskva,* no. 172, Jul. 30, 1925, 3.

64. "Mogily piati dekabristov," *Izvestiia,* no. 169 (2800), Jul. 25, 1926, 2.

65. "Pamiatnik kaznennym dekabristam," *Leningradskaia pravda,* no. 58, Mar 11, 1926, 4.

66. See Stites, 65–67; 88–92.

67. The poems "Piati" by T. Shilejko appeared in *Leningradskaia pravda,* no. 169, Jul. 25, 1926, 3 and "Kazn'" by I. Keller appeared in *Ural'skii rabochii,* Aug. 1, 1926. Ogarev's poetry on the Decembrists' execution was reprinted in *Krasnyi sever,* Jul. 25, 1926.

68. A. Olenin, "Mucheniki svobody, "*Rabochaia gazeta,* no. 170, Jul. 27, 1926, 2.

69. "K 100-letiu kazni dekabristov," *Leningradskaia pravda,* No. 169, Jul. 25, 1926, 4.

70. "Zakladka pamiatnika dekabristam," *Izvestiia,* no. 170 (2801), Jul. 27, 1926, 4.

71. "Pamiati piati," 5.

72. Nevelev, "Pushkin o meste," 181 n. 19.

73. "Pamiati piati," 5.

74. Levitt, "Pushkin in 1899," 192.

75. David Cannadine, "The Context, Performance and Meaning of Ritual: The British Monarchy and the 'Invention of Tradition,' c. 1820–1977" in Hobsbawm, 101–164.

76. The stamps were announced on December 11 and released December 20, 1925 ("Iubileinye pochtovye marki: 1825–1925 g. i 1905–1925 g," *Vecherniaia Moskva,* no. 283 [593], Dec. 11, 1925, 1). Although commemorative stamps were issued in honor of the 1905 revolution, it appears ceramics were not produced.

77. F. G. Chuchin, "K stoletnemu iubileiu dekabristov," *Sovietskii filatelist* 1(1926): 7–8.

78. Ibid., 8.

79. S. Chekhonin, "Khudozhestvennyi farfor," *Krasnaia niva,* No. 42, Oct. 17, 1926, 14–15. Unfortunately, I could not find statistics on the porcelain's production and sale.

80. Shtraikh, 9. The inclusion of Merezhkovskii's novel is surprising given its author's emigration, political affiliation and negative portrayal of revolution. See chapter 3.

81. Ibid, 15–16.

82. See, for example, Nechkina, *Griboedov i dekabristy* and "O Pushkine, dekabristakh i ikh obshchikh druziakh," *KS* 4, no. 65 (1930): 7–40; Lotman, "P. A. Viazemskii i dvizhenie dekabristov;"; Eidel'man, *Pushkin i dekabristy, Dekabristskii tsikl poem Nekrasova. Kurs lektsii* (1976); Frizman, *Dekabristy i russkaia literatura,* to name a few.

83. R. Uralov, "Vvedenie v iubileevedenie," *Voprosy literatury,* Jul. 8, 1960, 77–80.

84. Brodskii, 187–226; V. Figner, "Zheny dekabristov," *KS* 21 (1925): 227–237; Gessen, *Dekabristy pered sudom istorii. 1825–1925.*

85. Only in the 1930s does Griboedov become a central part of the canon through Nechkina's scholarship. Lotman later analyzes Chatskii's behavior as a "text" cluing the reader in to his revolutionary views in "The Decembrist," 73–76.

86. Brodskii lists: Pushkin's "Andre Chénier," "Arion," "Poslanie v Sibir," the epistle to Pushchin, *Eugene Onegin* (chapter 10 and Pushkin's reference to Ryleev's hanging), *The Bronze Horseman;* Odoevskii's response to Pushkin; Ogarev's "Pamiati Ryleeva," "S togo berega," "Kavkazkie vody," and "Radaev;" Lermontov's "I den' nastal," "Pamiati A. I. Odoevskogo;" Leskov's "Smekh i gore;" Korolenko's "Legenda o tsare i dekabriste;" Nekrasov's *Russkie zhenshchiny;* Tolstoi's "Dekabristy," *War and Peace;* Dostoevskii's

Besy (Stavrogin as the Decembrist Lunin), *Zapiski iz mertvogo doma* (on the wives); Merezhkovskii's *14 dekabria* (as "popular history"), Gippius's "14 dekabria 1917 goda;" Osip Mandel'shtam's poem "Dekabrist." Brodskii also mentions a number of obscure historical novels, poems, and plays written from the mid-nineteenth century to 1923 on the Decembrists.

87. Brodskii, 226.
88. Gessen, 290.
89. Nekrasov's contemporaries criticized his poems for their lack of historical orientation. Annenkov lamented that Nekrasov's did not depict the "noble aristocratic motives which moved the hearts of these women"; M. S. Volkonskii (Maria and Sergei Volkonskii's son) confirmed Trubetskaia was not a revolutionary (*buntarka*) but a "highly virtuous and gentle-hearted woman" (Frizman, 204).
90. Figner, 228–229.
91. Vera Zasulich, Sofia Perovskaia, and Elizaveta Kovalskaia, among other female revolutionaries, attested to the Decembrists' influence in their revolutionary engagement. See Barbara Alpern-Engel and Clifford N. Rosenthal, *Five Sisters: Women against the Tsar* (New York: Routledge, 1992), 69, 208 and B. Alpern-Engel, *Mothers and Daughters: Women of the Intelligentsia in Nineteenth-Century Russia* (Cambridge, MA: Cambridge University Press, 1983), 17–20, 56–57. There was also a generational link to the Decembrists among later revolutionaries: Olga Bulanova-Trubnikova (1858–1942), a member of Black Repartition who later joined the left SRs, was the Decembrist Ivashev's granddaughter (Engel, *Mothers and Daughters*, 201). Irina Kakhovskaia (1888–1960), a maximalist who later joined the SRs and assassinated General Eickhorn in during the Civil War was great-granddaughter of a Decembrist, and Petr Filippovich Iakubovich (1860–1911), organizer of the Young People's Will Party and poet who espoused agrarian and factory terror, was related to the Decembrist Iakubovich. On Kakhovskaia, see Amy Knight, "Female Terrorists in the Russian Socialist Revolutionary Party," *Russian Review* 38/ 2 (1979): 157; on Iakubovich, see B.N. Dvinianov, *Mech i lira: Ocherk zhizni i tvorchestva P. F. Iakubovicha* (Moscow: Nauka, 1967), 9–10.
92. Figner, 229.
93. Ibid., 237.
94. H. Hoogenboom, "Vera Figner and revolutionary autobiographies: the influence of gender on genre," in Rosalind Marsh (ed.), *Women in Russia and Ukraine* (Cambridge: Cambridge University Press, 1996), 90.
95. Stites, 76.
96. Ibid., 78.

Five   Centennial Representations in Fiction and Film

1. Iurii Tynianov, "Avtobiografiia" (1939), in V. Kaverin (ed.), *Iurii Tynianov. Pisatel' i uchenyi. Vospominaniia, razmyshleniia, vstrechi.* (Moscow: Molodaia gvardiia, 1966), 19.
2. Marich first published several chapters in journals and newspapers in 1925 then republished the work as a separate book in 1926 and 1927. The second volume came out in 1931. Each time the novel was reprinted she made changes to the text (cf. *Dictionary of Russian Women Writers,* eds. Marina Ledkovsky, Charlotte Rosenthal, Mary Zirin [Westport, CT: Greenwood Press, 1994], 410–411).
3. Kaverin, 115–117.
4. Clark, *Petersburg*, 192–193.
5. Gasparov, *Cultural Mythologies*, 11–12.

6. Kaverin, 20.

7. Andrew Wachtel, *An Obsession with History: Russian Writers Confront the Past* (Stanford, CA: Stanford University Press, 1994) 179. See 183–190 for discussion of Tynianov's theoretical writings and his fiction.

8. Angela Brintlinger, *Writing a Usable Past: Russian Literary Culture, 1917–1937* (Evanston, IL: Northwestern University Press, 2000), 25.

9. See Larry Joseph, "From Literary Theory to Fiction: An Interpretive biography of Iurii Tynianov in the 1920s" (Ph.D. diss., Stanford University, 1994), for the political allegory thesis.

10. Iur. S-v, *Vecherniaia Moskva*, No. 24, Jan. 30, 1926, 2.

11. E. Mustangov, *Zvezda* 2 (1926): 279. "There is no objective picture of the uprising and no revelation of its reasons and essences."

12. Claude Levi-Strauss, *The Savage Mind* (London: Weidenfeld and Nicolson, 1966), 257.

13. Iu. Tynianov, *Kiukhlia* (Voronezh: Izd. Voronezhkogo universiteta: 1987), 230–231. All further references will be made to this edition and included in the text.

14. See L. G. Muratov, "Petersburgskaia tema O. Forsh i Iu. Tynianova (K probleme preem-stvennoi sviazi mezhdu literaturoi i kinematografom 20kh-godov)," *Russkaia literatura* 4 (1982): 196–208.

15. Wachtel, 183.

16. See Joseph, 160–174, for discussion of amputated limbs and their significance as metaphors of social dysfunction and disaffection. Irina Reyfman suggests a different reading, invoking the biblical connotation of the sinful (separated) limb; in the New Testament, a sinful limb acts on its own and must be cast off in order to rid oneself of sin. See her *Ritualized Violence Russian Style: The Duel in Russian Culture and Literature* (Stanford, CA: Stanford University Press, 1999), 234–235.

17. Kaverin, 80.

18. Kaverin, 80. Kiukhelbeker, however, was incarcerated in two other fortresses (Dinaborg and Sveaborg) before being sent to Siberian exile.

19. "I overate at supper,/And Iakov mistakenly locked the door/Thus, my friends I felt/both kiukhelbekerish and nauseous" (*Kiukhlia*, 68).

20. Abram Terz, *Strolls with Pushkin*, transl. by Catharine Nepomnyashchy and Slava Yastremski, (New Haven: Yale University Press, 1993), 111.

21. G. Munblit, *Komsomolia* 4 (1926): 93.

22. Irina Reyfman, *Vasilii Trediakovsky: The Fool of the 'New' Russian Literature* (Stanford, CA: Stanford University Press, 1990), 11–12.

23. Reyfman, *Vasilii Trediakovsky*, 198–225.

24. Ibid., 237.

25. Tynianov returned to this scene in his unstaged drama "December 14," which he began at the end of the 1930s. In the play, he turns the scene into slapstick comedy.

26. Tynianov expands upon this scene in the aforementioned play, using it as a dramatic finale to the action.

27. Kaverin, 79.

28. Ibid., 67.

29. Ibid., 19.

30. Clark, 194. See Tynianov's essay "Mnimyi Pushkin" (1922) in which he criticized unschol-arly approaches to Pushkin. Much of the same criticism could be applied to scholarship of the Decembrist movement. For further commentary on the essay's influence on Tynianov's fiction, see Brintlinger, 47–51.

31. "Kinokartiny o dekabristakh," *Izvestiia TsiK SSSR*, Jan. 30, 1926, No. 24 (2655), 5.

32. Denise Youngblood, *Movies for the Masses: Popular cinema and Soviet society in the 1920s* (Cambridge: Cambridge University Press, 1992), 80.

33. Ibid, 80–81. Two sources cite the budget as 340,000 rubles, while another said the film brought Sevzapkino to the brink of bankruptcy at the cost of 250,000 rubles. See 197 n. 39.

34. "*Dekabristy*: K s'emke na Senatskoi ploshchadi," *Kino*, No. 9, Mar. 2, 1926, 1.

35. Advertisements for *Dekabristy* began in *Zhizn' iskusstva* a week before its release on Jan. 11, 1927. *Zhizn' iskusstva* featured film stills on the cover of the Jan. 25, 1927 issue, No. 4 (1135), and a picture of the director, A. Ivanovskii, on the cover of "Teatry i zrelishcha," a supplement to the same issue. *Dekabristy* played at four major theaters (Velikan, Gigant, Kolizei, and Pavil'on de Pari) in Leningrad and in four theaters in Moscow (Pervyi Sovkino, Ars, Kolizei, and Forum) for two weeks. After that, it continued its run through the first week of March 1927. A box-office run of this length was unusual for a domestic film; advertisements indicate that most Soviet films came and went in about two weeks and that even foreign films did not often enjoy such long success in theaters.

36. The title has been translated variously into English as "The Union of the Great Deed" or "The Club of the Big Deed;" into French as "Nieges sanglantes," and into German as "Der Bund die Grossen Tat." Throughout I will use the Russian acronym.

37. Iurii Tynianov, "O FEKSakh," *Sovetskii ekran*, Apr. 2, 1929, 10 translated in Richard Taylor and Ian Christie (eds.), *The Film Factory: Russian and Soviet Cinema in Documents, 1896–1939* (London: Routledge, 1988), 258.

38. Shchegolev's work on the Decembrists, begun in 1903, emphasized their lofty idealism as a part of their psychological composition. See Nevelev, *Dekabristy i dekabristovedy*, 218–225.

39. "A fine actress was needed for the role of the Frenchwoman Polina Gueble. When I was in Berlin, I met the actress Barbara von Annenkova. She turned out to be the great-granddaughter of Polina Gueble! I thought it would be good if the role of Annenkov's wife would be played by Annenkova, my heroine's direct descendant" (A. V. Ivanovskii, *Vospominaniia kinorezhissera* [Moscow: Iskusstvo, 1967], 202).

40. "Kak ia igraiu Polinu Gebl': ocherk pravnuchki dekabrista I. A. Annenkova—artistki V. P. Annenkovoi," *Ogonek*, No. 17 (161), Apr 25, 1926, 13.

41. Ivanovskii, 200. "We avoided the main question: why did the uprising fail and what reasons hampered its success."

42. "Dekabristy: Senatskaia ploshchad'," *Kino*, No. 6, Feb. 9, 1926, 1; "Senatskaia ploshchad'," *Kino*, No. 7, Feb. 16, 1926, 2. Photographs of the filming on Senate Square were featured in "Dekabristy v Kino," *Krasnaia Niva*, No. 13, Mar. 13, 1926, 22. *Sovetskii ekran* also documented the film's progress in two articles (V. Ardov's "Progulka v istoriu," No. 12, Mar. 23, 1926, including a photo of the Senate Square scene, and "Iug na severe," No. 31, Aug. 3, 1926, 2). *Krasnaia panorama* included a film still of Ryleev's country home with Professor N. Firsov's article, "Kto takie dekabristy?" No. 1 (95), Jan 1, 1926, 7.

43. Denise J. Youngblood, "History on Film: the historical melodrama in early Soviet cinema," *Historical Journal of Film, Radio and Television* 11, No. 2 (1991): 180.

44. See chapters 6 and 7.

45. "Iz epokhi dekabristov," *Kino*, No. 8, Feb. 23, 1926, 1. Before the revolution, Sabinskii worked with Pathé Freres, a French film distribution and production company that came to Russia in 1904.

46. The FEKS group published its manifesto, *Ekstsentrism* (Ekstsentropolis, byvshii Petrograd, 1922), listing its models and methods. See *Ekstsentrizm*, 4.

47. J. T. Heil, "Theme and Stylization and the 'Literary Film' as Avant-Garde," *Avant-Garde* 5–6 (1991): 137–162.

48. Enve, "S. W. D.," *Kino*, No. 35–36, Sep. 6, 1927, 2.

49. *Kino*, No. 35–36, Sep. 6, 1927, 1.

50. According to a brief notice (*Kino*, No. 25, Jun. 21, 1927, 3), the completed film's first negative was destroyed by fire during transport from the laboratory to the studio. Re-shooting

began in December 1926 and the film was completed a second time at the beginning of June 1927.

51. For Russian intertitles to *SVD* and their English translation, see Jerry Tyrone Heil, "The Russian Literary Avant-Garde and the Cinema (1920s and 1930s): The Film Work of Isaak Babel' and Jurij Tynjanov" (Ph.D. diss., University of California, Berkeley, 1984), 340–352. Heil claims the film is missing one-third of its original footage (parts 2–6 are lost), and originally ran 80 minutes but now runs 50 minutes.

52. Grigorii Kozintsev," Tynianov v kino," in *Vospominaniia o Iu. Tynianove: portrety i vstrechi* (Moscow: Sovetskii pisatel', 1983), 269.

53. *S. V. D. (Soiuz velikogo dela). Sovkino. Metodicheskie materialy k filme.* ed. B. Levman. (Moscow: Izdatel'stvo Roskino, n.d.).

Six Rewriting Russian History:
Stalin Era Representations

1. Lidiia Libedinskaia, *"Zelenaia lampa" i mnogoe drugoe* (Moscow: Raduga, 2000), 29. Writer and wife of author Iu. N. Libedinskii, Libedinskaia (1921–2006) was the daughter of the poet Tatiana Vechorka neé Tolstaia (d. 1965).

2. David Brandenberger, *National Bolshevism: Stalinist Mass Culture and the Formation of Modern Russian National Identity, 1931–1956* (Cambridge, MA: Harvard University Press, 2002), 44.

3. Brandenberger, 40. See also Karen Petrone, *Life Has Become More Joyous, Comrades: Celebrations in the time of Stalin* (Bloomington, IN: Indiana University Press, 2000), on the purges' effect on the Academy edition of Pushkin's work. See V. M. Esipov, *Pushkin v zerkale mifov* (Moscow: Iazyki slavianskoi kul'tury, 2006), especially 127–172, on how the ideological demands of the Soviet era were reflected in the textological work of the Academy edition.

4. "The official rhetoric of the centennial also contained a thinly veiled threat against those who resisted cooperation with the state" (Petrone, 114–115).

5. Brintlinger, 170. For more detail on the mixed messages of jubilee rhetoric, see Jonathan Brooks Platt, "Feast in the Time of Terror: Stalinist Temporal Paradox and the 1937 Pushkin Jubilee" (Ph.D. dissertation, Columbia University, 2008) and Stephanie Sandler, *Commemorating Pushkin: Russia's Myth of a National Poet* (Stanford, CA: Stanford Univeristy Press, 2004), 107–119.

6. Petrone, 132–135; 115. Petrone claims the 1937 celebration "was the mirror image of the 1899 government version," 299 n. 12. See also Levitt, "Pushkin in 1899," 188.

7. The articles in *Pravda* include: D. Blagoi, "Literaturnye druz'ia Pushkina," Feb. 4; M. Nechkina, "Pushkin i dekabristy," Feb. 7; D. Kosarik, "Pushkinskaia Kamenka," and Iu. Tynianov, "Lichnost' Pushkina," Feb. 10. Bubnov and Luppol's speeches, the centerpieces of the official celebration, both refer to Pushkin's association with the Decembrists (For the speeches' stenograms, see *Pravda* No. 41 [7007], Feb. 11, 1937, 2). *Izvestiia* printed D. N. Kardovskii's drawing "Pushkin among the Decembrists at Kamenka" (1925) on Feb. 10 (No. 36 [6198], 2) and M. Solov'ev's painting "Pushkin reads poetry to the Decembrists," on Feb. 5 (no. 32 [6194], 3).

8. "Pered Pushkinskimi dniami," *Pravda*, Feb. 6, 1937 No. 36 (7002), 6.

9. Nechkina, "Pushkin i dekabristy," 4. Though Western scholarship questions the evidence of the Green Lamp group's political engagement, Soviet scholarship closely associates the society and the proto-Decembrist organization, the Union of Welfare. See B. L. Modzalevskii, "K istorii 'Zelenoi lampy," in *Dekabristy i ikh vremia*, vol. 1, 1928.

10. Tynianov, "Mnimyi Pushkin," 78–92.
11. *Puteshestvie v Arzrum* (Lenfilm, Komintern Leningrada, 1937), 16.
12. D. Zaslavskii, "Pushkin na ekrane," *Pravda*, Feb. 4, 1937, No. 35 (7000), 6. S. Ginzburg exclaims: "Pushkin in the scenario and film is one of the Decembrists' leaders, and reads poetry in convenient situations. Pushkin the artist has disappeared from the film." See his article, "Obraz Pushkina na ekrane 'Iunost poeta'," *Iskusstvo kino* 3 (Mar. 1937): 39. A. Novogrudskii levels the same charge in his review (see n. 13).
13. A. Novogrudskii, "Film o velikom grazhdanine," *Iskusstvo kino* 3 (Mar. 1937): 37.
14. I am indebted to Karen Petrone, who shared her archival research on the film with me (cf. RGALI [State Archive of Literature and Art], f. 2450, op. 2, d. 1636, l. 41 and l. 55, "Zasedanie rezhiserrskoi kollega Lenfil'ma").
15. *Iunost' poeta* (Lenfilm, Komintern Leningrada, 1937).
16. *"Iunost' poeta* rezhisserskii tsenarii," RGALI, f. 2450 op 2 d. 1635 l. 10; l. 60.
17. A. Slonimskii, *"Iunost' poeta*: literaturnyi tsenarii," *Iskusstvo kino* 2 (Feb. 1937): 23.
18. See Libedinskaia, 91–97.
19. Petrone asserts the celebration mobilized both the intelligentsia and the people; for the masses Pushkin became "instrumental in their transformation into cultured Soviet men and women" and provided a model for emulation (116–117).
20. Brandenberger, 67.
21. A. V. Shestakov, *Kratkii kurs istorii SSSR* (Moscow: Gosudarstvennoe Uchebno-Pedagogicheskoe Izdatel'stvo, 1937), 85.
22. Brandenberger, 54.
23. Ibid., 55.
24. For discussion of composers' use of the Short Course, see Stanley Krebs, *Soviet Composers and the Development of Soviet Music* (New York: W. W. Norton & Company, 1970), 53–59.
25. David Brandenberger, "Who Killed Pokrovskii? (the second time): The Prelude to the Denunciation of the Father of Soviet Marxist Historiography, January 1936," *Revolutionary Russia* 11, no. 1 (Jun. 1998): 69–71.
26. M. Nechkina, "Vosstanie dekabristov v kontseptsii M. N. Pokrovskogo," in *Protiv istoricheskoi kontseptsii M. N. Pokrovskogo* (Moscow-Leningrad: Izdatel'stvo Akademii nauk SSSR, 1939), 303.
27. Nechkina, "Vosstanie dekabristov," 336.
28. *Istoriia SSSR*, ed. M. V. Nechkina (Moscow-Leningrad, Gosudarstvennoe izdatel'stvo politicheskoi literatury, 1949), 2: 152.
29. E. S. Seniavskaia, *1941–1945 Frontovoe pokolenie: istoriko-psikhologicheskoe issledovanie* (Moscow: Institut rossiiskoi istorii RAN, 1995), 164; 198–203, in Jeffrey Brooks, *Thank You, Comrade Stalin: Soviet Public Culture from Revolution to Cold War* (Princeton: Princeton University Press, 2000), 196.
30. Naum Korzhavin, *Vremena. Izbrannoe* (Frankfurt: Possev-Verlag, 1976), 13. All further citations will be to this volume.
31. Korzhavin immigrated to the United States in 1973.
32. Cited in Margaret Ziolkowski, *Literary Exorcisms of Stalinism: Russian Writers and the Soviet Past* (Columbia, SC: Camden House, 1998), 164. For the title of his poem, Solzhenitsyn used the Soviet name for the main road to Siberia by which convicts were transported to their places of imprisonment. Its prerevolutionary name was Vladimirskii trakt or Vladimirka. For more on Solzhenitsyn's work, see the following chapter.
33. Several memoirists recall jokes about how long Shaporin took to complete the opera. M. Chulaki relates the following lines (from "The History of Music from Adam to Aram"): "Oborin has already become famous / Shaporin was writing "Polina Gebl" / Deborin was already debunked / Shaporin was writing "Polina Gebl'," etc., etc." (E. Grosheva [ed.], *Iurii Aleksandrovich Shaporin: Stat'i, Materialy. Vospominaniia* [Moscow: Sovetskii kompozitor, 1989], 311).

34. Chulaki said the costumes and scenery disintegrated after so many performances and the gifted artists who performed the main roles retired (Ibid., 316). E. Svetlanov said the opera disappeared for "unknown and unmotivated reasons" and that its loss "inflicted injury on our art" (Ibid., 330).

35. Krebs, 137. See also E. D. Tolstaia, "L. V. Shaporina v rabote nad operoi 'Dekabristami," in Kiianskaia, 532–549. Tolstaia suggests that Shaporin's strained family circumstances impeded progress on the opera.

36. S. Levit, *Iurii Shaporin: ocherk zhizni i tvorchestva* (Moscow: Nauka, 1964), 118.

37. N. Malkov, "Polina Gebl'," *Zhizn' iskusstva* 12 (1926): 10, cited in Levit, *Iurii Shaporin*, 119.

38. B. Gorev, "Pamiati dekabristov," *Rabochii teatr*, Jan. 5 1926, No. 1 (68), 12.

39. Levit, 120.

40. V. Bogdanov-Berezovskii, "Stareishina sovetskoi muziki," in Grosheva, 302.

41. The other romances to rival theirs were the Volkonskys and Ivashevs. See Herzen's *Byloe i dumy* (8:58–59) for a romanticized version of Camille LeDantu and Vasilii Ivashev's courtship.

42. Annenkova's memoirs were first published in *Russkaia starina* in 1888 and reprinted in 1915 as a separate book by Prometei press. The memoirs were excerpted and republished during the 1925 centennial and again in 1929. Knowing aspects of the story by hearsay, Alexandre Dumas wrote a novel loosely based on the romance entitled *Le Maître d'Armes* (1851). Dumas's novel was read avidly by the Russian elite, purportedly including the Empress, despite the fact that it was banned in Russia (Alexandre Dumas, *En Russie*, 607, in Elizabeth Beaujour, "Dumas's Decembrists: *Le Maître d'armes* and the Memoirs of Pauline Annenkova," *Russian Review* 59, no. 1 [Jan. 2000]: 39). Beaujour contends that Annenkova's memoirs were written to rebut Dumas's novel.

43. For example, Shchegolev's "O Russkikh zhenshchinakh Nekrasova," published 1904, reprinted in *Perventsy russkoi svobody* (M: Sovremennik, 1987), 169–200. Shchegolev also published on the legal status of the wives in 1906. See Iu. N. Emel'ianov, *P. E. Shchegolev—istorik russkogo revoliutsionnogo dvizheniia* (M: Nauka, 1990), 428–429.

44. Emel'ianov, 428. For more on Shchegolev's work on the Decembrist movement, see especially 74–145.

45. James Bakst, *History of Russian-Soviet Music* (New York: Dodd, Mead and Co., 1966), 360.

46. I rely upon Bakst and Lyudmila Polyakova's *Soviet Music* (Moscow: Foreign Languages Publishers) for my review of 1920s-1930s' operas.

47. Bakst, 390 n. 18. The quote is from S. Prokofiev, *Rastzvet iskusstva*, 97–98, cited in T. Govdanova, *Natsionalnorusskie traditsii v muzyke S. S. Prokofiev* (Moscow: Sovetskii kompozitor, 1961), 5.

48. For more on socialist realism in Soviet music, see Krebs, 51–59, and Masayuki Yasuhara, "The Concept of Socialist Realism in Soviet Music," in *Socialist Realism Revisited* (1994), 73–83.

49. This montage corresponded to the libretto's second version and was excerpted as 17 different numbers. See S. Katonova, "Istoriia sozdaniia opery 'Dekabristy' Iu. A. Shaporina," *Uchenye zapiski. Sektor muzyki* (Leningrad: Gosudarstvennyi nauchno–issledovatel'skii institut teatra, muzyka i kinematografii, 1958), 2: 142–143.

50. B. Bogdanov-Beresovskii, *Vecherniaia krasnaia gazeta*, Oct. 3, 1932, quoted in Levit, 311.

51. Levit, 118; 304–319.

52. The original opera consisted of three acts with a total of seven scenes as per the libretto's second version; the first version was comprised of nine scenes (Katonova, 138–139, quote from 139).

53. Levit, 308.

54. Iu. Shaporin, "Mysli ob opernoi dramaturgii," *Sovetskaia muzyka* 10 (1940): 15.

55. Katonova, 147.

56. Levit, 308–311.
57. This recommendation was made at the Bolshoi as per the meeting minutes of Feb. 13, 1954 (Katonova, 147).
58. Katonova, 149.
59. See reviews by Georgii Khubov and Vl. Zakharov, respectively, in *Pravda*, Jul. 2, 1953, 3, and *Izvestiia*, Jul. 4, 1953, No. 156 (11227), 2.
60. E. Grosheva, "Traditsii vysokogo patriotizma: opera 'Dekabristy' v Moskve i Leningrade," *Teatr* 10 (Oct. 1953), 82.
61. Prince Dmitrii Aleksandrovich Shepin-Rostovskii (1798–1858) served as staff captain of the Moscow Regiment Life-Guards. He did not belong to the secret society though he attended the organizational meeting held at Ryleev's on the eve of the uprising and participated in the revolt on Senate Square. He was judged among the first category (*pervyi razriad*) of conspirators and sentenced to lifetime penal servitude in Siberia. His sentence subsequently was shortened to 20 years. There is no evidence that he had a fiancée or wife who followed him. See *Dekabristy: biograficheskii sbornik*, 205.
62. These lines come from an anonymous poem written in the 1830s that circulated widely in manuscript form at the time. See *PS*, 1:43.
63. E. Grosheva, " 'Dekabristy' (Opera Iu. Shaporina)," *Sovetskaia muzyka* 8 (Aug. 1953): 11.
64. Krebs, 172.
65. N. Sinkovskaia, "Rol' leitmotivov v "Dekabristakh" Shaporina," in Shaporin, *Literaturnoe nasledie*, 44.

Seven   The Decembrists and Dissidence: Myth and Anti-Myth from the 1960s–1980s

1. Dmitrii Sukharev (ed.), *Avtorskaia pesnia: antologiia* (Ekaterinburg: U-Faktoriia, 2002), 371. Okudzhava wrote this song in response to a request from a Moscow journal to discuss the nature of his writing. See B. Okudzhava, *65 pesen* (Ann Arbor: Ardis, 1980), 161.
2. Andrei Sinyavsky, *Soviet Civilization: A Cultural History* (New York: Arcade Publishing, 1990), 229.
3. Lotman, "Theater and Theatricality," 141–164.
4. Lotman, "The Decembrist," 71–123.
5. Lotman, "The Decembrist," 81.
6. Ibid., 116.
7. Ibid., 119.
8. Catherine Depretto-Genty, "N. Ja. Èjdel'man," *Revue des Étude Slaves* 62, no. 3 (1990): 708.
9. Katerina Clark, "Changing Historical Paradigms in Soviet Culture," in *Late Soviet Culture: From Perestroika to Novostroika* (Durham, NC: Duke University Press, 1993), 298.
10. Elena Mikhailova, "Natan Eidel'man: 'Volshebnoi palochki v istorii ne byvaet," *Daugava* 2 (1987): 102.
11. Hugh Ragsdale, "Russian Popular History in Fact and Fiction: Three Contemporary Styles," *Soviet Union/Union Sovietique* 17, No. 3 (1990): 282–286.
12. Ragsdale, 286.
13. Ludmilla Alexeyeva and Paul Goldberg, *The Thaw Generation: Coming of Age in the Post-Stalin Era* (Pittsburgh, PA: University of Pittsburgh Press, 1993), 242. Eidel'man inspired Nazarenko to use historical paintings to reflect contemporary concerns. Nazarenko's *The Decembrists. Chernigov Uprising* uses montage to elide different times and spaces, providing multiple viewpoints on the revolt and its era but also suggesting its links with the present. See Susan Reid, "The 'art of memory': retrospectivism in Soviet painting of the Brezhnev

era," in *Art of the Soviets: Painting, Sculpture and Architecture in a One-Party State, 1917–1992*, ed. Matthew Collerne Brown and Brandon Taylor (Manchester: Manchester University Press, 1993), 161–187.

14. Ziolkowski, *Literary Exorcisms* 166. Ziolkowski discusses Evtushenko's, Kushev's and other poets' works that have also been analyzed in Jay Bergman's article, "Soviet Dissidents on the Russian Intelligentsia, 1956–1985: The Search for a Usable Past," *Russian Review* 51 (Jan. 1992): 16–35.

15. Ziolkowski, *Literary Exorcisms* 153.

16. Alexeyeva and Goldberg, *Literary Exorcisms* 34–35.

17. Ibid., 97.

18. Ziolkowski, 163.

19. Alexander Galich, *Kogda ia vernius': Polnoe sobranie stikhov i pesen* (Frankfurt: Possev-Verlag, 1981), 29.

20. Alexeyeva and Goldberg, 218.

21. Vladimir Bukovsky, *To Build a Castle: My Life as a Dissenter* trans. Michael Scammell (New York: Viking Press, 1978), 142.

22. Fedor Razzakov, *Zvezdnye tragedii: zagadki, sud'by i gibeli*, 82–102, as excerpted on www.bard.ru/galich.

23. D. Andreeva, "Rossiia serdtse ne zabudet," *Grani* 109, cited in Galich, 14.

24. The novel circulated in samizdat and was well-known in translation abroad before its Russian publication in 1990.

25. Alexander Solzhenitsyn, *First Circle* (New York: Harper and Row, 1968), 215.

26. See Ziolkowski, 162–65 and Bergman, 25–33.

27. Ludmilla Alexeyeva, *Soviet Dissent: Contemporary Movements for National, Religious, and Human Rights* (Middletown, CT: Wesleyan University Press, 1987), 358–359. These actions in 1975 recall the 1964 group of Muscovite dissidents honoring the Decembrists called the "Ryleev Club." By 1968 that group began to publish a samizdat journal, *Russkoe slovo*, modeled along the lines of the Petersburg literary journal (Bergman, 21–25).

28. Irina Prussakova, "Bard, Khroniker, Letopisets," *Neva* 7 (1994): 266.

29. Evgenii Dvornikov, "A Talk with the poet B. Okudzhava," *Soviet Literature* 4, no. 493 (1989): 123.

30. Prussakova, 270.

31. Bulat Okudzhava, *Bednyi Avrosimov* (Moscow: PAN, 1999), 44. All further references will be made to this edition and included in the text.

32. "S istoriei ne rasstaius', *Literaturnaia gazeta,* May. 23, 1979, 4–5.

33. Galina Belaia, introduction to B. Sh. Okudzhava, *Izbrannye proizvedeniia* (Moscow: Sovremennik, 1989), 14.

34. The work's publication abroad did not create a scandal though it also circulated widely during the era in manuscript. When finally published in Russia during *glasnost* it was censored for obscene language and some objectionable scenes. See Helena Goscilo, "Introduction: A Nation in Search of its Authors," *Glasnost': An Anthology of Russian Literature Under Gorbachev* (Ann Arbor: Ardis, 1990), xxxi, xxxiii and Anindita Banerjee, "Venedikt Vasil'evich Erofeev," *Russian Writers since 1980* (Dictionary of Literary Biography, v. 285. Gale, 2003), 75.

35. Venedikt Erofeev, *Moscow to the End of the Line* trans. H. William Tjalsma (Evanston, IL: Northwestern University Press, 1992), 81.

36. Banerjee, 73. Vagrius re-issued the novel in 2000 in a separate edition as well as in Erofeev's collected works.

37. Anatolii Vishevsky, *Soviet Literary Culture in the 1970s* (Gainesville, FL: University of Florida Press, 1993), 5.

38. Ibid., 7.

39. Korzhavin plays on the name of Herzen's journal, *The Bell (Kolokol)* in this line.

40. This line paraphrases Lenin's famous response to his brother's execution for the assassination of Tsar Alexander II.

41. Here Korzhavin refers to Lenin's well-known article "Three sources, three component parts of Marxism" ("Tri istochnika, tri sostavnykh chasti marxizma," 1913).

42. Korzhavin, 379–380. This edition includes an author's note: "The story is not about the individual Herzen, for whom the author feels reverence and love, but only about his contemporary official reputation."

43. Okudzhava's fascination with the Decembrists continues into his later historical fiction, specifically in *The Adventures of Shipov (Pokhozhdeniia Shipova,* 1971), where he depicts the twisted artifice of Russian society and the devastation that the Decembrists' families and their sympathizers experienced.

44. Alexeyeva and Goldberg, 240.

45. Conferences took place in Irkutsk, Chita, Moscow, Tambov, Leningrad, Petrovsk-Zabaikalsk, Kiakhta, and Kemerovo. See A. N. Granina, E. M. Darevskaia, O. V. Shevereva, "Bibliograficheskii spisok gazetnykh statei, posviashchennykh 150-iu vosstaniia dekabristov" in *Sibir' i dekabristy,* 252–266.

46. "Oh victims of irrational thought! You hoped that your meager blood would perhaps be enough to melt the eternal snow! Hardly smoldering, it flared on the age-old mass of ice, the iron winter exhaled—and not a trace remained!" M.V. Nechkina, "Delo dekabristov," *Pravda,* Dec. 24, 1975, No. 363 (20967), 13.

47. Ibid.

48. Quoted in S. Koval', N. Tenditnik, "Pravda istorii—pravda obraza," *Vostochno-Sibirskaia pravda,* No. 17 (16706), Jan. 22, 1976, 4.

49. M. Bilinkis, "Zhenshchinam Rossii posviachaetsia," *Smena,* Dec. 19, 1975, 4.

50. Bilinkis, 4.

51. Vadim Erlikhman, "K cherty podrobnosti!," *Paradox,* Nov. 30, 2003, 14.

52. Motyl' asked Okudzhava to co-write the film scenario, but Okudzhava declined though he agreed to pen the musical motif for the Annenkov story-line. See Vladimir Motyl', "Poka zemlia eshche vertitsia," *Literaturnoe obozrenie* 3, No. 269 (1998): 21.

53. Koval', Tenditnik, 4.

54. "K 150-letiu so dnia vosstaniia dekabristov na ekrane," *Znamia kommunizma,* Dec. 28, 1975, 4.

55. Motyl' does not specify what impeded approval. See Oleg Dulenin, "Vladimir Motyl': Bez kharaktera v kinematograf sovat'sia nechego," *Kultura* No. 10, Mar 11, 2003, 16.

Eight   The Decembrists' DeSacralization during the *Glasnost* and Post–Soviet Eras

1. Cited in Irina Glushchenko, "Zhivoe i mertvoe," *Nezavisimaia gazeta* (EVNG), no. 9, Jan. 17, 1996, electronic version.

2. In R. W. Davies's words, "sometimes the earlier hostility to the tsarist period has even been replaced by a somewhat naïve enthusiasm" (*Soviet History in the Gorbachev Revolution* [Bloomington, IN: Indiana University Press, 1989], 11).

3. Eidel'man's principal works during this period were: *Tvoi vosemnadtsatyi vek* (Moscow: Kniga, 1986), *A. S. Pushkin: iz biografii i tvorchestva* (Moscow: Khudozhestvennaia literatura, 1987), *Obrechennyi otriad* (Moscow: Sovetskii pisatel', 1987, which contained a new edition of his 1970 book *Lunin*), *Russkii 1789* (1989), *Revoliutsiia sverkhu v Rossii* (Moscow: Kniga, 1989), and, posthumously, *Byt; mozhet za khrebtom Kavkaza: russkaia literatura i obshchestvennaia mysl' pervoi poloviny XIX v., kavkazskii kontekst* (Moscow: Nauka, 1990).

4. Michael Khlebnikov, a descendant of Ivan Pushchin, told me his impressions of this trip.
5. Mikhail Kuraev, *Night Patrol and other Stories* trans. Margareta O. Thompson (Durham, NC: Duke University Press, 1994), 85–86. All further references will be included in the text.
6. Goscilo, xxxv–xxxvi.
7. John B. Dunlop, *The Rise of Russia and the Fall of the Soviet Empire* (Princeton: Princeton University Press, 1995), 188.
8. Vladimir Sadovnikov, "V preddverii godovshchiny vosstaniia: dvizahenie dekabristov i sovremennost'," *Khronos*, http://www.hrono.info/statii/2004/sad_dekab.html, last accessed Mar. 29, 2009.
9. Elizabeth Rich, "Introduction: Russian Literature after Perestroika," *South Central Review* 12, Nos. 3–4 (Autumn–Winter 1995): 1.
10. Kama Ginkas and John Freedman, *Provoking Theater: Kama Ginkas Directs* (Hanover, NH: Smith and Kraus, 2003), 152.
11. Anatoly Smeliansky, *The Russian Theatre after Stalin* (Cambridge: Cambridge University Press, 1999), 177.
12. Smeliansky, 177.
13. For my description of the performance, I rely upon John Freedman, "Big Names Keep Moscow Moving: The 1995–1996 Season," *Slavic and East European Performance* 16, No. 3 (Fall 1996): 19–20.
14. Glushchenko, "Zhivoe i mertvoe."
15. Ginkas, 10.
16. Glushchenko, "Zhivoe i mertvoe."
17. Ibid.
18. Ginkas, 10–11.
19. *1825-i god: Zagovor: Risovannaia Kniga* (Moscow: Progress, 1990).
20. "The hostile whirlwinds blow above us / Dark forces evilly oppress us."
21. Zara Abdullaeva, "Popular Culture," in Dmitri N. Shalin (ed.), *Russian Culture at the Crossroads: Paradoxes of Postcommunist Consciousness* (New York: Westview Press, 1996), 234.
22. Gary Saul Morson, *Narrative and Freedom: The Shadows of Time* (New Haven, CT: Yale University Press, 1994), 148.
23. D. Shalin, "Intellectual Culture," in *Russian Culture*, 43.
24. Jim Collins, *Uncommon Cultures: Popular Culture and Post-Modernism*, New York: Routledge, 1989, 75.
25. V. Razdishevskii, "L'va Tolstogo—na mylo!," *Literaturnaia gazeta*, no. 13 (5595), Mar. 27, 1996.
26. Ibid.
27. Morson, 149.
28. Ibid., 118.
29. Ibid., 151.
30. Ibid.
31. Gleb Uspenskii, in Alessandra Stanley, "'War and Peace: the Sequel: Scholars see Scarlett," *New York Times*, Mar. 5, 1996, A4.
32. Ibid.
33. *Knizhnoe obozrenie*, no. 12, Mar. 19, 1996.
34. Several scholars in Russia during the summer of 1996 told me they heard a great deal about the literary scandal though I have not found other printed sources.
35. Vasil'eva stated, "It's not Tolstoy," but "People are stupid" (Stanley, A4).
36. Detective novels by Aleksandra Marinina (pseudonym of Maria Alexeyeva, a crime investigator who attained the rank of lieutenant colonel in the police force prior to resigning

to write novels full time) and historical detective novels of Boris Akunin (pseudonym of Grigorii Chkhartishvili, a translator of Japanese literature), have been described as "pulp for intellectuals." See *Russian Writers Since 1980*, 4.
37. Frederick Starr, "Conclusion: Toward a Post-Soviet Society," in *Russian Culture*, 316.
38. Ibid., 317.
39. "Dekabristy u paradnogo pod"ezda," *Limonka* online, Official site of the National Bolshevik Party, http://www.nbp-info.ru/subs/limonka/34_dekabristy.html. Last accessed Mar. 29, 2009.
40. Dmitrii Bykov and Maksim Chertanov have not attempted to conceal their authorship. Brein Daun, *Kod Onegina* (St. Petersburg: Amfora), 2006.
41. So far Vagrius released the following works on the Decembrists and their contemporaries: *Lunin, Bol'shoi Zhanno, Gran' vekov* (2004); *Apostol Sergei, Pervyi Dekabrist, Pushkin i dekabristy* (2005); *Prekrasen nash soiuz, Sekretnaia dinastia* (2006) and *V'evarum* (2007).
42. A. Iu. Shcherbatov, *Dekabristy: Zagovor protiv Rossii* (St. Petersburg: Neva, 2005) and Vladimir Briukhanov, *Mify i pravda o vosstanii dekabristov* (Moscow: Iauza, Eksmo, 2005). Manilov was a landowner in Gogol's *Dead Souls* who was characterized by his overly sweet, obliging behavior. Cf. Lenin's charge of Manilovism against bourgeois democrats in his 1905 essay "Revolutionary Office Routine and Revolutionary Activism," available online at: http://www.marxists.org/archive/lenin/works/1905/nov/20.htm#bkV10E030.
43. V. M. Bokova, "'Bolnoi skoree zhiv, chem mertv.' Zametki ob otechestvennom dekabristovedenii 1990-x godov," *14 dekabria 1825 goda* 4 (2001): 526–529. Bokova argues the term should be considered a biographical and not an ideological marker and should be limited to those who: (1) actually participated in either the December 14 or the Chernigov uprising; and/or (2) who actively belonged to a Decembrist group and not to one of the several other secret societies which might have been tangentially related. Bokova's *Epokha tainikh obshchestv* (Moscow: Realia press, 2003), further develops this point and provides valuable material on the wide variety of organizational groups in the early nineteenth century.
44. O. I. Kiianskaia, "'Nos amis de quatorze,' ili Dekabristovedenie i dekabristovedy XXI veka" in Kiianskaia, 9.
45. Kiianskaia, 11.
46. Clark, "Changing Historical Paradigms," 289.
47. Vladimir Berelovich, "Sovremennye uchebniki istorii. Mnogolikaia istina ili ocherednaia natsional'naia idea?" *Neprikosnovennyi zapas: debaty o politike i kul'ture* No. 24 (4/2002) http://www.nzonline.ru/index.phtml?aid=25010918.
48. Sherlock, 169 and 172. Sherlock cites Putin's address to historians at the Russian National Library on 27 November 2003. See 238 n. 72.
49. Orlando Figes, "Putin vs. the Truth," *New York Review of Books* 56, no. 7, Apr. 30, 2009, online edition, http://www.nybooks.com/articles/22642.
50. Ibid, and Sherlock, 179.

Epilogue: "The Decembrists Are Our All"

1. See http://www.gleza.livejournal.com/215341.html.
2. http://gzt.newsbis.ru/newizv/49931-novye-dekabristy-.-v-moskve-i-sankt-peterburge.html
3. Kiianskaia, 9 (my emphasis).
4. See http://www.og-irk.ru/vp97/v_irkutsk_priehali_potomki_dekabristov/view_556.html; http://www.newsprom.ru/print.shtml?lot_id=119644115387870; http://temadnya.com/news/V-Zabaikale-ptomki-dekabristov-provodjat-akciju-v-pamjat-predkov/.

5. S. E. Erlikh, "Dekabristy.ru. Istoriia v kiberprostranstve: pamiatnye imena i mesta pamiati," in Kiianskaia, 550–619.

6. Anecdote from Jul. 17, 2006. See also anecdotes dated Aug. 20, 2006, Jul. 19, 2005 on http://www.bibo.kz/anekdoti/89471-iz-shkolnykh-sochinenijj-dekabristy-vozbudili. html.

7. Herzen, *PSS*, 12:54, cited in Venturi, 3.

8. My thanks to Edward Dumanis and Liza Ginzburg, both of whom recounted this anecdote in 2000–2001.

9. The conference was sponsored by the St. Petersburg Division of the Russian Imperial Society and the Russian General Military Society with the participation of the editor of the newspaper *Monarchist (Monarkhist)*. See http://www.dekabristy.narod.ru for conference proceedings.

REFERENCES

Bibliographies

Chentsov, N. M. "Iubileinaia literatura o dekabristakh 1924–1926." *Vestnik Kommunisticheskoi Akademii.* Moscow: Gosudarstvennoe izdatel'stvo, 1927.

———. *Vosstanie dekabristov.* Moscow: Gosudarstvennoe izdatel'stvo, 1929.

Dekabristy: biograficheskii spravochnik. Moscow: Nauka, 1988.

Dekabristy i Sibir': bibliograficheskii ukazatel'. Irkutsk: Izdatel'stvo Irkutskogo universiteta, 1985.

Dvizhenie dekabristov: Ukazatel' literatury 1928–1959. Moscow: Izdatel'stvo vsesoiuznoe knizhnoi palaty, 1960.

Dvizhenie dekabristov: ukazatel' literatury 1960–1976. Moscow: Nauka, 1983.

Perventsy svobody: k 165-letiiu vosstaniia dekabristov: rekomendatel'nyi bibliograficheskii spravochnik. Moscow: Knizhnaia palata, 1989.

Selivanov, Vl. *Dekabristy, 1825–1925: sistematicheskii ukazatel' russkoi literatury.* Leningrad: Golos, 1925.

Primary Sources

Algasov, V. A. *Dekabrizm i dekabristy: 1825–1925. Khrestomatiia.* Kiev: Gosudarstvennoe izdatel'stvo Ukrainy, 1925.

Azadovskii, M. A., ed. *Vospominaniia Bestuzhevykh.* Moscow–Leningrad: Izdatel'stvo Akademii Nauk, 1951.

Bozherianov, I. *Dekabristy: khudozhestvennyi al'bom.* Petrograd: Tipografiia "Rus," 1917.

Bukovsky, Vladimir. *To Build a Castle: My Life as a Dissenter,* trans. Michael Scammell. NY: Viking Press, 1978.

Donesenie sledstvennoi komissii. Pechatano po vysochaishemu pozvoleniiu v voennoi tipografii glavnogo staba ego Imperatorskago Velichestva, 1826.

Dostoevsky, F. M. *Polnoe sobranie sochinenii v 30-ti tomakh.* Leningrad: Nauka, 1972–1985.

Erofeev, Venedikt. *Moscow to the End of the Line,* trans. H. William Tjalsma. Evanston, IL: Northwestern University Press, 1992.

Ginkas, Kama, and John Freedman. *Provoking Theater: Kama Ginkas Directs.* Hanover, NH: Smith and Kraus, 2003.

Herzen, Alexander. *Polnoe sobranie sochinenii*. Moscow: Izdatel'stvo Akademii Nauk SSSR, 1959.

Herzen, Alexander. *Poliarnaia zvezda, 1855*, facsimile ed. Moscow: Nauka, 1966.

Iakushkin, I. D. *Memuary, stat'i, dokumenty*. Irkutsk: Vostochno-Sibirskoe knizhnoe izdatel'stvo, 1993.

————. *Zapiski*. St. Petersburg: Obshchestvennaia pol'za, 1905.

Ivanovskii, A. V. *Vospominaniia kinorezhissera*. Moscow: Iskusstvo, 1967.

Kaverin, V., ed. *Iurii Tynianov: Pisatel' i uchenyi*. *Vospominaniia, razmyshleniia, vstrechi*. Moscow: Molodaia gvardiia, 1966.

Korf, M., Baron. *Vosshestvie na prestol Imperatora Nikolaia I-go*. 5th ed. 3rd for the public. St. Petersburg: Tipografiia II-ogo otdeleniia sobstvennoi ego Imp. Vel. Kantselarii, 1857.

————. "Iz zapiski barona M. A. Korfa." *Russkaia starina* 101 (Mar. 1900): 545–588.

Korzhavin, Naum. *Vremena*. *Izbrannoe*. Frankfurt: Possev-Verlag, 1976.

Krupskaia, N. K. *Vospominaniia o Lenine*. Moscow: Partizdat, 1932.

Kuraev, Mikhail. *Night Patrol and Other Stories*, trans. Margareta O. Thompson. Durham, NC: Duke University Press, 1994.

Lenin, V. I. *Polnoe sobranie sochinenii*. 5th ed. Moscow: Institut Marksizma i Leninizma, 1958–1965.

Libedinskaia, Lidiia. *"Zelenaia lampa" i mnogoe drugoe*. Moscow: Raduga, 2000.

Merezhkovskii, Dmitrii. *Sobranie sochinenii v 4-ti tomakh*. Moscow: Pravda, 1990.

————. *Perventsy svobody: istoriia vosstaniia 14 dekabria 1825g*. Petrograd: Narodnaia vlast', 1917.

Mezhdutsarstvie 1825 goda i vosstanie dekabristov v perepiske i memuarakh chlenov tsarskoi sem'i. Moscow-Leningrad: Gosudarstvennoe izdatel'stvo, 1926.

Nekrasov, N. A. *Polnoe sobranie sochinenii i pisem*. Moscow: Gosudarstvennoe izdatel'stvo khudozhestvennoi literatury, 1949.

Ogarev, N. P. *Izbrannye sotsial'no-politicheskie i filosofskie proizvedenniia*. t. 1–2. Moscow: Gosudarstvennoe izdatel'stvo politicheskoi literatury, 1952.

————. *Stikhotvoreniia i poemy*. Leningrad: Sovietskii pisatel', 1956.

Okudzhava, B. *Bednyi Avrosimov*. Moscow: PAN, 1999.

————. *Izbrannye proizvedeniia: v 2-kh t*. Moscow: Sovremennik, 1989.

Pisateli-dekabristy v vospominaniiakh sovremennikov. Moscow: Khudozhestvennaia literatura, 1980.

Posledovanie blagodarstvennago i molebnago peniia ko Gospodu Bogu, darovavshemu svoiu pomoshch' Blagohestneishemu Gosudariu nashemu imperatoru Nikolaiu Pavlovichu, na isproverzhenie kramoly, ugrozhavshiia mezhdousobiem i bestviiami Gosudarstvu Vserossiiskomu. Moscow: Sinodal'naia Tipografiia, 1826.

Pushchin, I. I. *Zapiski o Pushkine, Pis'ma*. Moscow: Pravda, 1989.

Pushkin, A. S. *Polnoe sobranie sochinenii*. Moscow: Izdatel'stvo Akademii Nauk, 1937–1959.

Rozen, A. E. *Zapiski dekabrista*. Irkutsk: Vostochno-Sibirskoe knizhnoe izdatel'stvo, 1984.

Shestakov, A. V. *Kratkii kurs istorii SSSR*. Moscow: Gosudarstvennoe uchebno-pedagogicheskoe izdatel'stvo: 1937.

Shteingel', V. I. *Sochineniia i pis'ma*. Irkutsk: Vostochno-Sibirskoe knizhnoe izdatel'stvo, 1985.

Staroi, Vasilii. *P'er i Natasha*. Moscow: Vagrius, 1996.

S. V. D. (Soiuz velikogo dela). Sovkino. Metodicheskie materialy k filme. Moscow: Izdatel'stvo Roskino, undated.

Tolstoi, L. N. *Polnoe sobranie sochinenii v 90-ti tomakh (iubileinoe)*. Moscow-Leningrad: Goslitizdat, 1925–1958.

Tynianov, Iu. N. *Kiukhlia, rasskazy*. Voronezh: Izdatel'stvo Voronezhskogo universiteta, 1987.

————. *Sochineniia v trekh tomakh*. Moscow: Terra, 1994.

Trubetskoi, S. P. *Zapiski dekabrista kniazia S. P. Trubetskogo.* St. Petersburg: Vsemirnyi vestnik, 1906.

Ustav Obshchestva Pamiati dekabristov. Petrograd: M. G. Mazur, 1917.

Veresaev, V. *Pushkin v zhizni.* Moscow: Novaia Moskva, 1926.

Secondary Sources

14oe dekabria: sbornik k stoletiu vosstaniia dekabristov. Leningrad: Gosudarstvennoe izdatel'stvo, 1925.

14oe dekabria 1825 goda i ego istolkovateli: Gertsen i Ogarev protiv Barona Korfa. Moscow: Nauka, 1994.

Alexeyeva, Ludmilla. *Soviet Dissent: Contemporary Movements for National, Religious, and Human Rights.* Middletown, CT: Wesleyan University Press, 1987.

———, and Paul Goldberg. *The Thaw Generation: Coming of Age in the Post-Stalin Era.* Pittsburgh, PA: University of Pittsburgh Press, 1993.

Arkhipova, A.V. *Literaturnoe delo dekabristov.* Leningrad: Nauka, 1987.

Azadovskii, M. K. *Stranitsy istorii dekabrizma.* Irkutsk: Vostochno-Sibirskoe knizhnoe izdatel'stvo, 1992.

Bagby, Lewis. *Alexander Bestuzhev-Marlinsky and Russian Byronism.* University Park, PA: The Pennsylvania State University Press, 1995.

Bakst, James. *History of Russian-Soviet Music.* New York: Dodd, Mead and Co., 1966.

Bazanov, V. G. *Literaturnoe nasledie dekabristov.* Leningrad: Nauka, 1975.

———. *Ocherki dekabristskoi literatury: publitsistika, proza, kritika.* Moscow: Khudozhestvennaia literatura, 1953.

Beaujour, Elizabeth. "Dumas's Decembrists: *Le Maitre d'armes* and the Memoirs of Pauline Annenkova." *Russian Review* 59 (Jan. 2000): 38–51.

Berelovich, Vladimir. "Sovremennye uchebniki istorii. Mnogolikaia istina ili ocheredniaia natsional'naia idea?" *Neprikosnovennyi zapas: debaty o politike i kul'ture* No. 24 (4/2002): online edition. http://www.nzonline.ru/index.phtml?aid=25010918.

Bergman, Jay. "Soviet Dissidents on the Russian Intelligentsia, 1956–1985: The Search for a Usable Past." *Russian Review* 51 (Jan. 1992): 16–35.

Bethea, David, ed. *Pushkin Today.* Bloomington, IN: Indiana University Press, 1993.

Bokova, V. M. " 'Bolnoi skoree zhiv, chem mertv.' Zametki ob otechestvennom dekabristove-denii 1990-x godov." *14 dekabria 1825 goda* 4 (2001): 497–561.

Brandenberger, David. *National Bolshevism: Stalinist Mass Culture and the Formation of Modern Russian National Identity, 1931–1956.* Cambridge, MA: Harvard University Press, 2002.

———. "Who Killed Pokrovskii? (the second time): The Prelude to the Denunciation of the Father of Soviet Marxist Historiography, January 1936." *Revolutionary Russia* 11, no. 1 (Jun. 1998): 69–71.

Brintlinger, Angela. *Writing a Usable Past: Russian Literary Culture, 1917–1937.* Evanston, IL: Northwestern University Press, 2000.

Brooks, Jeffrey. *Thank You, Comrade Stalin: Soviet Public Culture from Revolution to Cold War.* Princeton, NJ: Princeton University Press, 2000.

Burbank, Jane. *Intelligentsia and Revolution: Russian Views of Bolshevism, 1917–1922.* Oxford: Oxford University Press, 1986.

Cherniavsky, Michael. *Tsar and People: Studies in Russian Myths.* New Haven, CT: Yale University Press, 1961.

Clark, Katerina. *Petersburg: Crucible of Cultural Revolution*. Cambridge, MA: Harvard University Press, 1995.

———. "Changing Historical Paradigms in Soviet Culture." in *Late Soviet Culture: From Perestroika to Novostroika*. Durham, NC: Duke University Press, 1993.

Debreczeny, Paul. "'Zhitie Aleksandra Boldinskogo': Pushkin's Elevation to Sainthood in Soviet Culture." *South Atlantic Quarterly* 90, no. 2 (Spring 1991): 269–292.

Dekabristy: k stoletiu zagovora, 1825–1925. Moscow: Molodaia gvardiia, 1925.

Depretto-Genty, Catherine. "N. Ja. Èjdel'man." *Revue des Étude Slaves* 62, no. 3, (1990): 708.

Druzhinin, N. M. "S. P. Trubetskoi kak memuarist." *Dekabristy i ikh vremia*, t. 2, Moscow: Izdatel'stvo Vsesoiuznoe obshchestva politkatorzhan i ssyl'noposelentsev, 1932.

Dunlop, John B. *The Rise of Russia and the Fall of the Soviet Empire*. Princeton, NJ: Princeton University Press, 1995.

Dvinianov, B. N. *Mech i lira: Ocherk zhizni i tvorchestva P. F. Iakubovicha*. Moscow: Nauka, 1967.

Dvornikov, Evgenii. "A Talk with the poet B. Okudzhava." *Soviet Literature* 4, no. 493, (1989): 123.

Eidel'man, Natan. *Pushkin i dekabristi*. Moscow: Vagrius, 2005.

Eikhenbaum, Boris. *Lev Tolstoi (kniga vtoraia: 60-ye gody)*. Moscow-Leningrad: Gosudarstvennoe izdatel'stvo khudozhestvennoi literatury, 1931.

Emel'ianov, Iu. N. *P. E. Shchegolev—istorik russkogo revoliutsionnogo dvizheniia*. Moscow: Nauka, 1990.

Engel, Barbara Alpern. *Mothers and Daughters: Women of the Intelligentsia in Nineteenth-Century Russia*. Cambridge: Cambridge University Press, 1989.

Enteen, George. *The Soviet Scholar-Bureaucrat: M. N. Pokrovskii and the Society of Marxist Historians*. University Park, PA: Pennsylvania State University Press, 1978.

Esipov, V. M. *Pushkin v zerkale mifov*. Moscow: Iazyki slavianskoi kul'tury, 2006.

Feuer, Kathryn B. *Tolstoy and the Genesis of War and Peace*. Ithaca, NY: Cornell University Press, 1996.

Fitzpatrick, Sheila, and Yuri Slezkine, eds. *In the Shadow of Revolution*. Princeton, NJ: Princeton University Press, 2000.

Foucault, Michel. *Discipline and Punish: The Birth of the Prison*, trans. Alan Sheridan. NY: Vintage Books, 1995.

Freedman, John. "Big Names Keep Moscow Moving: The 1995–1996 Season." *Slavic and East European Performance* 16, no. 3 (Fall 1996): 19–20.

Friedberg, Maurice. *Russian Classics in Soviet Jackets*. NY: Columbia University Press, 1962.

Frizman, L. G. *Dekabristy i russkaia literatura*. Moscow: Khudozhestvennaia literatura, 1988.

Gessen, Sergei. *Dekabristy pered sudom istorii*. Moscow-Leningrad: Petrograd, 1926.

Ginzburg, Lidiia. *O lirike*. Moscow-Leningrad: Sovetskii pisatel', 1964.

——— (Lydia). *On Psychological Prose*, trans. by Judson Rosengrant. Princeton, NJ: Princeton University Press, 1991.

Girard, René. *Violence and the Sacred*, trans. Patrick Gregory. Baltimore, MD: Johns Hopkins University Press, 1977.

Goldenveizer, A. B. *Vblizi Tolstogo*. Moscow: Kooperativnoe izdatel'stvo, 1922–1923.

Goncharova, T. I. "Istoricheskie vechera." *Prepodavanie istorii v shkole* 3 (1984): 44–49.

Gorbachevich, K. S. and E. P. Khaldo. *Pochemu tak nazvany? O proiskhozhdenii nazvanii ulits, ploshchadei, ostrovov, rek i mostov v Leningrade*. Leningrad: Leninizdat, 1967.

Goscilo, Helena, ed. *Glasnost': An Anthology of Russian Literature under Gorbachev*. Ann Arbor, MI: Ardis, 1990.

Grosheva, E., ed. *Iurii Aleksandrovich Shaporin: Stat'i, Materialy. Vospominaniia*. Moscow: Sovetskii kompozitor, 1989.

———. "Traditsii vysokogo patriotizma: opera 'Dekabristy' v Moskve i Leningrade." *Teatr* 10 (Oct. 1953): 81–94.

Heil, Jerry Tyrone. "The Russian Literary Avant-Garde and the Cinema (1920s and 1930s): The Film Work of Isaak Babel' and Jurij Tynjanov." Ph.D. diss., University of California, Berkeley, 1984.

———. "Theme and Stylization and the 'Literary Film' as Avant-Garde." *Avant-Garde* no. 5/6 (1991): 137–162.

Hobsbawm, Eric J., ed. *The Invention of Tradition.* Cambridge: Cambridge University Press, 1983.

Hoogenboom, Hilde. "Vera Figner and revolutionary autobiographies: the influence of gender on genre." In *Women in Russia and Ukraine,* ed. Rosalind Marsh. Cambridge: Cambridge University Press, 1996.

Iakushkin, V. E. *O Pushkine: Stat'i i zametki.* Moscow: Izd. M. i S. Sabashnikov, 1899.

Joseph, Larry. "From Literary Theory to Fiction: An Interpretive Biography of Iurii Tynianov in the 1920s." Ph.D. diss., Stanford University, 1994.

Katonova, S. "Istoriia sozdaniia opery 'Dekabristy' Iu. A. Shaporina." *Uchenye zapiski. Sektor muzyki.* t. 2. Leningrad: Gosudarstvennyi nauchno-issledovatel'skii institut teatra, muzyka i kinematografii, 1958.

Kerzhentsev, P. M. *Tvorcheskii teatr.* Moscow: Gosudarstvennoe izdatel'stvo, 1923.

Khin, M. M. "Zheny dekabristov." *Istoricheskii vestnik* 18 (1884): 651–683.

Kiianskaia, O. I. (ed.) *Dekabristy: aktual'nye problemy i novye podkhody.* Moscow: RGGU, 2008.

Knight, Amy. "Female terrorists in the Russian Socialist Revolutionary Party." *Russian Review* 38/2 (1979): 139–159.

Kornblatt, Judith. *The Cossack Hero in Russian Literature: A Study in Cultural Mythology.* Madison, WI: University of Wisconsin Press, 1992.

Krebs, Stanley. *Soviet Composers and the Development of Soviet Music.* New York: W. W. Norton & Company, 1970.

Lednicki, Waclaw. *Pushkin's Bronze Horseman: The Story of a Masterpiece.* Berkeley, CA: University of California Press, 1955.

Leonov, N. "Dekabristy: po khudozhestvennoi literature i dokumentam." *Narodnyi uchitel'* 12 (1925): 100–105.

Levi-Strauss, Claude. *The Savage Mind.* London: Weidenfeld & Nicolson, 1966.

Levinson, N.R. *Pushkinskaia Moskva: putevoditel'.* Moscow: Moskovskii rabochii, 1937.

Levit, S. *Iurii Shaporin: ocherk zhizni i tvorchestva.* Moscow: Nauka, 1964.

Levitt, Marcus C. "Pushkin in 1899." In *Cultural Mythologies of Russian Modernism: From the Golden Age to the Silver Age,* ed. Boris Gasparov. Berkeley, CA: University of California Press, 1992.

———. *Russian Literary Politics and the Pushkin Celebration of 1880.* Ithaca, NY: Cornell University Press, 1989.

Liashenko, K. G. "1917 g. Obrashchenie Obshchestva pamiati dekabristov k grazhdanam Rossii." *Sovietskie arkhivy* 6 (1991): 71–73.

———. "Listovki RSDRP o vosstanii dekabristov." *Voprosy istorii* 12 (December. 1975): 198–202.

———. "Sotsial-demokraticheskaia listovka pamiati 14 dekabria 1825 goda." *Sovietskie arkhivy* 6 (1976): 23–24.

Lincoln, W. Bruce. *Nicholas I: Emperor and Autocrat of All the Russias.* DeKalb, IL: Northern Illinois University Press, 1989.

Lotman, Iu. M. and Uspenskii, B. A. *The Semiotics of Russian Culture.* Ann Arbor, MI: Michigan Slavic Contributions, No. 11, 1984.

Lozinskaia, T. *Dekabristy—Ekskurziia.* Leningrad: Izdatel'stvo knizhnogo sektora LGONO, 1925.

Makogonenko, G. P. *Tvorchestvo A. S. Pushkina v 1830-e gody (1833–1836).* Leningrad: Khudozhestvennaia literatura, 1982.

Malia, Martin. *Alexander Herzen and the Birth of Russian Socialism, 1812–1855.* Cambridge, MA: Harvard University Press, 1961.

Marin, Louis. *The Portrait of the King,* trans. Martha Houle. Minneapolis, MN: University of Minnesota Press, 1988.

Mazour, Anatole G. *The First Russian Revolution, 1825, the Decembrist Movement: Its Origins, Development, and Significance.* Stanford, CA: Stanford University, 1937.

———. *Women in Exile: Wives of the Decembrists.* Tallahassee, FL: The Diplomatic Press, 1975.

Mikhailova, Elena. "Natan Eidel'man: 'Volshebnoi palochki v istorii ne byvaet." *Daugava* No. 2 (1987): 102.

Morson, Gary Saul. *Narrative and Freedom: The Shadows of Time.* New Haven, CT: Yale University Press, 1994.

Murav, Harriet. "'Vo glubine Sibirskikh rud': Siberia and the Myth of Exile." In *Between Heaven and Hell: The Myth of Siberia in Russian Culture,* eds. Galya Diment and Yury Slezkine. New York: St. Martin's Press, 1993.

Nechkina, M. V. *Dekabristy.* Moscow: Nauka, 1982.

———. *Griboedov i dekabristy.* Moscow: Khudozhestvennaia literatura, 1977.

———, ed. *Istoriia SSSR.* Moscow–Leningrad: Gosudarstvennoe izdatel'stvo politicheskoi literatury, 1949.

———. "Portreti 'predkov': iubilei dekabristov za rubezhom." *Pechat' i revoliutsiia* 8 (Dec. 1926): 28–38.

———. "Vosstanie dekabristov v kontseptsii M. N. Pokrovskogo." in *Protiv istoricheskoi kontseptsii M. N. Pokrovskogo.* Moscow–Leningrad: Izdatel'stvo Akademii nauk SSSR, 1939.

Nevelev, G. A. *Dekabristy i dekabristovedy.* St. Petersburg: Technologos, 2003.

———. *"Eksizy raznykh lits . . .": Dekabristy v risunkakh A. S. Pushkina.* St. Petersburg: Izdatel'stvo IKS, 1993.

———. "Pushkin o meste pogrebeniia dekabristov." *Voprosy istorii* 5 (1984): 179–184.

Obshchestvennye dvizheniia v Rossii v pervoi polovine XIX veka. t. 1. St. Petersburg, 1905.

O'Meara, Patrick. *K. F. Ryleev: A Political Biography of the Decembrist Poet.* Princeton, NJ: Princeton University Press, 1984.

———. *The Decembrist Pavel Pestel: Russia's First Republican.* New York: Palgrave Macmillan, 2003.

Oleinikov, D. I. "Don Kikhot i Gamlet kak tipy istoricheskogo samosoznaniia pokolenii dekabristov i idealistov 30-kh godov." *Ekonomicheskaia i obshchestvennaia zhizn' Rossii novogo vremeni,* ch. 2, Moscow: Rossiiskaia akademiia nauk, Institut Rossiiskoi istorii, 1992, 167–178.

Ol'minskii, M. "Razrushennye legendy." *Vestnik zhizni* 3 (Mar. 1907): 72–83.

Pavliuchenko, E. A. *V dobrovol'nom izgnanii: o zhenakh i sestrakh dekabristov.* Moscow: Nauka, 1986.

———. *Zhenshchiny v russkom osvoboditel'nom dvizhenii.* Moscow: Mysl', 1988.

Petrone, Karen. *Life Has Become More Joyous, Comrades: Celebrations in the Time of Stalin.* Bloomington, IN: Indiana University Press, 2000.

Piksanov, N. K. "Dvorianskaia reaktsiia na dekabrizm." *Zven'ia,* vyp. II, Moscow–Leningrad: Academiia, 1933.

———. *Griboedov i staroe barstvo.* Moscow: Nikitinskie subbotniki, 1926.

Platt, Jonathan Brooks. "Feast in the Time of Terror: Stalinist Temporal Paradox and the 1937 Pushkin Jubilee." Ph.D. diss., Columbia University, 2008.

Plekhanov, G. "Rech' proiznesennaia na russkom sobranii v Zheneve 14/27 dekabria 1900 goda." *14-oe dekabria 1825 goda*. Petrograd: Gosudarstvennoe izdatel'stvo, 1921.

Pokrovskii, M. N. *Dekabristy: Sbornik Statei*. *Legenda i deistvitel'nost'*. Moscow–Leningrad: Gosudarstvennoe izdatel'stvo, 1927.

———. "Nuzhno li prazdnovat' iubilei dekabristov?" 19–32, in *Dekabristy: K stoletiu zagovora. 1825–1925*, ed. S. Ia. Shtraikh. Moscow: Molodaia gvardiia, 1925.

Pokrovskii, V. I. *Zheny dekabristov*. Moscow: G. Lissner i D. Sobko, 1906.

Pugachev, V. V. "Onegin-dekabrist ili Onegin 'chaadaevets'?," *Studia Slavic Hung*. 37 (1991–1992): 273–285.

Prussakova, Irina. "Bard, Khroniker, Letopisets." *Neva* 7 (1994): 266.

Raeff, Marc. *The Decembrist Movement*. Englewood Cliffs, NJ: Prentice Hall Inc., 1966.

———. *Origins of the Russian Intelligentsia: The Eighteenth Century Nobility*. New York: Harcourt Brace Jovanovich, 1966.

Ragsdale, Hugh. "Russian Popular History in Fact and Fiction: Three Contemporary Styles" *Soviet Union/Union Sovietique* 17, no. 3 (1990): 282–286.

Reyfman, Irina. *Vasilii Trediakovsky: The Fool of the "New" Russian Literature*. Stanford, CA: Stanford University Press, 1990.

Russian Writers since 1980. Dictionary of Literary Biography, v. 285. Florence, KY: Gale Press, 2003.

Sandler, Stephanie. *Commemorating Pushkin: Russia's Myth of A National Poet*. Stanford, CA: Stanford University Press, 2004.

Shalin, Dmitri N., ed. *Russian Culture at the Crossroads: Paradoxes of Postcommunist Consciousness*. New York: Westview Press, 1996.

Sherlock, Thomas. *Historical Narratives in the Soviet Union and Post-Soviet Russia*. New York: Palgrave Macmillan, 2007.

Shchegolev, P. E. "Podvig russkoi zhenshchiny." *Istoricheskii vestnik* 96 (1904): 530–550.

Shtraikh, S. Ia. *K iubileiu dekabristov*. Moscow: Transpechat', 1925.

Sinyavsky, Andrei. *Soviet Civilization: A Cultural History*. New York: Arcade Publishing, 1990.

Slonimskii, A. L. "Pushkin i dekabr'skoe dvizhenie." in A. S. Pushkin, *Polnoe sobranie sochinenii*, ed. S. A. Vengerov. St. Petersburg: Izdanie Brokgauz-Efron, 1908, 503–528.

———. *Iunost' poeta*. Leningrad: Tipografiia Komintern, 1937.

Smeliansky, Anatoly. *The Russian Theatre after Stalin*. Cambridge: Cambridge University Press, 1999.

Spierenburg, Pieter. *The Spectacle of Suffering. Executions and the Evolution of Repression: from a Pre-industrial Metropolis to the European Experience*. Cambridge: Cambridge University Press, 1984.

Stites, Richard. *Revolutionary Dreams: Utopian Vision and Experimental Life in the Russian Revolution*. Oxford: Oxford University Press, 1989.

Tertz, Abram. (Sinyavsky, Andrei.) *Strolls with Pushkin*, trans. Catharine Theimer Nepomnyashchy and Slava Yastremski. New Haven, CT: Yale University Press, 1993.

Tomashevskii, B. V. "Desiataia glava *Evgeniia Onegina* (Istoriia razgadki)" in Tomashevskii, B. V. *Pushkin* (Moscow-Leningrad: Izd. Akademii Nauk SSSR, 1961), 2:208.

Tsiavlovskii, M. A. "Dekabristy. Istoriia pisaniia i pechataniia romana," In L. N. Tolstoi, *Polnoe sobranie sochinenii* (1936), 17: 468–513.

Turner, Victor. *Dramas, Fields, and Metaphors: Symbolic Action in Human Society*. Ithaca, NY: Cornell University Press, 1974.

———. *The Ritual Process: Structure and Anti-Structure*. Ithaca, NY: Cornell University Press, 1969.

Tumarkin, Nina. *Lenin Lives! The Lenin Cult in Soviet Russia*. Cambridge, MA: Harvard University, 1983.

Venturi, Franco. *Roots of Revolution: A History of the Populist and Socialist Movements in Nineteenth-Century Russia.* London: Weidenfeld and Nicolson, 1960.

Vishevsky, Anatolii. *Soviet Literary Culture in the 1970s.* Gainesville, FL: University of Florida Press, 1993.

Verdery, Katherine. *The Political Lives of Dead Bodies: Reburial and Postsocialist Change.* New York: Columbia University Press, 1999.

Volk, S. S. *Istoricheskie vzgliady dekabristov.* Moscow: Izd. Aklademii Nauk SSSR, 1958.

Von Geldern, James. *Bolshevik Festivals: 1917–1920.* Berkeley, CA: University of California Press, 1993.

Vsesoiuznoe obshchestvo politicheskikh katorzhan i ssyl'no-poselentsev. *1825–1905–1925. Sto let politicheskoi katorgi. 2-oi vsesoiuznyi s'ezd politkatorzhan.* 26–29 dek. 1925 g. Moscow, 1926.

Wachtel, Andrew Baruch. *An Obsession with History: Russian Writers Confront the Past.* Stanford, CA: Stanford University Press, 1994.

Wood, Alan. "Crime and Punishment in the House of the Dead," in *Civil Rights in Imperial Russia,* ed. Olga Crisp. Oxford: Clarendon Press, 1989.

Wortman, Richard S. *Scenarios of Power: Myth and Ceremony in Russian Monarchy.* vol. 1. Princeton, NJ: Princeton University Press, 1995.

Yasuhara, Masayuki. "The Concept of Socialist Realism in Soviet Music." in *Socialist Realism Revisited.* Hamilton, Ontario: McMaster University, 1994, 73–83.

Youngblood, Denise J. "'History' on film: the historical melodrama in early Soviet cinema." *Historical Journal of Film, Radio and Television* 11, no. 2 (1991): 173–184.

———. *Movies for the Masses: Popular Cinema and Soviet Society in the 1920s.* Cambridge: Cambridge University Press, 1992.

Zimmerman, Judith E. *Mid-passage: Alexander Herzen and European Revolution, 1847–1852.* Pittsburgh: University of Pittsburgh Press, 1989.

Ziolkowski, Margaret, "Hagiography and History: The Saintly Prince in the Poetry of the Decembrists." *Slavic and East European Journal* 30 (Spring 1986): 29–44.

———. *Hagiography and Modern Russian Literature.* Princeton, NJ: Princeton University Press, 1988.

———. *Literary Exorcisms of Stalinism: Russian Writers and the Soviet Past.* Columbia, SC: Camden House, 1998.

INDEX

voiced by, 146. *See also* "In Memory of Herzen: A Ballad of Historic Sleep-Deprivation"
Kostolevskii, Igor, 158
Kotliarevskii, N. A., 58
Kovalskaia, Elizaveta, 202n.91
Kozintsev, Grigorii, 112, 114, 116
Krachkovskii (academician), 86
Kramarov, P., 71
Kudelli, Praskovia, 80–81, 88
Kupchenko, Irina, 159
Kuraev, Mikhail, 162–165; *Captain Dikshtein*, 162, 163; individual in history as concern of, 163; *Night Patrol*, 163–165
Kuzma of Khvalynsk, 165

last words, 48–50
Lean, David, 158
LeDantu, Camille, 188n.7
"Legend of the Tsar and the Decembrist, The" ("Legenda tsaria i dekabrista") (Korolenko), 89
Le Goff, Jacques, 43
Lenfilm, 122, 123, 162
Lenin, Vladimir Ilyich: collected works of, 95; death of, 74; on Decembrists as gentry revolutionaries, 124, 126; in Decembrists' mythologization, 54, 55, 56–57, 68, 74, 93; on Decembrists rousing Herzen, 56, 153, 155, 186; Erofeev's *Moscow to the End of the Line* on, 152; jubilee articles cite, 83; Korzhavin's "In Memory of Herzen" on, 153, 155; on monuments for Decembrists, 58, 85; Nechkina cites, 157–158; Pokrovskii cites, 72; Staroi's *Pierre and Natasha* steals from, 178; "Varshavianka" as favorite song of, 175
Lenin corners, 76, 81
Leningrad. *See* Petersburg (Leningrad)
Lermontov, Mikhail, 14
Lerner, Nikolai, 90
Levin, Moisei, 122

Levi-Strauss, Claude, 97
Liatskii, E. A., 58
Libedinskaia, Lidiia, 119, 123, 205n.1
"Liberty" ("Vol'nost'") (Pushkin), 5, 123
literature: Herzen's literary genealogy, 14; literary prizes, 182; as medium for Decembrist myth, vii, 1. See also *authors and works by name*
Litovskii, Valentin, 123
Lomonosov, Mikhail, 107, 108
Lorer, N. I., 37
Lotman, Iurii, 142–145; "The Decembrist in Everyday Life," 143–144; Decembrists as men of action for, 145; on Decembrists' using literary and historical models, ix, 44, 143–144; on Decembrists' wives inspired by literary model, 24; on Griboedov's *Woe from Wit*, 201n.85; on psychology of Decembrist era, 39, 143; "The Theater and Theatricality as Components of Early Nineteenth-Century Culture," 142
Lunacharskii, A., 87
Lunin, Mikhail, 11, 145

Magarill, Sophia, 115
Maiboroda, A. I., xvii
Malia, Martin, 16
Mandelshtam, Nadezhda, 126
Mandelshtam, Osip, 59, 126, 178
Maria Fedorovna, Dowager Empress, 48
Marich, Maria, 95–96, 202n.2
Marin, Louis, xxv
Marinina, Aleksandra (Maria Alexeyeva), 211n.36
"Matvei Radaev" (Ogarev), 23
Meditations (*Dumy*) (Ryleev), 44
Merezhkovskii, Dmitrii, 57, 63–68, 80, 88–89, 90, 171, 173
Michael Pavlovich, Grand Prince, xvii, xviii, xxi, xxvii, 102
Miiakovskii, V. V., 82
Miloradovich, M. A., xvii, xxi, 172, 183